GOUN
540

Contesting Global Governance

This book argues that increasing engagement between international institutions and sectors of civil society is producing a new form of global governance. The authors investigate 'complex multilateralism' by studying the relationship between three multilateral economic institutions (the IMF, World Bank, and World Trade Organization), and three global social movements (environmental, labour, and women's movements). They provide a rich comparative analysis of the institutional response to social movement pressure, tracing institutional change, policy modification and social movement tactics as they struggle to influence the rules and practices governing trade, finance and development regimes. The contest to shape global governance is increasingly being conducted upon a number of levels and amongst a diverse set of actors. Analysing a unique breadth of institutions and movements, this book charts an important part of that contest.

ROBERT O'BRIEN is Assistant Professor of Political Science in the Institute for Globalization and the Human Condition, McMaster University.

ANNE MARIE GOETZ is a Fellow of the Institute of Development Studies, University of Sussex.

JAN AART SCHOLTE is Reader in International Studies at the University of Warwick.

MARC WILLIAMS is Professor of International Relations at the University of New South Wales.

D0188032

CAMBRIDGE STUDIES IN INTERNATIONAL RELATIONS: 71

Contesting Global Governance

Editorial Board

Steve Smith (*Managing editor*)
Thomas Biersteker   Chris Brown   Alex Danchev
Rosemary Foot   Joseph Grieco   G. John Ikenberry
Margot Light   Andrew Linklater   Michael Nicholson
Caroline Thomas   Roger Tooze

Cambridge Studies in International Relations is a joint initiative of
Cambridge University Press and the British International Studies
Association (BISA). The series includes a wide range of material,
from undergraduate textbooks and surveys to research-based
monographs and collaborative volumes. The aim of the series is to
publish the best new scholarship in International Studies from
Europe, North America and the rest of the world.

Series list continues at the end of the book

Contesting Global Governance

Multilateral Economic Institutions and Global Social Movements

Robert O'Brien
McMaster University

Anne Marie Goetz
Institute of Development Studies

Jan Aart Scholte
University of Warwick

Marc Williams
University of New South Wales

CAMBRIDGE
UNIVERSITY PRESS

PUBLISHED BY THE PRESS SYNDICATE OF THE UNIVERSITY OF CAMBRIDGE
The Pitt Building, Trumpington Street, Cambridge, United Kingdom

CAMBRIDGE UNIVERSITY PRESS
The Edinburgh Building, Cambridge CB2 2RU, UK
40 West 20th Street, New York, NY 10011-4211, USA
10 Stamford Road, Oakleigh, VIC 3166, Australia
Ruiz de Alarcón 13, 28014 Madrid, Spain
Dock House, The Waterfront, Cape Town 8001, South Africa

http://www.cambridge.org

© Robert O'Brien, Anne Marie Goetz, Jan Aart Scholte, Marc Williams 2000

This book is in copyright. Subject to statutory exception
and to the provisions of relevant collective licensing agreements,
no reproduction of any part may take place without
the written permission of Cambridge University Press.

First published 2000
Reprinted 2000, 2001

Printed in the United Kingdom at the University Press, Cambridge

Typeset in 10/12.5 Palatino   [CE]

A catalogue record for this book is available from the British Library

ISBN 0 521 77315 6 hardback
ISBN 0 521 77440 3 paperback

Contents

Preface

The origins of this book lie in a 1994 research programme on global economic institutions (GEI) launched by the Economic and Social Research Council (ESRC) of Great Britain. The programme encouraged researchers to discuss how existing global economic institutions and regimes, 'shape international interaction, within the context of important changes underway in the world economy' (ESRC 1995). Feeling that initial ESRC projects reflected a narrow field of investigation, we (at that stage all colleagues at the University of Sussex) formulated a research project that would help discover the nature of the evolving relationship between the major public multilateral economic institutions and the world's population. From our perspective, early ESRC GEI projects were dominated by economistic methodologies and a view of the global political economy which excluded civil society actors. Although claiming that changes in the world economy posed great challenges for economic institutions, the methodology and units of analysis used in the projects were hardly innovative. Our view was not that the funded projects were unimportant or unworthy, but that as a group they seemed oblivious of recent theoretical and empirical developments in the fields of international relations, sociology and politics.

It was our hope that the research we produced would supplement and challenge both the findings and the intellectual assumptions of other GEI projects. The initial goal was to determine what relationship there might be between this grand developing architecture of inter-state (and sometimes interfirm or state–firm) economic institutions and the non-elite majority of the world's population. It was an interesting, but over-ambitious undertaking given the temporal (two years) and financial (£56,700) constraints on the project. To fulfil the demands of the funding agency for timely completion, scholarly output and relevance to users we were required to be selective in our study and limit our focus. We decided to focus upon the actions of three multilateral economic institutions (the International Monetary Fund, World Bank, and the World Trade Organization) and three social movements (women's movements, environmentalists and labour). We have used insight gained from these studies to reflect more widely on multilateral governance.

During the course of our research we have accumulated many debts. First, we thank the ESRC for funding our project (grant L120251027). Second, we are grateful to a number of academic colleagues for providing sound advice and supporting us over the evolution of this project. This group includes Robert Cox, Stephen Gill, Richard Higgott, Craig Murphy, Roger Tooze and Caroline Thomas. A graduate student, Chris Slosser, helped in the preparation of this manuscript for publication. Third, we thank many people in our selected international institutions and social movements who have given freely and openly of their time and views on the subject matter. Their number is too great to thank them individually here, but their contribution has been essential to the final product.

Fourth, a number of academics, institutional officials and social movement activists participated in a one-day workshop in February 1998 to discuss our interim report. This group included Jo Marie Griesegraber of the Center of Concern in Washington, Sheila Kawamara of the Ugandan National NGO Forum, Ricardo Melendez of the International Centre for Sustainable Development and Trade in Geneva, Elizabeth Morris-Hughes of the World Bank, Susan Prowse of the International Monetary Fund, Stephen Pursey of the International Confederation of Free Trade Unions, Laura Fraude Rubio of the Mexican section of Women's Eyes on the Bank, Gary Sampson of the World Trade Organization, Caroline Thomas of Southampton University, and David Vines of Oxford University. Their insights were greatly appreciated. Despite the fact that there are sections of the book that each of them would challenge we hope that they are stimulated by the final product.

The research for and writing of this book was undertaken as a joint project. Our aspiration was that it would read as a single work rather than an edited collection. Robert O'Brien acted as coordinator and took the lead on the introduction, conclusion and the WTO chapter. Anne Marie Goetz researched and wrote the chapter on the World

Bank, Marc Williams was responsible for the environmental chapter, and Jan Aart Scholte conducted the IMF study. We have faced scheduling difficulties and intellectual disagreements, but we believe a coherent and persuasive study has emerged from our efforts.

Abbreviations

AFL–CIO	American Federation of Labor–Congress of Industrial Organisations
BothENDS	Environment and Development Service for NGOs
CEM	Country Economic Memorandum (World Bank)
CTE	Committee on Trade and Environment
DAWN	Development Alternatives with Women for a New Era
Development GAP	The Development Group for Alternative Policies
EAs	Environmental assessments (World Bank)
ED	Executive Director (of the IMF)
EGCG	External Gender Consultative Group (World Bank)
EI	Education International
ENGOs	Environmental NGOs
ESAF	Enhanced Structural Adjustment Facility
ESDVP	Environmentally Sustainable Development Vice President (World Bank)
ESM	Environmental social movement
ESW	Economic and sector work (World Bank)
EURODAD	European Network on Debt and Development
EXR	External Relations department (IMF)
FAD	Fiscal Affairs department (IMF)
FOE	Friends of the Earth
GAB	General Arrangements to Borrow
GAP	Gender Analysis and Policy (World Bank)
GATT	General Agreement on Tariffs and Trade

GEMIT	Group on Environmental Measures and International Trade (GATT)
GSM	Global social movements
HIPC	Highly Indebted Poor Countries (debt-relief initiative)
IBRD	International Bank for Reconstruction and Development
ICFTU	International Confederation of Free Trade Unions
ICHRDD	International Centre for Human Rights and Democratic Development
IDA	International Development Authority
IFC	International Finance Corporation
IIF	Institute of International Finance
ILO	International Labour Organisation
ILRF	International Labor Rights Fund
IMF	International Monetary Fund
ITGLWF	International Textile, Garment and Leather Workers' Federation
ITS	International Trade Secretariats
MD	Managing director (of the IMF)
MEI	Multilateral economic institution
MIGA	Multilateral Investment Guarantee Agency
NGLS	Non-Governmental Liaison Service (of the United Nations)
NGO	Non-governmental organisation
ODs	Operational Directives (World Bank)
PAs	Poverty Assessments (World Bank)
PAD	Public Affairs Division (of IMF's EXR)
PDR	Policy Development and Review department (of the IMF)
PSI	Public Services International
Res rep	Resident representative (of the IMF)
SAF	Structural Adjustment Facility
SAP	Structural adjustment programme
SAPRI	Structural Adjustment Policy Review Initiative
SCDO	Swiss Coalition of Development Organisations
SDR	Special Drawing Right
TPRM	Trade policy review mechanism
TWN	Third World Network

1 Contesting governance: multilateralism and global social movements

In May 1998 a crowd swarmed through Geneva attacking McDonald's restaurants and vandalising expensive hotels as part of their protest against the World Trade Organization (WTO). In preparation for the same WTO meeting a global peasant alliance cemented relations and declared their opposition to the goal of trade liberalisation. In Indonesia social unrest in response to subsidy cuts agreed between the government and the International Monetary Fund (IMF) contributed to the downfall of a government. In the same year the IMF was subject to fierce criticism for its handling of the East Asian debt crisis by Indonesian trade unionists and the prime minister of Malaysia. In South Korea unions engaged in strikes in order to combat IMF and World Bank restructuring prescriptions. The closing years of the twentieth century have been marked by increasing opposition to the operation of multilateral economic institutions.

Although the US scholarship ignores the distributional effect of international institutions, preferring to debate their theoretical relevance to the study of international relations (Martin and Simmons 1998), there is little doubt that for hundreds of millions of people institutions such as the IMF, World Bank and WTO matter a great deal. The terms of IMF structural adjustment programmes influence the life chances of people in developing countries, a World Bank decision to prioritise girls' education can open the possibility for personal and community development; and the ability of the WTO to balance environmental concerns with trade liberalisation may save or condemn an ecological system. The operations of these institutions have serious ramifications for many people far from the decision-making centres of Washington and Geneva. It is little wonder that the people on the receiving end of these institutions' policies are increasingly mobilised to influence the structure and policies of the institutions themselves. The collision between powerful economic institutions and social movements in many countries has led to a contest over global governance. The contest takes place both over the form of the institutions (their structure, decision-making procedures) and over the content of their policies (free market oriented or a balancing of social values). It is this contest that is the subject of this book.

Contesting global governance

Governance, according to the Commission on Global Governance (1995: 2), is the sum of the many ways that individuals and institutions, public and private, manage their common affairs. Since world politics is characterised by governance without government (Rosenau and Czempiel 1992), the process of governance encompasses a broad range of actors. In addition to the public (interstate) economic organisations such as the IMF, World Bank and the WTO, states retain a key decision-making role. Indeed, most of the international relations literature that deals with regimes views states as the only significant actor (Hasenclever, Mayer and Rittberger 1997). Large scale private enterprises or multinational corporations also participate in governance by attempting to influence the activity of international organisations and states. In some cases, private enterprises have created their own systems of regulation and governance (Cutler, Haufler and Porter 1999). This study focuses on the relationship between multilateral economic institutions (MEIs) and global social movements (GSMs) as one aspect of a much wider global politics (Shaw 1994a) and governance structure. Where possible, we take account of other actors and their relationship to the objects of this study.

Since the early 1980s there has been a gradual change in the functioning of key MEIs. Although the extent of this change has varied across institutions, the pattern of increasing engagement with social groups is noticeable. MEIs are moving beyond their interstate mandates to actively engage civil society actors in numerous countries. In order to gauge the significance of such developments this book investigates the interaction between three MEIs and three GSMs.[1] The MEIs are the IMF, the World Bank, and the WTO while the GSMs are the environmental, labour and women's movements.

---

[1] This project was funded by a grant from the Economic and Social Research Council of Great Britain, grant L120251027.

We argue that there is a transformation in the nature of global economic governance as a result of the MEI–GSM encounter. This transformation is labelled 'complex multilateralism' in recognition of its movement away from an exclusively state based structure. To date the transformation has largely taken the form of institutional modification rather than substantive policy innovation. Such changes expli citly acknowledge that actors other than states express the public interest. While signalling a clear alteration to the method of governance, the change in the content of governing policies and the broad interests they represent is less striking. In the short run the MEI–GSM nexus is unlikely to transform either institutional functions or their inherent nature to any significant degree. In the longer run, there is the possibility of incremental change in the functioning and ambit of these key institutions. Complex multilateralism has not challenged the fundamentals of existing world order, but it has incrementally pluralised governing structures.

The relationship developing between MEIs and GSMs highlights a contest over governance between old and new forms of multilateralism. The 'old' or existing dominant form of multilateralism is a top down affair where state dominated institutions are taken as given and minor adjustments in their operation are suggested (Ruggie 1993). The 'new' or emerging multilateralism is an attempt to 'reconstitute civil societies and political authorities on a global scale, building a system of global governance from the bottom up' (Cox 1997: xxvii). The new multilateralism offers a challenge to existing multilateralism not just because it entails institutional transformation, but because it represents a different set of interests.

The concept of a state centric multilateralism as form of international organisation has been outlined by John Ruggie. In an attempt to re-establish the importance of cooperative international institutions to the study of International Relations, Ruggie and a number of colleagues have argued that 'multilateralism matters'. He defines multilateralism as 'an institutional form that coordinates relations among three or more states on the basis of generalized principles of conduct' (Ruggie 1993: 11). There are two elements of this definition which help us understand the tension between existing and new forms of multilateralism in the MEI–GSM relationship. The first is the limiting of multilateralism to 'three or more states' and the second is the status of 'generalized principles of conduct'.

The conduct of the IMF, World Bank and the General Agreement on

3

Tariffs and Trade (GATT) before the 1980s was indicative of this state form of multilateralism. The organisations were dominated by member states, had little institutionalised connection to civil societies within member states and were intent upon generalising a particular set of principles. Under increased pressure from some elements of civil society for transparency and accountability the institutions have in the 1990s embarked upon a strategy of incremental reform. The intent is to extend and universalise existing multilateralism while blunting opposition through coopting hostile groups. Existing multi-lateralism can be universalised through geographic extension to new countries as well as a strengthening of the generalised rules of conduct. An example of the first is bringing China into the WTO while an example of the second is a strengthening of the WTO dispute settlement mechanism. One method of blunting opposition to this extension is to create links with hostile groups and integrate them into a governing structure so that their outright opposition is diminished.

This form of multilateralism has recently been challenged by a strategy termed 'new multilateralism' by its proponents. The concept, and political project, of new multilateralism has emerged from a four-year project on Multilateralism and the United Nations System (MUNS) sponsored by the United Nations University (Cox 1997; Gill 1997; Krause and Knight 1994; Sakamoto 1994; Schechter 1998a, 1998b). Its goal is to foster a form of multilateralism which is built from the bottom up and is based upon a participative global civil society. It differs in three major respects from existing multilateralism. Firstly, the new multilateralism is an emerging entity that does not yet exist in its final form. It is slowly and painfully being created through the interaction of numerous social groups around the world. Secondly, while engaging with existing multilateralism, it attempts to build from the bottom up by starting with social organisations independent of the state. It does not view the state as the sole representative of people's interests. Thirdly, the new multilateralism is an attempt at post-hegemonic organising. This last point requires some clarification.

A hegemonic approach to multilateralism takes a dominant set of assumptions about social life and then attempts to universalise these principles through expanding key institutions. For example, hege-monic assumptions might include the primacy of free markets in the allocation of resources or the naturalness of patriarchal social relations. A post-hegemonic approach to multilateralism must begin with far more modest assumptions. It acknowledges the differences in assumptions about the social world and attempts to find common ground for cooperation. In the place of universalistic principles of neoclassical economics one is aware of alternative methods of social organising and cultural diversity.

The advent of a new multilateralism is itself marred by uncertainties. The challenging of states' legitimacy to act on behalf of peoples raises questions about the relationship between other forms of representation or advocacy. Is the dominance of Northern interests reproduced in the new multilateralism? Does it weaken the power of all states or have a disproportionate influence upon those states that are already weak? Does it excessively complicate the functioning of existing multilateral institutions or provide an opportunity for them to serve the interests of a broader community? The exercise of power by dominant states, institutions or social groups remains an issue of concern.

Our argument is not that the various organisations and groups encountered in this book would necessarily identify themselves as defenders of an established, state centric multilateral system or part of the new multilateralism project, but that their actions are contributing to just such a contest. On one side an effort is being made to reform existing MEIs so that they can better perform their liberalising agenda. On the other side is an attempt to transform the institutions so that policy process and outcomes are radically different. Our research captures a particular moment in the meeting of old and new forms of multilateralism. The relative opening of MEIs to GSMs reveals their attempt to adjust to a new structural environment. However, this opening is often limited by a preference to maintain policy effectiveness and pre-empt a far reaching restructuring of multilateralism or transformation of the principles underlying existing policies. Although the nature of interaction varies across the MEI–GSM nexus, the obstacles to mutual accommodation are large. The developments sketched in this book are likely to be only a brief chapter in the struggle to influence the structures of global governance.

The evidence of our investigations suggest that we are witnessing the development of a hybrid form of multilateralism. We call this hybrid *complex multilateralism*. It is discussed in more detail in the final chapter, but its outlines can be sketched here. Complex multilateralism has five central characteristics. The first characteristic is varied institutional modification in response to civil society actors.

International public institutions are modifying in response to pressure from social movements, NGOs and business actors, but this varies across institutions depending upon institutional culture, structure, role of the executive head and vulnerability to civil society pressure. A second characteristic of this institutional form of international relations is that the major participants are divided by conflicting motivations and goals. The goal of the institutions and their supporters is to maintain existing policy direction and facilitate its smoother operation while the goal of many civil society actors, and certainly social movements, is to change the policy direction of the institutions.

The clash of rival goals leads to a third characteristic, namely the ambiguous results of this form of organisation to date. If accomplishments are defined in terms of the actors achieving their own goals, both institutions and social movements have enjoyed only limited success. A fourth characteristic of complex multilateralism is its differential impact upon the role of the state depending upon the state's pre-existing position in the international system. It tends to reinforce the role of powerful states and weaken the role of many developing states. A fifth aspect of complex multilateralism is a broadening of the policy agenda to include more social issues. MEIs are finally being forced to address the social impacts of their policies.

Context of the MEI–GSM relationship

The MEI–GSM relationship is embedded in a broader context that provides the opportunities and incentives for increased interaction. This section briefly reminds the reader of the context. Three areas are noteworthy. The first is a series of structural changes in the global political economy that are often referred to as 'globalisation' which has laid the groundwork for greater MEI–GSM interaction. The second is a transformation of the mandate and roles of the MEIs. New mandates and greater responsibilities of the IMF, World Bank and WTO have increased the importance of these institutions for civil society actors. A third development is the increasing significance of global social movement politics.

Structural transformations in the global political economy

Five of the most significant structural changes in the global political economy which provide a background to increased MEI–GSM contact are: the liberalisation of economies; innovation in information technology; the creation of new centres of authority; instability in the global financial system; and changes in ideology. Let us briefly consider how each of these affects our area of study.

Liberalisation of economies

The decade of the 1980s witnessed a three pronged advance of economic liberalisation in the global political economy. In developed countries a process of deregulation, including financial deregulation and globalisation, liberalised OECD economies. Although this was much more pronounced in Britain and the United States, other countries have also been opening up their markets and deregulating. In the developing world the search for capital following the debt crisis resulted in the 'triumph of neoclassical economics' in many states (Biersteker 1992). This involved the liberalisation of economies following IMF/World Bank structural adjustment programmes, as well as unilateral liberalisation. Finally, the collapse of communism in Eastern Europe and the former Soviet Union brought vast new areas into the global economy that had been relatively insulated for at least forty years. Even in China a process of selected opening to Western investment added to the liberalisation bandwagon. The exposure of increased numbers of people to market forces has also led to greater concern about how such markets will be regulated.

Increase in information technology

An increase in the ability of people to communicate with each other over vast distances has had two significant effects. Firstly, it has facilitated liberalisation by providing an infrastructure for increased capital mobility. This has occurred both in the area of linking financial markets and in facilitating the operation of multinational companies. Secondly, developments such as faxes, the Internet and e-mail have facilitated the networking of groups in civil society. The rise of the network society (Castells 1996) lets groups that were formerly isolated communicate with each other and share information about common concerns. In some dramatic instances this has facilitated political mobilisation and democratisation (Jones 1994).

New centres of authority

A third factor has been the creation of new centres of authority beyond the state (Strange 1996). Some of the centres have been in the private sector, such as bond rating agencies (Sinclair 1994) while some have taken the form of regional regulation such as the European Union or NAFTA. In other cases it can be seen in the increased importance of MEIs in making authoritative statements about how state economic policy should be conducted. This dispersal of authority across national, regional and global levels has implications for citizens. In order to influence such authorities citizens must either force their states to engage actively with these new centres or they must attempt to engage the authorities directly. In practice both options may be pursued. In some cases this necessitates the trans-nationalisation of citizen activity.

Global financial instability

The 1990s has seen a series of financial crises sweeping over Mexico, Russia, Brazil and East Asia. This instability has led to a questioning of the principles and institutions governing global finance. The East Asian crisis, in particular, has created calls for reflection and action. In the second half of 1997 a financial crisis began in Thailand and swept its way through a number of South and Southeast Asian countries including Indonesia and South Korea. Countries that had only recently been regarded as development miracles by the World Bank (1993a) suddenly seemed very fragile. A currency crisis turned into a financial crisis, threatening the health of a number of countries and the stability of the international financial system. This had three important implications for our study. Firstly, the damage inflicted by rapid capital movements on formerly thriving countries led to an intense debate over the desirability of capital controls (Wade and Veneroso 1998). The relative insulation of countries which had systems of capital control such as India and China encouraged other states to consider and implement controls. This challenged MEI economic orthodoxy and provided the context for a much wider debate about MEI policy and policy formation.

Secondly, the crisis revealed the extent to which MEIs were vulnerable to civil society pressure. In developed states the IMF's seemingly inadequate response to the crisis unleashed a wave of criticism and necessitated a strong defence (Feldstein 1998; Fischer 1998, Kapur 1998). In developing countries the IMF and the World Bank were forced to seek strategic social partners that might help them implement their economic packages. The political vulnerability of financial reform packages became apparent to MEIs and provided an unprecedented opportunity for civil society groups to influence institutional policy. Details of this process are contained in the case studies later in the book.

The third implication was that the financial uncertainty arising from the economic crisis fed a broader reconsideration of ideological positions. A limited, but significant ideological shift can be detected in MEIs and amongst state elites in the late 1990s.

Ideological shifts

By the mid-1990s leaders in several Western states were turning away from the pure liberal principles of the Thatcher/Reagan years. In pursuit of the 'radical centre' President Bill Clinton in the United States and Prime Minister Tony Blair in the United Kingdom sought to facilitate the restructuring of their economies in a way that would make them more competitive, but with some attempt to temper market excesses. Although continuing to give emphasis to the market, they called for new methods of regulation and policy prescriptions to temper the excesses of the market or to carve out competitive niches within the market. Labour, environmentalist and women's groups encountered a more friendly reception in the halls of power even though their agendas were not automatically taken up.

In the international arena a number of voices, sometimes from unlikely sources, called attention to the issue of social provision and the reregulation of markets. After making a fortune through financial speculation, financier George Soros became a leading figure calling for increased social and financial regulation (Soros 1997). By 1998 a Senior Vice President of the World Bank could be found making speeches about the failure of the 'Washington consensus' (neoliberal policy prescriptions) to assist in development (Stiglitz 1998). During the 1999 annual meeting of the World Economic Forum the UN Secretary General added his voice to the growing numbers of prominent people calling for social regulation to soften the impact of globalisation (Annan 1999). Concern was expressed at the social costs and political fragility of neoliberal globalisation. This marked a significant shift from earlier agendas of preaching rapid liberalisation as the solution to the world's problems.

Thus, from a perspective of what resonated with governing ideology, by the end of the 1990s more interventionist policies could once again be considered. This was not a return to Keynesianism, but it was a more open arena for people suggesting that neoliberalism should be tempered in the interest of domestic and/or global society. Although a far cry from the favoured policies of environmentalists, labour unions or women's movements, the shift in governing rhetoric to calls for a tempered form of liberalism provided a more inviting space for the social movement advocates that feature in this study.

Institutions in transition

MEIs have been transforming in response to structural changes in the economy. In general, they have taken a more prominent role in governing the economy and expanded or modified their mandates for action. For example, following the outbreak of the debt crisis in 1982 the IMF took on a significant role in guiding the restructuring of indebted countries so that private capital would renew flows to such countries. This process involved the negotiation of structural adjustment programmes (SAPs) with debtor governments. SAPs advocated the liberalisation of economic policies and the privatisation of many state owned industries and some government services. In the 1990s the IMF has also served as a key institution in attempting to stabilise an increasingly volatile financial system as short term capital movements undermined the Mexican economy in 1994 and attacked East Asian economies in 1997. With the end of the Cold War the IMF began to play a prominent role in the transition economies in Eastern Europe and the former Soviet Union. The East Asian crisis of 1997 also expanded the IMF's geographic scope as it shifted its attention from the debtors of the 1980s to the tiger economies of Asia. It has also brought it into negotiating the liberalisation of these states' economic policies and the restructuring of their financial sectors to achieve greater transparency.

The World Bank has also gone through an extensive transition in the past twenty years. It has moved away from financing particular development projects to supporting policies which facilitate structural adjustment (Gilbert *et al.* 1996). Investment in physical infrastructure was increasingly replaced with investment in economic infrastructure in the form of 'appropriate' policies and sectoral restructuring. It has moved closer to the IMF's role of reorganising domestic economies so that they are more competitive in the international market. Conditionality attached to loans has become the key mechanism for ensuring compliance with this restructuring imperative. Since 1997 the Bank has begun lending directly to subnational units, such as Brazilian and

Indian state governments, to finance privatisation and economic adjustment.

In the case of the founding of the WTO, a new institution was created to replace GATT. The key features of the WTO are an expansion in its mandate to new areas of economic activity and a strengthened legal structure (Croome 1995; Jackson 1998). Because of the Uruguay Round agreements, the WTO has expanded to take in the liberalisation of agriculture, services and investment and the protection of intellectual property rights. It has also established a working party to examine competition policy issues. On the legal front, a strengthening of its dispute settlement mechanism endows the WTO with greater coercive powers over incompatible state policies.

In summary, the IMF, the World Bank and the WTO have undergone several changes since the early 1980s which have increased their importance for global governance. This troika of multilateral economic institutions is a cornerstone of the liberal world economy. Assisting in the governance of financial and production structures, they exercise considerable influence on the daily lives of the world's population. In the category of multilateral public institutions they are notable because their rule-creating and rule-supervisory decisions have important immediate consequences for states and peoples around the world. Their importance and power contrasts with institutions such as the International Labour Organization (ILO) or the United Nations Conference on Trade and Development (UNCTAD) which must rely upon moral suasion and argument (Cox and Jacobson 1974: 423–36). In recent decades the institutions have become more intrusive in the lives of citizens as their policy pronouncements influence a wide range of state activities.

From a research perspective, the World Bank/IMF/WTO combination offers a useful contrast in institutional structure and engagement with non-state, non-firm actors. The Bretton Woods institutions (IMF and World Bank) date back to the early post-war era while the WTO is a more recent creation (1995). Although all three institutions provide services to their members and act as public forums, the WTO's role is less in service provision and more in the field of negotiating forum. It is also distinctive because of its legalistic nature and possession of a dispute settlement mechanism. Whereas the World Bank has since the early 1980s had considerable experience with social organisations, the IMF has a more insulated history and the WTO has just begun to define its relationships with non-state actors. Formal decision making also varies between the institutions. The Bretton Woods pair are formally controlled by their wealthiest member states through weighted voting, but the WTO strives to operate upon a unanimity principle.

The significance of global social movements

Recent scholarship has pointed to the increasing activity of non-state actors operating across national borders. There is no agreement upon what this signifies or even how it should be classified. Leading terms employed to describe this activity include: global society (Shaw 1994b), global civil society (Lipschutz 1992), international society (Peterson 1992), world civic politics (Wapner 1995), transnational relations (Risse-Kappen 1995), NGOs (Charnovitz 1997), transnational social movement organisations (TSMOs) (Smith, Chatfield and Pagnucco 1997), global social change organisations (Gale 1998) and transnational advocacy networks (Keck and Sikkink 1998). Each term refers to a slightly different subject of study with a wider or narrower scope and is selected in response to a specific research question. They reveal differences about the centrality of the state in each investigation and assumptions about the appropriate method for investigating such phenomena. This study focuses on global social movements so we will clarify what we mean by this term and why we use it.

Social movements are a subset of the numerous actors operating in the realm of civil society. They are groups of people with a common interest who band together to pursue a far reaching transformation of society. Their power lies in popular mobilisation to influence the holders of political and economic power (Scott 1990: 15). They differ from state elites in that they do not usually utilise the coercive power of the state. They lack the resources of business interests who may rely on the movement of capital to achieve their purposes. They can be distinguished from interest groups in that their vision is broader and they seek large scale social change. Social movements, by definition, are not members of the elite in their societies. They are anti-systemic. That is, they are working to forward priorities at odds with the existing organisation of the system. They rely on mass mobilisation because they do not directly control the levers of formal power such as the state.

A global social movement is one which operates in a global, as well as local, national and international space. In this study we refer to global as a plane of activity which coexists with local, national and international dimensions (Scholte 1997). It is an area of interaction which is less bounded by barriers of time and space than the local or national and goes beyond the interstate relations of the international. It refers to the transnational connections of people and places that were formerly seen as distant or separate. Thus, one can think of a global financial structure which connects financial centres around the world into a rapid and unceasing market. One can also think of a 'global' social movement. The term global social movement refers to groups of people around the world working on the transworld plane pursuing far reaching social change.

There are difficulties with the appropriating of notions of civil society and social movements from the domestic context. The global civil society concept goes against the basic ontology of most international relations literature. The traditional international relations approach to 'international society' has been to speak of a society of states (Bull and Watson 1994). This leaves no room for discussion of civil society, because non-state actors are defined out of society. While traditional international relations scholarship may reject the notions of global civil society and GSMs because of its state centric approach, others will raise doubts about the existence of a global civil society and GSMs in the absence of a global state (Germain and Kenny 1998: 14–17). Civil society and social movements have always been defined in the context of a relationship with a national state. It is the sphere of public activity amongst a bounded community within the reach of a particular state. The logic seems to be that if there is no overreaching global state, there can be no global community and therefore no global civil society and no global social movements.

It is important to acknowledge that the concept of civil society does not make a smooth transition from the domestic to the international sphere if one expects them to have identical characteristics. However, if one accepts that moving to another level implies a qualitative shift in the concept, then there is less of a problem. The adjective 'global' implies that civil society and social movements are more differentiated than their domestic counterparts. Because there is no single world state and no single world community, GSMs are less cohesive than their national counterparts. A GSM's local characteristics and interests may clash with other local manifestations of the movement. Despite this, there are some transnational connections between the various parts of the movement and there is some sense of a common identity and the need for coordinated if not identical action.

Analysts of GSMs must be particularly aware of making broad statements that assume an identity of interests or purposes between elements of the movement located in different parts of the world. The theory and study of social movements, especially new social movements, and global civil society has on the whole tended to generalise from the experience of Western Europe and the United States (Walker 1994). This poses difficulties for national social movement theory, but poses dangers for global social movement analysis. Three clear problems arise. First, such an intellectual history may assume that the characteristics of Northern or Western social movements are shared by social movements in other parts of the world. Second, it may assume an identity of interest between Western social movements and those in other parts of the world that does not actually exist. Finally, the neglect of social movements in other areas may prevent researchers asking difficult questions of Northern-dominated social movements.

The difficult questions are particularly important in the North–South context. Southern social movements operate in a different local environment from their Northern counterparts (Wignaraja 1993). In addition to having fewer financial resources, they may be much more concerned with local organising and activity. Their relationship with the state may be more ambivalent. While Southern states may be actively oppressing local social movements, they may still be seen as worthy of support against dominant Northern interests. They may welcome assistance from sections of Northern based social movements, but not at the cost of adopting a Northern agenda. We are interested in the degree to which the concerns of Southern social movements have been filtered through Northern based global NGOs. What impact might this have on the issues taken up or ignored? Does the prominence of Northern NGOs influencing MEIs undermine the domestic legitimacy of Southern social movements? Does MEI conditionality influenced by Northern NGOs serve to weaken the Southern state and harm the prospects of those they seek to help?

One should also be wary about characterising global civil society as a place where society is civil or developed. For example, John Hall (1995: 25) describes (national) civil society as 'a particular form of society, appreciating social diversity and able to limit the depredations of political power ...' Lipschutz's (1992) analysis comes close to reducing global civil society to the activity of environmental, development, human rights and aboriginal movements. Not only does he overlook the more sinister social movements (e.g. neo-Nazis), but powerful economic forces do not seem to be active in civil society. Rather than viewing global civil society as a normative social structure to be achieved, it is more accurate to see it as an arena for conflict that interacts with both the interstate system and the global economy.

While social movements may extol the virtues of global civil society, that space has been and is largely dominated by the extensive formal and informal contacts of transnational business and their allies.[2] Social movements are not moving into an empty space. Indeed, discussion about democracy in a globalising era needs to be clear about the forces driving the process in its present direction. Transnational business already has privileged access to those governments whose cooperation would be required to implement reform of multilateral institutions.[3] An arrangement that limited the prerogatives of global business would encounter great resistance.

In research terms it is difficult to capture the diversity that is contained within a particular social movement. How does one interview a global social movement? Social movements are, by definition, fluid and large. They evolve, transform and usually lack a permanent institutional structure. There is no central core where one could go to study the environmental movement as one might begin an investigation of the IMF in Washington. The best that can be accomplished is to identify organisational nodes within the movement on the understanding that these represent only particular tendencies of the whole.[4] Within a broad based movement, one may encounter numerous organisational forms or nodes. One can discuss the rise of environmentalism as a social movement and yet distinguish between a number of organisations within that movement such as the Sierra Club, Kenya's Greenbelt Movement and Friends of the Earth. These green organisations may all share a commitment to the environment, but differ widely upon policy issues and programmes. For example,

---

[2] On the concept of a transnational managerial class and its relationship to other classes see Cox (1987: 355–91). Gill's (1990) study of the Trilateral Commission offers an example of an influential global civil society actor linked with transnational business interests. From a business studies perspective Stopford and Strange (1991: 21) refer to a transnational business civilisation.

[3] Charles Lindblom's (1977: 170–88) neo-pluralist work could now be reformulated to stress the privileged position of *trans*national business in domestic political systems. Milner (1988) has detailed the influence of transnational corporations on US and French trade policy.

[4] Blair (1997) takes a similar approach when he attempts to 'operationalise' civil society by focusing upon NGOs.

the distance between conservationists such as the Sierra Club and rejectionists such as Deep Ecology activists is immense. The former seeks to conserve the environment within the present system while the latter rejects the existing industrial structure.

The key organisational node in global social movements are the ubiquitous (non-profit) non-governmental organisations (NGOs). NGOs have been particularly active at building global civil society around UN world conferences (Clark, Friedman and Hochstetler 1998). Alger (1997) has gone further to note that international NGOs (INGOs) seeking social transformation (TSMOs in his terms) operate on a number of levels to influence global governance. INGOs create and activate global networks, participate in multilateral arenas, facilitate interstate cooperation, act within states and enhance public participation. This leads to the question of the relationship between particular NGOs and the more broadly based social movements under consideration in this study. With the growth of some organisations such as Greenpeace into sizeable actors with considerable financial resources, questions of accountability and representativeness of NGOs themselves must be addressed. To what degree do they speak and act on behalf of the wider movement? Some NGOs claim that because they do not seek state power themselves they have no need to be bound by demands for representativeness (UNGLS 1996b: 64). This claim needs to be challenged if such groups are pressing for a more inclusive role in policy making.

If it is true that it is much easier to study an NGO than a GSM and that there is doubt about the cohesion of GSMs in different countries, is there any sense in deploying the concept of a global social movement? Despite its acknowledged weaknesses, we believe it can still serve a useful function. Our study is not about particular NGOs or NGOs in general, but captures the activity of a collectivity of people and organisations concerned with the social impacts of the three MEIs. Some of these people are in well known NGOs, but others work on a more local basis while some work inside the institutions themselves. They are more than an interest group in that they draw upon social mobilisation of numerous forms of organisation from neighbourhood associations to formal organisations. They are different from firms or business organisations in that their primary function is not to amass profit, but to transform society so that it protects their social interests. The term GSM is elastic enough to capture this collectivity of people.

We concentrate on three social movements: women, environmentalists and labour. They have been active in engaging MEIs on a number of policy issues and also provide a useful contrast because they have varying degrees of financial resources, institutionalisation and differing priorities for engaging MEIs. Two of them are often labelled as 'new' social movements while the third is usually seen as an 'old' social movement, if it even qualifies for the social movement label. The distinction between old and new is not actually a chronological one, but is based upon the divisions around which they organise. Old social movements are class-based such as workers' or peasants' groups. New social movements refer to the post-war development of movements around non-class issues such as gender, race, peace and the environment. They are usually associated with political and cultural change in advanced industrialised countries since the 1960s.

This is not an exhaustive list of social movements engaged with MEIs. In particular it does not take account of groups which do not fit easily our environmental–labour–women's typology. For example, a number of groups organise around the theme of development. They may address environmental, women's and labour issues. These organisations make an appearance in our study when they intersect with the MEIs and GSMs that are the focus of our book.

Key questions

In pursuing our case studies we tried to answer three principal questions. These questions served to focus our investigations and provided coherence across the case studies in addition to helping us gauge the significance of the MEI–GSM relationship.

How have the MEIs modified?

The first question that we explore is 'What have MEIs done to accommodate the desires of social movements interested in increased relations, including influence in policy making?' How have the IMF, World Bank, and WTO changed or adapted their institutional structures to communicate with social movements? To what degree have they undertaken institutional modifications to accommodate the concerns of social movements? In some cases this question is rather

17

preliminary and need not detain us for long. The task is simply to describe the forms of institutional mechanisms that have been established and may be established to facilitate MEI–GSM interaction.

As the case studies will demonstrate, the contribution of this study in answering this question is significant. In the case of the IMF, it is the first study of its kind. Although there has been similar work undertaken on the World Bank and work is emerging on the WTO, we believe this is the first comparative study of the three institutions. This allows us to draw some conclusions about why the institutions have followed different paths in their engagement of social movements.

The detailed answer to this question is contained in each case study chapter with a comparative overview in the final chapter. All three institutions have developed mechanisms to increase their engagement with social movements ranging from providing more information to informal channels of communication to the creation of new departments to deal with social movement concerns. This process has been most developed at the Bank, with much more modest developments at the IMF and WTO.

What are the motivations driving MEI–GSM engagement?

The increasing engagement of MEIs and GSMs requires some explanation. Constitutionally, MEIs are the creation of states and are responsible to states. Traditional practice in world politics has been to recognise states as the legitimate voice of the people within its boundaries. Why have these institutions felt the need to move beyond state structures of interaction? A number of possibilities come to mind.

Rather than begin by assuming that MEIs are inherently committed to openness and democratisation, we suspect that social movements have something that the MEIs need. Since the MEIs and GSMs surveyed in this study are often engaged in a hostile relationship, the question becomes why do MEIs, which occupy positions of power in comparison to the social movements, bother to interact with GSMs? The IMF, World Bank and WTO are engaged in a process of liberalising the world economy and subjecting more social and economic areas to the discipline and imperative of market forces. GSMs are often engaged in a defensive movement against such coercion. In many cases, they challenge the underlying neoliberal philosophy and material interests behind MEI policy. Indeed, elements of the GSMs we examine are anti-systemic in that they can challenge the principles upon which existing MEI multilateralism is built.[5]

MEIs find GSMs useful in two areas – policy implementation and in broader political terms. In regard to policy implementation, GSMs might assist or frustrate MEI policies. MEIs may want to tap GSMs' specialised local knowledge that is unavailable to the staff of the institutions. For example, GSMs may be able to shed light on the impact of particular policies on the ground. GSMs are often familiar with the micro aspects that the macro institutions address. MEIs are often unfamiliar with vulnerable sectors of society such as the poor or women. Parallel to this is the possibility that MEIs might hope to use GSMs as tools to implement favoured policies. This may take the form of privatising tasks formerly done by the institutions such as infor mation collection or having the movements pressure states to follow MEI policy lines. In the case of the World Bank, NGOs can assist in the delivery of development services. In the case of the IMF, it is hoped that labour will exert pressures on states to limit corruption and maintain good governance.

The other side to this is that GSMs may be able to frustrate MEI initiatives on the ground. For example, social mobilisation in India may result in the cancellation of a World Bank dam-building project. Another example would be social movement lobbying against trade liberalisation measures whether they be intellectual property rights in India or environmental concerns in the United States. IMF riots such as those in Venezuela in 1989 which left over three hundred dead may make it extremely difficult to implement particular structural adjust- ment policies.

In broader political terms GSMs may influence key governmental actors which control the fate of the MEIs. The most relevant example would be the influence of environmental groups upon the US Congress which in turn influences funding decisions for the World Bank. Similarly, civic groups have lobbied the US Congress since the early 1980s to put conditions upon funding designated for the IMF. In the case of the GATT, member states started to recognise the import- ance of NGOs when environmentalists threatened to derail the Uruguay Round agreements in the USA. The present WTO leadership hopes that by opening relations with NGOs it will secure public

---

[5] Discussion of anti-systemic movements can be found in Arrighi, Hopkins and Wallerstein (1989).

support for a new round of liberalisation in the early years of the twenty-first century.

MEI accommodation of social movements may be a result of the direct demands of the most powerful governments or as a strategy to pre-empt the wrath of particular states. A slightly different angle is that those interested in seeing the expansion of MEI activity, be it the bureaucrats themselves, a policy community, or a leading state, may want to build public support for new initiatives. Good relations with social movements may make for smoother acceptance of an expanding governing role for the institutions.

Turning to social movements, why and how have they increasingly engaged MEIs? Why have elements of some social movements decided to target MEIs? The explanations vary across social movement and institution, but in general GSMs are concerned about the growing influence of MEI activity upon their constituency. With regard to the IMF, there is concern about the neoliberal approach to structural adjustment programmes, as well as criticism of its expansion past the bounds of monetary relations. GSM concern with the World Bank is focused upon its lending policies and projects. The WTO is seen as an institution creating new international economic law and enforcing liberalisation programmes in a number of new areas. In each case, GSMs offer a challenge to the liberal economic approach of the governing institutions.

In some cases, particular NGOs link up with MEIs because they will benefit directly. For example, the World Bank may contract selected NGOs to assist in policy implementation. This allows some NGOs to forward their agenda and privileges them over other groups. In other cases NGOs may feel international organisations will give them a better hearing than national states. The attempt by some social movements and NGOs to lobby MEIs may be a recognition that governance is now a multilayered affair requiring participation at the local, national, international and global levels.

We also hope to suggest what kinds of strategies and tactics social movements have found to be most effective. Is the priority to influence institution officials or the purse holders in the developed states? What does this mean for their relationship with their home states? How do they order priorities between various levels of activity? Conversely, why have some elements of the social movements refused to engage with MEIs?

What is the significance of the MEI–GSM relationship?

The significance of the MEI–GSM relationship lies in three areas: policy change, democratic governance and political sustainability. The first area for evaluation is the degree to which this relationship is shaping policy outcomes. In cases where we have found some changes in this field we will highlight them. Prominent examples include environmental assessments of World Bank projects, increased attention to gender issues in development, the creation of social dimensions to structural adjustment programmes and the high-lighting of core labour standards. Each of these policy changes shifts resources in the global economy, affecting the health and livelihood of target populations. In some cases, such as the construction of social safety nets, these can be questions of life and death. Potentially, the MEI–GSM relationship can be very significant for the vulnerable sectors of global society.

The second aspect is to determine what effect the relationship is having on the method of governance in terms of democratisation. The operation of MEIs is a concern for global democracy. The activity of these institutions is increasingly affecting the daily lives of hundreds of millions of people. The lead role the IMF and World Bank have played since the debt crisis of the early 1980s has guided the structural adjustment policies in many developing countries. The World Bank's lending policies have guided development projects, often causing considerable controversy amongst local inhabitants. Article IV con-sultations of the IMF have subjected the member states to detailed critical review. The new powers of the WTO herald an era of increased scrutiny of national economies by the international community in the area of trade policies. In Northern states some groups are concerned that the ideology of these institutions subordinates issues such as environmental protection, gender equality and labour rights to a liberalisation drive. In Southern countries these concerns are accom-panied by fears of the increasing gap generated between developed and developing countries in a liberal global economy. People in both Southern and Northern countries have expressed fears about the dilution of state sovereignty by these institutions and the interests they represent.

Some theorists have pointed to the activity of social movements working beyond state borders as a method of increasing democratic practice. They see a contradiction between the fact that the structures of power and issues of concern are firmly rooted in a global context, but participation, representation and legitimacy are fixed at the state level (Connolly 1991; Walker 1993: 141–58). Rather than stressing the rebuilding of state-like institutions at an international level, new social movements are advanced as the best hope for global democratic practice. These movements are said to have a global vision, proposing transnational solutions. One of the primary tasks of such movements and the way in which they might contribute to increasing democracy is by creating a global political community which has a sense of common problems (Brecher, Childs and Culter 1993; Thiele 1993). Does this work in practice? Does the MEI–GSM relationship contribute to a democratisation of global governance? The answer developed in our conclusion is a tentative and qualified 'yes'.

Finally, the MEI–GSM relationship is significant because it highlights the issue of the political sustainability of global governance. In addition to debates about the most desirable economic strategy, attention must be given to the political foundation upon which these institutions rest. The study argues that the foundations of global governance go beyond states and firms to include social movements. Proposals for change in the institutions' structures and roles should be cognisant of this dimension of their activity.

Research method and plan of the study

We have combined several research methods. In addition to a survey of secondary sources we have undertaken interviews with officials from the three institutions under study. Where possible we have also consulted their libraries and files. A similar approach was adopted with regard to social movements and NGOs. We also acted as observers at events where MEI–GSM interaction took place, such as the 1995 UN Summit for Social Development (Copenhagen), the 1995 Fourth World Conference on Women (Beijing), the 1996 World Congress of the ICFTU (Brussels), the 1996 IMF/World Bank Annual Meetings (Washington), the 1996 WTO Ministerial Meeting (Singapore), the 1997 Asia Pacific Economic Cooperation meeting (Vancouver) and the 1998 WTO Ministerial Meeting (Geneva). Field work has also taken place in Romania and Uganda. A draft report was circulated to a selection of people involved in the activities of MEIs and GSMs. In February 1998 we hosted a small workshop where participants from MEIs and GSMs were able to voice their criticisms and offer suggestions for improvements to the report. This book is a response to those helpful suggestions.

This introductory chapter is followed by four case studies and a conclusion. The case studies reflect the varied degree of activity in the MEI–GSM relationship. On the institutional side, the World Bank has had the most involvement with GSMs. On the GSM side, environmentalists have had more success than labour and women's groups. As a result, although each institution has its own chapter focusing upon engagement with a GSM (Bank and women, WTO and labour, IMF and GSMs) we also have a chapter which offers a comparative analysis of the environmental campaign at the Bank and the WTO. The conclusion provides an overview of the MEI–GSM engagement and develops the complex multilateralism concept.

2   The World Bank and women's movements

This chapter examines the ways in which women's movements have engaged with the World Bank in order to challenge the neoliberal economic development paradigm which the Bank promotes, and which some feminists claim is responsible for accelerating rates of female immiseration in developing countries. Feminist critiques have made inroads at the World Bank in terms of diverting some development resources to support women's education, health, and access to micro-credit. But the feminist critique has barely grazed neoliberal prescriptions for market led economic growth in spite of evidence that failures in economic reform policies and structural adjustment have been caused in part by ignorance about the ways gender affects household level responses to production incentives. The outcomes of engagement between women's movements and the World Bank reflect on characteristic features of the Bank's institutional culture, cognitive framework, and decision-making structures which make it relatively indifferent to the gender justice and equity argument. Outcomes of this engagement are also shaped by characteristic features of women's organisations which have, until recently, limited their capacity for building global coalitions around women's economic rights.

The World Bank: what it is, what it does, how it works

The World Bank is the world's biggest development bank, providing finance, research and policy advice to developing countries, with an annual turnover in new loan commitments to developing nations of

24

over $20 billion.[1] Up to the 1980s Bank loans were primarily for specific development projects, but in response to national crises in economic management in the 1980s it embarked on the more controversial course of policy-based lending, attaching conditions on loan disbursement which resembled the IMF's economic austerity conditions.[2] This influence over how loans are spent gives the Bank an important position in setting the terms of development policy discourses, which is why the Bank's policies are of such great interest to global social movements and alternative development practitioners.

The Bank's operations are divided across four main institutions: the International Development Authority (IDA) for concessional lending to the poorest countries, the International Bank for Reconstruction and Development (IBRD) for regular loans, the International Finance Corporation (IFC) for private sector commercial lending, and the Multilateral Investment Guarantee Agency (MIGA) to insure private foreign direct investors against 'political risks' in developing countries. IDA loans are funded by regular voluntary contributions by developed countries ('Part I' countries in Bank terminology), and increasingly from IDA repayments and IBRD profits. IBRD loans are funded through the sale of Bank bonds on international capital markets ($15 billion a year compared to $6 billion a year for IDA). The operations of the IFC and the MIGA are the least subject to conditionalities and quality controls, but are just as much of concern to gender equity advocates. The Bank's support to the private sector through the IFC and the MIGA is the fastest growing component of Bank lending, and it has a 'multiplier' effect, in that Bank activity in the private sector of a given country acts as a green light to other commercial investors. Bank critics therefore target Bank activities in the private sector as an arena in which labour and environmental standards, and gender equity concerns, could be modelled as standards for the commercial sector.

The World Bank is not a monolithic or monological institution, for

---

[1] However, the importance of Bank lending has diminished with increased private capital flows – e.g. in the Latin American region public capital flows have dropped from 50 per cent to 20 per cent of total capital flows in the last five years. In the last seven years, the flow of private sector funds to developing countries has increased fivefold (World Bank 1997b: 7, 13).

[2] The Bank's adjustment loans are actually only a small proportion of its loans. In 1995, it made 130 adjustment loans (average size $140 million) and 1,612 project investment loans (average size $80 million) (Alexander 1996).

all it may seem so to its critics. It has always been somewhat torn between two competing identities. On the one hand, it is a bank, an institution driven by a 'disbursement imperative for capital-driven growth-oriented lending' (Nelson 1995: 171). On the other, it is a development organisation with a stated objective of poverty reduction through economic growth. These two identities can clash, when new development ideas diverge from financial management requirements. The tension between the two identities actually creates space within the Bank for pockets of resistance and the development of alternatives to dominant neoliberal economic development paradigms. This tension is also productive of the periodic sea-changes in the Bank's approach to its development mandate. In the 1950s and 1960s the Bank promoted strong state-led investment in developing economies and poverty reduction programmes. From the late 1970s this approach was virtually reversed with a new neoliberal economic orthodoxy prescribing state withdrawal from markets. By the late 1980s as the human costs of structural adjustment programmes emerged, the Bank recommitted itself to its poverty reduction mission, and although it has not deviated from its neoliberal policies on market liberalisation, it is devoting more attention to human capital development and social development more generally. Since 1990, and very markedly since President James Wolfensohn took office in June 1995, there has been a shift, at least in the Bank's rhetoric, to promoting 'participatory development'. One of Wolfensohn's first acts in office was to launch a report by the Bank's 'Learning Group on Participatory Development', thus enormously validating the importance of participation in policy and project development, giving a fillip to the efforts of NGOs to make the Bank's work more transparent and accessible to those most affected by it (World Bank 1994h: 1). A partner to this agenda is the Bank's new concern with promoting good governance, and although its Articles of Agreement forbid any explicit promotion of political change – such as transitions to democracy – its approach to good governance aims to encourage greater participation in national institutions of governance, and to improve the accountability of these institutions, all of which should encourage a deepening of democracy in some contexts.

Formal power at the Bank rests with its owners – its member states. These are represented on the Board of Governors, a body which meets just twice a year and delegates decision making to the Bank's twenty-four-member Executive Board, which meets twice a week to review, approve, or reject Bank project proposals, as well as to review Bank policy. The president of the Bank chairs the Executive Board on which he has the casting vote in the event of a tie. The five largest shareholders in the Bank (the USA, Japan, Germany, United Kingdom and France) each appoint an Executive Director; the remainder of the Board is elected by the other member governments every two years. The Board operates on a weighted voting basis but most decisions are based on consensus. There is an obvious North–South power division between the rich, non-borrowing countries on the Executive Board who make the capital contributions which support the IDA, and the poor, borrowing countries. Within Part I countries the US Treasury exercises the most power, as it controls the biggest single-country contribution to the IDA. As a result the most effective way of influencing the Bank from the outside is by lobbying Congress to threaten funds released through the US Treasury to the Bank; precisely the strategy used to great effect by environmental groups in the mid-1980s. Another effective strategy is to lobby Executive Directors and the national legislatures to which they report to act as advocates for certain issues when scrutinising Bank policy.

The Executive Board is not the only site of power in the institution. Another important locus of power in the Bank in terms of setting policy priorities is the Bank's president and top management team. As Williams (1994: 107) points out, the ability of the management and staff of the bank to shape policies and decisions – and indeed, to enjoy a high degree of autonomy in relation to its Board of Directors, arises from a combination of the Bank's relatively 'independent financial base, the impressive technical and intellectual reputation of its staff, its pre-eminent position among multilateral lending agencies and the activities of successive presidents to develop and preserve organisational autonomy'. This relative autonomy extends to the rank and file of economists and other specialists working in the operational and technical divisions of the Bank in the sense that they have some room for manoeuvre in pursuing new ideas. This facilitated, for instance, the creation in 1990 of a Bank-wide Learning Group on Participatory Development – on the face of it a rather counter-cultural subject for the Bank. This kind of elasticity in the Bank's institutional culture has been very important to the relative successes of advocates of gender equity in development.

Bank–NGO relations

No formal place existed in the Bank's original institutional structure for the representation of the interests of non-state actors such as social movements. Since 1982, however, there has been an increasing degree of dialogue and cooperation between the Bank and development NGOs. The 1990s have seen increasing reference to the importance of 'dialogue' with 'stakeholders' and 'civil society' in the Bank's discourse. Such sentiments appear in particular in the Bank's new governance documents (World Bank 1994a) and in its discussion papers on participatory development and development partnership (World Bank 1998a).[3] 'Civil society' is very broadly defined in these kinds of documents, as are the range of actors which are embraced by the notion of 'stakeholders' in any particular set of economic reform policies or sectoral investment programmes. These might include trade unions, business associations, social movements and so on, but in the Bank's actual engagement with non-state actors, this has boiled down to NGOs involved in development.

Outreach to and incorporation of NGOs is prompted by two concerns. First, there is increasing recognition of the 'comparative advantage' exercised by NGOs over state bureaucracies in delivering development resources to the poor – and thereby in enhancing development effectiveness. Second, there is a growing recognition of the effectiveness of NGOs in determining the climate of public opinion, particularly in the North, about the Bank's work – and thereby threatening some of the Bank's operating funds, let alone the environment of good will for its work. There is also recognition of their role in developing countries in channelling and expressing popular frustrations with the sometimes painful social impact of economic reform policies, a role which can contribute to an often already weak national sense of ownership of these policies. Developing a partnership with NGOs is seen as helpful in enhancing the social sustainability of the Bank's work.

In this sense Bank–NGO dialogue has been stimulated by internal critiques of the quality of the Bank's work. In 1993 Wili Wapenhans, a

---

[3] Note that the notion of partnership is intended mainly to apply to more effective partnerships with borrowing country governments, as a step towards establishing more effective in-country ownership and management of economic reform processes. This, it is hoped, will overcome the tendency of borrowing countries to see economic reform agendas as an external imposition.

retiring bank vice-president, led an evaluation of the Bank's portfolio which charged that the preoccupation with 'moving money' had seriously undermined the quality of the Bank's work (World Bank 1993b). There is no automatic accountability check on the Bank's work because loans must be repaid whether or not the projects they finance are successful. The declining performance of the Bank's loan portfolio was undermining its credibility, as was Wapenhans' discovery that few of the conditions on loans were complied with by borrowers. This made it imperative to enhance local commitment and ownership of Bank-funded development work, which is where NGOs were seen to have a contribution to make.

The first official channel for World Bank–NGO dialogue predated this development, however. It was established in 1982 in the formal NGO–World Bank Committee of twenty-six NGO leaders from around the world, but this has been seen by many NGOs as a rather tame forum which is over-controlled by the Bank. In reaction to this, NGOs have created a forum for more critical and open dialogue: the NGO Working Group, in which representative non-governmental institutions from the world's regions participate through a staggered election process allowing for rotation and diversity of the NGOs represented.

During the 1980s the presence and importance of NGOs in development work increased rapidly, as did their impact on policy debates and their often strident opposition to the neoliberal 'Washington consensus'. Within the Bank, attention was paid to this phenomenon in Michael Cernea's 1987 paper 'Nongovernmental Organisations and Local Development', where he argued that NGOs were 'builders of organisational capacity and ... social (rather than financial) mobilisers in development work' (Cernea 1987: 8). This influenced the Bank's appreciation of the utility of NGOs in promoting project effectiveness, as suggested in a speech in 1988 by Moeen Quereshi, then Senior Vice-President for Operations, who noted: 'In the last few years NGO influence on Bank policies has grown ... I have asked our staff to look for more situations where NGOs could help us elicit participation of poor people in planning public projects and policies' (Nelson 1995: 7). This declaration suggests an internally driven process of outreach. But in fact, the Bank's engagement with NGOs has always been just as much in response to increasingly effective NGO campaigns to elicit reform of the Bank.

There have been tensions in Bank–NGO relations. Many NGOs

viewed the formal NGO–World Bank Committee with suspicion. Since the 1990s, as Bank–NGO interactions have become broader and more generally accepted, the Committee no longer appears to be performing any useful function. It was not, for instance, involved in the joint Bank–NGO initiative to research the impact of structural adjustment on the poor: the Structural Adjustment Participatory Research Initiative (SAPRI) launched in late 1996. This engages the Bank to work with NGO activists and researchers in seven countries experiencing economic reform to research the impact of adjustment (using participatory methods) and to enhance the participation of civil society groups in the design of policies. Over 1,000 NGOs all over the world have signed upto this initiative.

Bank–NGO interactions are structured around operational colla- boration, economic and sector work (ESW), and policy dialogue. There has been a great increase in the number of Bank projects which involve NGOs; they were an average of fifteen a year in the early and mid-1980s, but by 1991/92, 89 of the 156 projects approved involved NGOs in their design and implementation. NGO participation has been over 30 per cent in every year in the 1990s, and up to 50 per cent in 1994 (World Bank 1996b: iii). In most of these cases, the NGOs are involved primarily as service providers, as intermediaries in imple- menting projects, not as policy makers. Classically, they are contracted to provide targeted services to the poor to ease the impact of adjust- ment measures, without themselves having a chance to challenge the Bank's adjustment agenda.

This is changing, however, with the increasing involvement of NGOs in providing research-based inputs to the Bank's ESW, and to its in-country policy dialogues. ESW provides the analytical founda- tions for Bank policy work and project lending. It informs the 'policy dialogue' between the Bank and its clients via a central policy document: the Country Assistance Strategy (CAS), whose production and negotiation with governments has been, until recently, a secretive process. NGOs have been involved, however, in consultations over the documents which feed into the CAS, such as country economic memoranda (reports which are prepared for each borrower country analysing its economic prospects and suggesting broad policy directions), poverty and social assessments, public expenditure reviews, and environmental action plans.

Involvement of NGOs in policy dialogue has gradually become more meaningful in the sense that the Bank is slowly relinquishing aspects of its culture of secrecy to enable NGOs to inform themselves better of Bank–borrower-country dealings. The NGO–World Bank Committee is intended as a forum for policy dialogue, and topics discussed include poverty, participation, social development, environment, the management of the Bank and information disclosure. NGOs have lobbied persistently for a relaxation of the Bank's notorious secrecy around policy development and project preparation, and this paid off in the 1990s with a Public Disclosure Policy in January 1994 to open bank project documents (prepared after January 1994) to the public. In addition, an Independent Inspection Panel was created in September 1994 to improve accountability to 'affected parties of an action or omission by the Bank' (World Bank 1994b: 17, 74) – in effect, to give those who feel they have been harmed by the Bank a chance to hold the Bank accountable to its own operational policies.[4]

More directly, the Bank now speaks of establishing partnerships with civil society (along with the private sector) to encourage participation in the design and implementation of national development strategies. In part, this has involved convening huge in-country fora to discuss policy reform with civil society representatives. Inevitably such jamborees leave many participants unsatisfied because of the impossibility of including all interested parties, and because of the difficulty of establishing more than superficial exchanges. In part the notion of partnerships and dialogue with civil society has involved plans to finance a programme of 'education of civil society', to be managed by the Bank's Economic Development Institute (which focuses on research and training). This would mean a programme to 'build understanding of economic and social issues among organisations of civil society – NGOs, labour unions and the media – as well as among parliamentarians and other government officials' (Bread for the World 1997a: 6). Such activities are intended to build public consensus and support for economic reform, not to generate or pick up on popular critiques of the Bank's work.

Before discussing the history of the engagement of women's movements with the Bank, and their impact, we turn to a discussion of important features of women's movements which have determined their critique of economic policies and the nature of their engagement with multilateral economic institutions such as the Bank.

---

[4] For a more detailed history of Bank–NGO relations see UNGLS (1997).

Women's movements

There is no single international women's movement, nor such a thing as global feminism. Although women's movements have proliferated the world over, they differ across and between nations on the grounds of race, class, ethnicity, geopolitical location, and of course ideological orientation. However, there is no doubt that from the plurality of women's movements it makes sense to talk of 'women's movements' as national and international actors articulating new political and economic agendas based upon critiques of inequities in gender power relations.

Women's movements project a vision of a new social order which is more radical than the social change projects of other 'new' social movements globally, in that the gender equality which feminists propose would fundamentally change current approaches to social organisation. The condemnation of inequalities in relations between the sexes is a radical challenge to social relations which are still often seen as a matter of nature, not human choice and social design, not matters for politics. It is important, however, not to assume that all movements organised by women autonomously from male-dominated organisations are based upon a critique of gender relations; upon what could very broadly be described as a feminist social analysis. Many forms of women's activism are organised around struggles for democracy, national self-determination, environmental protection and human rights. Some women's movements such as religious fundamentalist and right-wing groups take a decidedly conservative perspective on gender relations, seeking to preserve, rather than challenge or change, unequal relations between women and men. This chapter, however, is concerned with women's movements which pursue justice in gender relations, and in particular, which propose alternative perspectives on economic development to challenge the Washington consensus on neoliberal economic policies.

Unorthodox organisational forms and tactics characterise women's civil society associations and their political struggles. This is because of structural constraints on women's activism which are caused by gender divisions of labour and power. These constraints include women's limited time for political activism because of their double duty of work in productive and reproductive arenas, and women's lack of financial and social resources and political experience. Women's movements rarely possess capacities to impose sanctions for failure to respect gender equity agendas or laws. Women's subordination to men means that they may have weak 'fallback' positions to retreat to as a threat in negotiations. They tend to lack independent sources of income and social support, and their physical subordination to men makes it difficult to effect a 'strike' from performing domestic and sexual duties.[5] More crucially, relations between the sexes in the family tend to be regarded as matters of cooperative and affective or loving values which are much less open to bargaining and compulsion than other forms of social relations, such as those between classes, or workers and employers. As a result, when it comes to challenging inequities in gender relations, women's movements employ complex, subtle, and sometimes very low-profile tactics which aim to reshape gender identities, methods of socialising children and cultural expectations in male–female interactions.

These structural features of many women's movements – low political leverage and loose organisational forms – affects their terms of engagement with multilateral economic institutions. As will be shown, they must seek constructive engagement and 'entry' into institutional processes and cognitive frameworks, rather than employing more overtly political tactics of capturing the resources and undermining the public image of such institutions in the way the environmental movement has been able to do (see chapter 4). Women's movements simply, to date, lack the collective power for such tactics. Above all, they tend to lack a broad base of public sympathy – or a broad constituency – because the challenge to 'natural' gender relations is experienced as deeply threatening in all societies, and because feminist politics are assumed to be the concern of a very small, elite and unrepresentative group of women.

Pursuing women's interests in the international arena

Multilateral organisations concerned with global governance, peace-keeping and human rights have proven important arenas in which women have been able to legitimise their rights claims and develop

---

[5] The 'strike' tactic has been attempted, though, for example the women's 'strike for peace' across the USA in the mid-1960s in protest at fallout from atmospheric testing of nuclear weapons. This spread to Canada and Europe, with national chapters of the Women's International League for Peace and Freedom providing a networking function in an early example of transnational women's activism. See Boulding (1993: 13) for a description.

transnational networks. Indeed, women's movements have had much more success in securing recognition (although not enforcement) of their rights in the UN's social institutions than in multilateral economic institutions. This owes in part to the differing cognitive frameworks and official ideologies of the different institutions. International organisations set up to enhance cross-national dialogue espouse values of tolerance and respect for human rights which women's movements can call upon when seeking equal respect for women's concerns. In contrast, multilateral economic institutions monitoring and supporting stability in national budgets, such as the World Bank and the IMF, or promoting the interests of transnational capital, such as the WTO, are governed by a set of values drawn from neoliberal economics, within which women's concerns with social justice can sometimes be seen as attempts to impose market distortions.

The four UN Conferences on Women (Mexico, 1975; Copenhagen, 1980; Nairobi, 1985; Beijing, 1995) have acted as great catalysts to the development of women's organisations and movements nationally and internationally. At each conference a parallel forum for NGOs was set up, at which the numbers of women participating multiplied over the years. There were 6,000 women representing NGOs at the Mexico City conference in 1975, and 23,000 twenty years later at the Beijing conference, with thousands more women registered but unable to attend owing to China's anxiety over the huge influx of visitors, its inadequate facilities and its outright obstruction of women's efforts to obtain visas.

The high profile of the UN conferences has encouraged a tendency to assume that women's movements are products of modernisation and development, animated primarily by middle-class urban women, and inspired by Western feminism. These conferences certainly helped to consolidate women's movements in many countries as they prepared for participation in NGO fora or as they lobbied their governments. But suggestions that women's movements are products of 'modernisation' and globalisation have been rejected by women in developing countries, who point to extensive pre-colonial histories of women's activism, and show that the bulk of women's associational energies in their countries is rooted in the concerns of rural women and of working-class urban women, not in the concerns of urban elites.

The notion that women's activism globally is inspired by Western liberal feminism has also been deeply resented and has triggered profound convulsions and divisions in international women's movements (Mohanty 1991). Women in developing countries, as well as poor women and women of colour in industrialised countries, have charged Western liberal feminists with ignoring differences of class and race between women; differences which generate profound inequalities between women, let alone between women and men. For example a statement from the Association of African Women for Research and Development (AAWORD), an international organisation established in 1976, argues: 'While patriarchal views and structures oppress women all over the world, women are also members of classes and countries that dominate others and enjoy privileges in terms of access to resources. Hence, contrary to the best intentions of 'sisterhood', not all women share identical interests' (AAWORD: 1992).

The painful debates between First and Third World feminists have had a fruitful outcome: they triggered the articulation of a new gendered political economy by socialist feminists and feminists in the South, a fundamental critique of economic development which now animates the position of many women's movements in relation to multilateral economic institutions.

Women's movements and alternative economics

Until recently, economic development policy has been a policy arena fairly closed to feminist critiques, with its technical language and its impervious international institutions maintaining high entrance barriers to the participation of women (let alone feminists). Western feminist critiques of economic development processes initially did not challenge the conceptual framework of economics; rather, the 'Women in Development' (WID) critique which developed out of the work of feminist development practitioners in Northern bilaterals in the early 1970s saw the problem as the exclusion of women from access to new development resources and opportunities (Tinker 1990).

A rather different critique of the development process itself (as opposed to women's apparent exclusion from it) had been emerging from feminist anthropologists, and socialist feminists, including women in developing countries, often developing out of critiques of colonial exploitation, post-colonial neo-imperialism, and consequent dependency. This critique was expanded by a new international network of women researchers from the economic South: Development Alternatives with Women for a New Era (DAWN), founded in

1984 on the eve of the NGO and official conferences marking the end of the UN Decade for Women. Their starting point was to establish that the problem of women's disprivilege was not caused by exclusion from the development process, but by their inclusion in a process which relies upon gendered divisions of labour and power (as well as systems of class and national inequality) to fuel processes of growth (Sen and Grown 1987). As Peggy Antrobus, one of DAWN's General Coordinators, noted with reference to current neoliberal economic development policies: 'The problem with structural adjustment policies is not that they assume women are outside of development and need to be brought in, but that they are actually grounded in a gender ideology which is deeply and fundamentally exploitative of women's time, work, and sexuality' (Antrobus 1988).[6]

Feminist critiques of economic development have proceeded from this point, exposing the unacknowledged assumptions made in economic theory about the low or zero value of women's labour. Economists such as Diane Elson (1991), Gita Sen (Sen and Grown 1987), and Nancy Folbre (1986) have elaborated principles of feminist economics which begin from new perspectives on household economic behaviour to endow women's work with value in spite of being unpaid, and which recognise that relations of power between women and men (and people of different age groups or life-cycle stages) within the household mean that members of households do not share equally in economic opportunities and wealth. This critique is a strong challenge to assumptions made by economic planners because it demonstrates that people will not respond to economic or market signals in a 'free', rational way unencumbered by social relations. The fact that gender relations ascribe female labour to domestic tasks means that this female labour is immobilised in activities which are not responsive to market signals. Thus price signals, so key to neoliberal economic planning, will not necessarily change the way a household allocates its labour. The non-attribution of economic value or cost to household work leads planners mistakenly to assume that women's time has a zero opportunity cost, and that women can therefore be called upon to expand their labour input to paid production or voluntary community activity with no negative impact on human reproductive activity – on the well-being of children, for example, or on the stability of the household.

---

[6] Also cited in Dayal and Mukhopadhyay (1995).

In the context of the structural adjustment policies promoted by the World Bank and IMF since the late 1970s, these feminist economic principles explain the unequal impact of economic reform on women and men. Adjustment policies have sought to stabilise economies and reduce balance of payments deficits by devaluing the currency, reducing government expenditures, increasing interest rates and controlling credit expansion, reducing the role of the state, privatising national industries, liberalising markets and removing government subsidies and minimum wages. A measure which has an immediate impact on women is the reduction of state expenditures on social services, with women expected to expand their domestic responsibilities to compensate for decreasing state investment in children's education or health. The introduction of charges to recover costs of social services can exacerbate gender biases in household decisions about which children to educate or bring to the clinic, with girls often losing out. In some cultures, gendered expectations about appropriate responsibilities for the sexes can mean that it is women's incomes which are expected to cover social service costs, not men's.[7] In effect, women are expected to bear the 'invisible' costs of adjustment:

> there is the risk that what is perceived in conventional economic analysis as efficiency improvements may in fact be a shift in costs from the visible (predominantly male) to the invisible (predominantly female) economy ... Gender bias (or 'neutrality') in the underlying concepts and tools of economics has led to invisibility of women's economic and non-economic work and to an incomplete picture of total economic activity.   (World Bank 1994e)

However, it is the positive growth programme proposed in neoliberal economic reform policies which have had more profoundly negative impacts upon women's well-being and household survival. Adjustment measures in productive sectors aim to encourage production for the market and for export. Price signals sent out by liberalised markets encourage this shift. But the capacity of producers to respond to these signals is affected by gender relations. Women's labour may be subject to the control of men, and in addition, their unequal rights and obligations mean they have differential access to and control over economically productive resources (such as land, labour, credit, extension services, transport infrastructure). In many

---

[7] This problem is discussed in the context of poverty in Uganda in Goetz, Maxwell and Maniyire (1994).

parts of Sub-Saharan Africa, where women dominate agricultural production, these constraints have led to a much lower response than expected to economic incentives – what has become known as the lack of a 'supply response' to the signals of increased 'demand' sent out by liberalised markets.[8] Alternatively, men have demanded increased inputs of women's labour on crops sold for cash and export, which has detracted from women's investment in food crops, undermining the food security of their families (Floro 1994; World Bank 1990). Some of the consequences of the strains which economic reform has put on women's time are becoming evident in family breakdown and increasing female household headship in urban areas of Latin America and Asia (Dayal and Mukhopadhyay 1995: 18), in women's deteriorating health and in girls' withdrawal from school to support mothers with household work (Sparr 1994).

A large number of women's development associations have taken up these issues, expressed variously through grass-roots struggles to defend women's economic rights or through national, regional, and international networks of researchers and activists articulating increasingly sophisticated analysis of economic policy. Just a few examples of regional networks besides DAWN include the African Women's Economic Policy Network (AWEPON), which critiques structural adjustment policies in Sub-Saharan Africa, and Women in Development Europe (WIDE), a network of feminist activists from research institutions and European non-governmental development organisations (NGDOs) which is analysing European Union trade policies from a gender perspective. The New York-based Women's Environment and Development Organization (WEDO) has developed extensive networks on gender and environment- development issues.

It is striking, however, that effective *global* coalitions of feminist economic development associations are much less developed than global coalitions promoting other gender issues, such as women's rights as human rights (the International Women's Rights Action Watch, the Asia-Pacific Forum on Women, Law and Development, Women in Law and Development in Africa, and the Latin American Committee for the Defence of Women's Rights) (Thompson 1997) and

[8] A World Bank discussion of this problem in terms of the 'missed' economic potential of women, whose productivity could be tapped for economic growth, is provided in Saito (1992).

women's reproductive rights (FINNRAGE, Women's Reproductive Health Coalition). This has had consequences for the nature and success of efforts by women's movements to challenge multilateral economic institutions.

A nascent feminist economic rights coalition does exist called the Women's Global Alliance for Development Alternatives. It is developing a holistic feminist critique of macroeconomic and trade policies, but it has some problems as a lobbying system which stem from some of the tensions in cross-national feminist activism mentioned in the previous section. The coalition has no structure, no secretariat, no address; just a mailing list linking about ten networks of women's associations which has at its core the strong regional networks provided by DAWN, WEDO, and WIDE.[9] It has developed in response to the need to have, to some degree, a united voice at UN conferences, and has come together in an *ad hoc* way, starting with DAWN/WEDO collaboration at the 1992 Rio Conference. Its greatest success was to create a platform for the feminist critique of economic austerity programmes at the Social Summit in Copenhagen in 1994. It coordinated feminist economic analyses to feed into national positions for the Beijing conference (particularly at the ECE preparatory conference for Beijing), and was a key actor at the Economic Justice NGO linkage caucus at Beijing which fed NGO perspectives to official conference participants.

However, the Alliance has been primarily reactive rather than proactive in setting an agenda for global change from the perspective of women's movements. There are several reasons for this. Like women's associations everywhere, it lacks resources, and this undermines effective communications with the extended web of women's groups which form its membership base. It is in debate internally

---

[9] The other networks comprise two from the USA: Alternative Women in Development (Alt-WID, a Washington-based network for women activists in development organisations), and the Center for Women's Global Leadership (a research, training, and advocacy group); two from Canada: the National Action Committee (representing 730 women's groups), and the Canadian Research Institute for the Advancement of Women (with 700 individual members from NGOs and research institutions), and several organisations which are neither dominated by women nor solely concerned with gender issues: Eurostep (European Solidarity towards Equal Participation of People), which coordinates the lobbying activities of twenty-one European non-denominational NGOs, and the Society for International Development (SID), a group of institutions and individuals concerned with development, involving 6,000 members in 115 countries.

about whether its members, North and South, have a common agenda and critique around economic reform, or whether it is instead a solidarity network to support its members from the South. This issue has been put on the table by Alt-WID, a US-based network of Women in Development activists, and also by women of the South. As one member of this Alliance said: 'the Southern members of the Alliance are not convinced that they need to be in a global alliance. We know that it is our countries which are taking the damaging decisions and we take responsibility for changing our own governments.'[10] There has been a challenge to acknowledge the complicity of women in the North in the sufferings of women in the South, for instance where the preservation of women's consumption standards and employment in the North results in environmental damage or loss of women's labour rights in the South. This tension points to the main problem in developing a shared global perspective amongst women's movements on economic change. The fact is that the economic interests of women in the South can directly conflict with those of women in the North. Cheap female labour in the South can draw jobs away from women in the North, for example.

Although all global women's coalitions must confront North–South power differences between women, the conflicts of economic interest which, though surmountable, challenge the coherence of the Alliance, demonstrate the particular challenges to cross-national coalitions on economic justice issues. Conflicts of interest of this sort do not muddy many of the other issues over which women have come together cross-culturally. For example, the great success of global women's movements to date has been politicising violence against women as a crime and a human rights violation. This is an issue which unites women across a vast ideological spectrum, and where gains in the physical security and human rights of particular groups of women are seen as gains for all, not as potentially detracting from the opportunities of others.

A recent initiative has sought to galvanise women's movements globally into scrutinising the impact of the World Bank's policies on women and monitoring the process of institutionalising gender equity concerns to the Bank's structure. The 'Women's Eyes on the Bank' campaign was launched at the Beijing conference with a petition

---

[10] Interview, NGO, Washington DC, 9 September 1997. Interviews were conducted on a non-attributable basis and hence no names will be furnished here.

signed by 900 activists, which was presented to the World Bank's President Wolfensohn. The petition called on the Bank to implement fully the Beijing Platform for Action and to expand NGO involvement in Bank activities. There were four specific demands:

- to increase the participation of grass-roots women in economic policy making;
- to institutionalise a gender perspective in the design and implementation of Banks' policies and programmes;
- to increase the Bank's investments that reach women, particularly in basic education, health, and credit programmes;
- to increase the number and diversity of senior women at the bank.

The campaign represents a sea-change amongst women's movements, because it is based on a perspective which, though challenging the Bank's policies, also sees it as a potential ally in dialogues between women's groups and their own governments. The campaign has had some success in triggering a response from the Bank, particularly since it is building on internal changes already underway to promote gender equity concerns in the Bank's work, as will be shown below.

Bank insiders say that the size of this response reflected Wolfensohn's impression that a coherent and massive global women's movement was pressing these demands. This speaks to the value of civil society efforts to develop a united front on economic reform issues, however difficult it may be to establish or maintain.

Gender issues in the Bank's work

It has been extremely difficult for women's movements to gain direct access to the Bank. Its Washington offices are inaccessible to most women's associations around the world unless they are represented by powerful Washington-based NGOs with an established relationship with the Bank. The Bank's economistic policy language is highly technical and can seem deliberately arcane and indecipherable to many women critics. In any case, its policy documents such as the important Country Assistance Strategy papers have been, until very recently, inaccessible to readers in civil society, protected by a comprehensive embargo on outside scrutiny. Above all, the Bank does not recognise women's movements as legitimate interlocutors in economic policy making; until very recently its policy dialogue process has been conducted exclusively between the Bank and the borrowing country.

The Bank has been markedly slow in its response to the concerns of women's movements. Most development agencies such as bilaterals and regional development banks were spurred into an institutional and policy response to the gender issue by the series of UN Conferences on Women. Most began putting in place institutional infrastructure to house Women in Development concerns after the Mexico City conference in 1975. Most had a policy directive to promote gender equity in development planning by the end-of-decade conference in Nairobi; those which did not issued policy statements shortly afterwards. At the World Bank, although the idea of developing a gender equity policy statement was first mooted in 1975, a Policy Paper: *Enhancing Women's Involvement in Economic Development*, was not issued until 1994.

In the mid-1970s, the Bank was criticised by women's movements for failing to include women in its development projects. And indeed, from FY 67 to FY 86 only 7 per cent of Bank projects included 'gender-related activities' (World Bank 1994f: 37). These activities formed a relatively small part of project objectives, and were also hardly oriented towards achieving gender equity; they tended merely to target women's reproductive roles, often just by providing contraceptives in family planning projects (World Bank 1994f: 37). Since FY 86 there has been a greater proportion of Bank projects with 'gender-related actions'; up to almost 30 per cent of Bank operations in 1995, although as we will see, women's groups question the quality of these actions. During the 1980s, the focus of critiques by women's movements shifted to a condemnation of the negative impact of Bank structural adjustment measures on women's livelihoods and on gender relations. Feminist critics charged that the Bank ignores gender issues in its important Economic and Sector Work (ESW) which includes the Bank's macroeconomic policy analysis and its research on development sectors such as finance, industry, agriculture, and infrastructure, as well as cross-cutting concerns such as poverty and the environment (Women's Eyes on the World Bank 1997).

Institutionally, the Bank has found it difficult to find a home for the gender equity concern. A lone woman advisor on Women in Development was appointed in 1977, who, lacking resources to develop policy or to monitor gender equity concerns in Bank projects, focused on defending the Bank's work to outside critics (Kardam 1991: 77). There was certainly no question of endowing this position with powers of influence over the Bank's work – such as a veto over inappropriate policies. This problem of inadequate resources for the gender equity concern within the Bank, and a lack of effective powers over Bank policies and processes, has plagued subsequent efforts to 'mainstream' a Women in Development focus in the Bank's work (Kardam 1991; Razavi and Miller 1995). In 1986, a three-person WID office was established, and the following year placed within the Population and Human Resources Department. By 1988 the WID office had become a division with eight staff. In 1990 each region was given funding to establish a full-time WID Coordinator post. This was an important step towards bringing WID issues into the operational part of the Bank, but rather pales in comparison to the expansion occurring simultaneously in another area related to the quality of Bank loans: the environment. Between 1983 and 1987 professional staff assigned to monitor environmental concerns multiplied from six to sixty; there were environmental divisions in the regional departments, and a full department for the environment in the technical support services of the Bank (Rich 1994).

In the 1990s, particularly since the UN Conference on Women in Beijing, the pace of change and enhanced commitment to gender equity concerns at the Bank has been accelerating. In 1993 after a Bank-wide reorganisation, a Gender Analysis and Policy (GAP) thematic group was set up in the Education and Social Policy Department of the new vice-presidency for Human Resources Development and Operations Policy. In 1995, the Bank's new president, James Wolfensohn, attended the Beijing conference, the first time a World Bank president had done so. The nature of his participation, in which he consulted with women's civil society groups at the NGO linkage Caucus on Economic Justice, and accepted a petition from the Women's Eyes on the Bank Campaign for policy reform at the Bank, signalled an important new opening to global women's movements. Wolfensohn, who is noted for his concern with the social impact of economic reform, responded to the Women's Eyes on the Bank campaign by setting up an External Gender Consultative Group (EGCG) composed of fourteen women who are members of women's movements around the world. Top management at the Bank has consulted with this group on an annual basis since Beijing. In spite of tremendous obstacles to regular communication among members, or to the development of a common strategy or set of concerns, the

EGCG has taken steps in areas which are relatively new for the feminist critique of the Bank. For instance, it has pressed the Bank to apply its principles on gender equity to its work in private sector development. Wolfensohn also demanded regional gender action plans of all Bank regional operations (most had been completed by mid-1997), asked the Bank to produce annual reports on progress in addressing gender issues in development, launched gender flagship projects,[11] and included gender equity in the institutional change process at the Bank which is intended to produce a new mission for the Bank based on fostering social as well as economic development. As part of a general effort to open up civil society participation in the design and implementation of some programmes, a commitment has been made to consult women in the Bank's economic and sector work, particularly the Country Assistance Strategy process.

In 1997, after yet another massive reorganisation, a Gender Sector Board was set up in one of the four new Technical Networks which represent restructured thematic support services to country-level operations. The Gender Sector Board is intended to operate as a family of gender specialists across the Bank, anchored by a core group in the Poverty Reduction and Economic Management Technical Network, whose other concerns include public sector management and poverty.[12] Locating the gender equity interest in this Technical Network is a coup for the internal Bank gender advocates who lobbied for this. It signals that gender equity is not considered a 'soft' sector issue related mainly to reproductive concerns. However, there has been no change to the fact that the gender unit at the Bank has little command over the incentive system and cannot therefore enforce compliance with gender equity goals in Bank lending. Indeed, outside observers suggest that the new system may make it even more difficult to impose a whole range of quality-related concerns on Bank project design, including social assessments, poverty reduction and participation. The new system is demand-driven, which means that

---

[11] These are sectoral investment programmes which are intended to be particularly productive in terms of enhancing women's or girls' development, such as the Tanzania Girls' Secondary Education Support Project, or the Zimbabwe Health Sector Projects.

[12] The other three Technical Networks are: Human Development (population, health, nutrition, education); Private Sector and Infrastructure (small and medium-sized businesses, banking and capital markets, telecoms, transportation, sanitation, energy); Environment, Rural and Social Development (participation, NGOs and post-conflict work).

gender specialists will have to rely upon project designers, or 'task team managers' in country departments, to call upon their services, but these managers will be under no strict obligation to do so (Bread for the World Institute 1996: 20). This puts the onus on gender specialists to 'sell' their services in ways which will attract project designers – and in a neoliberal economic environment this means stressing the business case for gender equity, not the social justice case, which has tended to be the stronger suit of gender advocates.

On the surface, the Bank appears to have taken gender equity concerns seriously. Many feminist critics, however, are sceptical about the Bank's commitment to these measures. A post-Beijing assessment of gender equity at the World Bank by the US chapter of the Women's Eyes on the Bank campaign lists a range of shortcomings in the Bank's approach to gender equity concerns. It charges that the Bank's 1994 gender policy is not actionable, because 'Bank gender initiatives have yet to translate into concrete actions that address gender inequalities and break down gender barriers in a majority of its policies' (Women's Eyes on the World Bank 1997: 2). It charges that the Bank has failed to recognise gender-specific constraints on the participation of women from civil society in Bank policy dialogues, pointing out that it makes no allowance for the greater time needed for 'partici-pation' where vast differences of power exist and where women's groups may be unfamiliar with economic planning languages. What is more, the Bank is accused of disingenuousness, of claiming credit for a greater degree of sensitivity to gender issues than it actually reflects in practice. For example, the Bank is satisfied that its economic and sector work addresses gender issues when its documents merely make mention of women or gender, rather than incorporate a gender-sensitive perspective into economic analyses. For instance, a Country Assistance Strategy for Indonesia was cited by the Bank as addressing gender issues, on the rather shallow basis that it mentions 'women' three times and 'gender' once, yet lacks either a gender analysis or strategies to address gender inequalities. The same problem applies to projects which are said to contain 'gender-related actions'; by and large, these actions do not challenge inequities in gender relations (Women's Eyes on the World Bank 1997: 3). The Bank is charged with persistently refusing to entertain a gendered critique of its macroeconomic policy framework; and with failing to alter its approach to structural adjustment to minimise its negative impact on poor women. The Bank has been described as 'conspicuously noncommittal' in response to pressure from the External Gender Consultative Group to bring gender issues into its more commercial arms, the IFC and MIGA, described by Wolfensohn as 'a much harder nut to crack' than the IDA (Women's Environment and Development Organization 1997: 14).

The Bank's opening to consultation with women's movements through the External Gender Consultative Group has also attracted criticism. The legitimacy of the EGCG is challenged by some women's groups on the grounds that as a body it is neither representative nor accountable – a very similar criticism as that levelled by many NGOs at the NGO–World Bank Committee when it was set up in 1982. Neither the criteria for nor process of selecting members was transparent, with only a narrow stratum of women's groups consulted for advice on suitable candidates. Very few of the fourteen members come from associations involved in day-to-day Bank monitoring and some are therefore not sufficiently familiar with Bank procedures to provide the kind of recommendations and advice which could result in real changes in the Bank. It has no resources and no clear mandate, nor are members certain about their expected term of tenure in the group. Not all members have extensive links with women's movements. It was not until June 1998 that a secretariat for the EGCG was created (based at the NGO Tools for Transition in Netherlands), with funds from the World Bank. The Women's Eyes on the Bank campaign has questioned the group's legitimacy, particularly as it is assumed to represent global women's movements. It has been described by one feminist activist in Washington DC as 'just a bone which Wolfensohn threw them [women's movements]',[13] and by a gender advocate within the Bank as 'Bank defined, managed, and implemented. Low-level and low-brow [...] and handled like a damage limitation measure'.[14]

Some of these criticisms have hit home. In mid-1998 the Bank announced that it was about to undertake a policy review report on gender for the first time, to be finalised in December 1999. This kind of review is intended to be a state-of-the-art assessment of the subject area as well as a Bank position statement. The Bank has invited broad civil society participation in this review, a process launched by an *ad hoc* working group of representatives from civil society and the

[13] Interview, NGO, Washington DC, 9 September 1997.
[14] Interview, World Bank, Washington DC, 11 September 1997.

Bank convened in mid-1998 by the EGCG. The Bank also announced that it would finally dedicate one of its important annual *World Development Reports* (*WDR*) to gender. These very broadly distributed annual reports establish a snapshot of current thinking on important development issues and themes, and are influential in shaping the dominant development discourse. A *WDR* on gender is badly overdue, and many felt one should have been produced for the 1995 UN Conference in Beijing. Instead, it is to be produced in 2004, as a contribution to the 2005 Fifth UN Conference on Women.

However promising recent developments may seem, the gender equity issue has had a troubled time at the Bank. In order to explain this it is important to understand aspects of the Bank's cognitive framework and its power structure. The Bank's cognitive framework affects the ways new development concerns like gender equity have been entertained by its staff, and determines the arguments used by external critics to plead their case. Its power structure affects its sensitivity to external critique and determines lines of entry or attack by outsiders.

The World Bank's cognitive framework: the 'business case for gender equity'

The Bank's cognitive universe – its framework for understanding human behaviour – is neoclassical economics. As the political scientist Yusuf Bangura notes: 'Perhaps the greatest barrier to the institutionalisation of gendered development is the inflexible nature of the dominant neo-liberal discourse [...] wide gaps exist between the fundamental premises, values and goals of neo-liberalism and the broad gender discourse' (Bangura 1997: 20).

The two policy discourses could not be more different. Neoliberal economics pitches its analyses at the level of the macro economy, whereas feminist economics begins in the microeconomics and politics of decision making between women and men in the household. The driving concern of neoliberal economics is to improve market efficiency, which, optimally, will lead to fairness in the allocation of resources and rewards. To create market efficiency, measures such as limited state intervention, private ownership of assets, trade liberalisation, and unregulated competition are encouraged. In contrast, the driving concern of feminist economics is gender justice, righting the wrongs experienced by women because of their sex, including the

47

derogation of the value of their work, the limits on their rights to property ownership, unequal access to education, employment, or positions of public power, and even the denial of women's rights to control their bodies and sexuality. This approach relies upon interventions to assign value to women's work and to mitigate distortions caused by gendered ideologies in institutions such as households, markets and state bureaucracies. There is some premium on the interventionist role of the state as an agent to challenge some of the tyrannies of private-sphere patriarchy. Neoliberal economists base their predictions of people's responses to economic signals on assumptions about the rationality of individuals keen to maximise personal advantage, with society simply the aggregate of these choices. Feminist economists are trying to find ways of working the politics of gender relations into economics so as to acknowledge the constraints on individual choices created by social structure, belief systems and ideologies.[15]

In interactions between gender equity advocates and the Bank, the terms of discourse are set by the Bank, as the more powerful interlocutor, obliging feminist critics to work within the framework of the neoliberal concern with efficiency. At the May 1997 meeting between the Bank and the EGCG, Minh Chau Nguyen, the acting head of the Bank's Gender Sector Board, described this as putting the onus on gender equity advocates to 'make the business case for gender and sell it to staff' (World Bank 1997b: 4). At this same meeting, phrases such as 'the business case for gender', as well as 'the economic rationale for investing in gender' were reiterated frequently by a series of senior Bank managers, including the president. This is nothing new, and gender equity advocates have become adept at demonstrating women's productive efficiency, which has resulted in a highly instrumental perspective on women's contribution to development, rather than the contribution of development to women's empowerment.

The case for the efficacy of investing in women has been made most effectively in the arena of human capital development. Research has demonstrated higher social pay-offs (or 'social externalities') to investing in women's rather than men's health and education; the results are lower fertility rates, higher life expectancy, better nutrition

---

[15] This comparison of the two approaches to economic analysis is summarised from Bangura (1997: 20–1).

levels and overall education levels. This evidence has persuaded the Bank to increase its investments in girls' education and women's health. Over the last twenty-five years, of the 615 Bank projects (out of 5,000) which included 'gender-related components',[16] 46 per cent were in the health, population and education sectors (Alexander 1996: 5; also ODA/ICRW 1995). These are relatively non-controversial areas in which to invest; they support women's reproductive roles[17] and do not overtly challenge gender roles. As an independent assessment of the Bank's record on gender equity explains, 'Development thinking has more easily embraced women's reproductive roles because ... an emphasis on motherhood validates widely held beliefs about women's role in society' (Razavi and Miller 1995: 2).

Gender equity advocates have had much less success in challenging the framework of the Bank's economic and sector work. Gender equity concerns have tended to receive scant mention in investment strategies for 'hard' sectors like agricultural or industrial planning, or industry, energy and transport which absorb the bulk of Bank sectoral loans, where women's differential resources and options as producers and homemakers are ignored.[18] Gender equity concerns do not even penetrate very deeply into the Bank's work on poverty reduction; its country-specific Poverty Assessments (PAs) by and large fail to disaggregate the experience of poverty by gender.[19] The important exception is the Bank's new programme of loans and grants to institutions offering micro-credit to the very poor: the Consultative Group to Assist the Poorest (C-GAP). The majority of borrowers in

[16] By the Bank's own admission, the rating system which identifies projects as having 'gender-related components' is insensitive to the quality and 'depth' of those components, not differentiating between whether the project addresses gender equity issues in a substantive or superficial way. See the Bank's two progress reports to date (World Bank 1996a, 1997c). Note that for all regions except for the Middle East, over half of these 'gender-related' projects were approved only very recently, between 1989 and 1993. Before then, 'gender-related components' in Bank projects were very scarce. The Bank's Operations and Evaluations Division estimated that between FY 79 and FY 84, the height of the UN Decade for Women, only 7 per cent of the investment portfolio could be said to relate to gender equity concerns (World Bank 1994g).

[17] Quite literally. The bulk of the Bank's early research on women was preoccupied with establishing the determinants of fertility, underlining the strong association between women and biological reproduction. See Razavi and Miller (1995: 35).

[18] 'Hard' sector loans totalled $18 billion in 1995 compared with $4 billion loaned to the social sectors (Alexander 1996: 7).

[19] Important exceptions are the PAs for Cameroon, Kenya, and Uganda. See the study of the World Bank's Poverty Assessments in IDS (1994).

many of these micro-credit programmes are women. Investing in women's access to micro-credit coheres comfortably with efficiency and poverty-reduction agendas without raising issues of social change because of the very individualised and home-based nature of micro-enterprise activities.

Two problems hold back the potential impact of the feminist critique on the Bank's economic and sectoral work. The most fundamental is the clash in the two cognitive frameworks. Forced to make the business case for investing in women's economic productivity, the feminist case has floundered somewhat. It is perfectly plausible to argue that women's productivity could be increased tremendously by enhancing women's human capital endowments and rights to factors of production and inputs (Saito 1992). Indeed, the Bank is prepared to support the project of 'investing in and releasing the economic potential of women' to enhance their contribution to economic development.[20] But this argument seems to be suggesting that gender inequalities would be eradicated if market imperfections were removed, and ignores the persistence of gendered power inequities which can keep women from controlling the fruits of their increased productivity. In addition, any increase in women's productivity in income-generating work represents a loss of their time for work within the home. In a policy environment which refuses to legitimate or to finance the costs of compensating for the loss of women's investment household reproduction, women will be expected to work harder in 'productive' and 'reproductive' arenas, depleting their productivity in both. Thus the arguments sometimes offered by gender equity advocates that 'investing in women's productivity is economically efficient', or that 'economic growth requires women's participation' are a little unconvincing.[21] One does not have to be a great cynic to note that economic growth in the West took place without rewarding women's participation, and indeed, probably profited from the unpaid subsidy provided by women's work.

The second problem has to do with the ethics and ideologies

---

[20] The quoted phrase is the subtitle of a special Bank memorandum for the Fourth UN Conference on Women (World Bank 1994d).

[21] Although research by the Bank and others has convincingly demonstrated the high returns to investing in women's education and health, according to the Bank, efforts to show that countries which invested heavily in women experienced more rapid economic growth has not been done in a 'rigorous and convincing' manner (Razavi and Miller 1995: 73).

surrounding judgements about what is 'unfair' in gender relations. Gender relations are seen as cultural matters, and the condemnation of inequities in gender relations is assumed to reflect a narrow, highly ideological, Western feminist perspective. The Bank therefore demurs on assessing justice in gender relations because this is seen as cultural interference. Its Operational Directive to all staff to integrate gender equity concerns into their work carries an important let-out clause: staff are enjoined to pay 'due regard to cultural sensitivity' (World Bank 1994c). No similar delicacy is expected of staff when dealing with other subjects which can interfere with cultural matters, such as population policy, privatisation, poverty reduction measures, policies to educate girls and so on. Nor does the Bank acknowledge the highly ideological nature of its own cognitive framework. As William Claussen, Bank president from 1981 to 1986, said: 'the Bank is not a political organisation, the only altar we worship at is pragmatic economics' (Razavi and Miller 1995: 31).

Power systems at the World Bank: few points of access or influence

As noted at the beginning of this chapter, the Executive Board is locus of formal decision making at the Bank, and as such it has been a very important channel for the expression of the concerns of global women's movements, depending on their success at lobbying certain member country governments. Nordic governments have been particularly critical in introducing 'social conscience' themes to the Bank, including poverty reduction, social sector lending, debt management reform, and gender equity, even though they have a weak position on the Executive Board in terms of their voting power. The UK, Canada, and the Netherlands have also been particularly sympathetic on gender equity matters. It was criticism from the Executive Board that triggered renewed efforts in the Bank in 1990 to institutionalise the gender and development interest.

In 1994, when the Bank presented its first full Policy Paper on gender to the Board, some Executive Directors again pressed the Bank to push its analysis further, particularly in terms of investigating the feminist critique of its macroeconomic work. According to the minutes of the 14 April Board meeting, the Executive Directors for Germany, the UK, and the Netherlands expressed surprise and concern that the gender differential effects of macroeconomic

measures such as structural adjustment loans had not been mentioned, and urged the Bank to address this. In a written statement, the
Dutch Executive Director quoted the reaction of the UK Executive
Director to the policy paper: 'It portrays gender in terms of a series of
special problems to be addressed through specific interventions,
rather than a social relation which underlies and needs to be
addressed in all Bank operations, policy dialogue, and ESW' (Herfkens 1994: 1).

Not all Executive Board members represent this kind of constructive
lobbying resource for the feminist case in macroeconomic planning.
Some Executive Directors find even the Bank's cautious approach to
gender equity issues to be too radical; at the same 1994 meeting, the
Executive Director for Korea asked that the policy paper be 'toned
down', and both he and the Executive Director for Saudi Arabia
implied that an interest in reducing gender disparities was a Western
concern which violated their countries' cultural sensitivities. This
familiar 'cultural' objection to gender equity concerns gives the Bank a
defence for its caution on the gender issue. Ambivalence from some
Executive Directors over gender equity issues reflects either the
weakness of domestic women's movements in influencing their
governments, or it can reflect a lack of democracy in state–civil society
relationships, which may be obstructing the expression of women's
interests in national politics. This makes it important for women's
movements to have access to international NGOs that can represent
their views to the World Bank, an issue to which we return in a
moment.

Women's movements have not attempted the most powerful
lobbying manoeuvre in relation to the governance and financing of
the World Bank, which is to lobby the more wealthy countries'
Treasuries to withhold replenishment funding for the IDA in the way
the environmental movement has done. Women's movements tend to
have a much narrower base of support than environmental movements and hence cannot exercise the same degree of political leverage.
Most importantly, the gender and development concern has not been
taken up by the US women's movement in a strong enough way to
support an assault on the Bank's funds through Congress. The US
environmental movement was central to the success of campaigns by
global environmental movements because it is well resourced, has a
wide base of domestic support and is familiar with the legislative and
lobbying dynamic in Washington. But in the case of the US women's

movement, even though it is the largest and most powerful women's movement in the world, its focus is squarely domestic, not international. It has not put its weight and political resources behind gender and development concerns. In addition, there is a great reluctance to tamper with US government funds for development since most women's groups in the USA which are involved in development issues rely heavily upon USAID for funds, and have no wish to threaten its Congress allocation, something which could occur as a side-effect of challenging the quality of World Bank spending of Congress allocations.

Beyond the Executive Board, as noted earlier, the Bank's president and top management have considerable autonomy in determining the Bank's policy directions. A 1994 evaluation of gender at the Bank by its Operations Evaluation Department found that although outside pressure and internal advocates were catalysts for change, it was the leadership of senior management at the Bank which most affected the amount of funds devoted to gender equity and its credibility in the organisation (World Bank 1994g).

In this respect President Wolfensohn is regarded by gender equity advocates both within and outside the Bank as a tremendous positive resource for change. One internal gender specialist pronounced him 'the Bank's biggest institutional asset, responding to the big social issues of the day'.[22] Wolfensohn does appear to have a genuine interest in democratising policy-making processes in the Bank, and also in encouraging sensitivity to the social sustainability of the Bank's work, which means paying attention to issues of poverty, human rights, gender equity, governance and participation. He is also under pressure to do so from the non-governmental development community. He took office in June 1995, at the climax of the 'Fifty Years Is Enough' global campaign by NGOs to rethink the role and relevance of the Bretton Woods financial institutions. This, as well as the battering the Bank has taken since the mid-1980s over its environmentally destructive grand infrastructure projects, has meant that he has inherited an institutional structure much more sensitive about its public image than ever before. He is presiding over sweeping changes in Bank structure to make it more transparent, consultative, and teamwork-based, with staff performance measured by 'results on the ground' rather than speed in moving money. This process has

---

[22] Interview, World Bank, Washington DC, September 1997.

involved establishing a new 'strategic compact' or corporate strategy with the Board of Directors to justify significant Bank expansion into new, key areas: social development, rural development, financial sector services, anti-corruption initiatives and knowledge-based exchanges.

However, it is difficult to reform any institution, particularly one with such a solidly homogeneous culture of economic rationality, professionalism, exclusiveness, and excellence, as well as a history of secrecy in its intellectual processes and products, with many policy documents embargoed from public scrutiny. From this perspective considerable power rests in the hands of the Bank's professional staff in Operations, the six regional departments and the individual country management units where the loans and sectoral projects are designed, negotiated and supervised. At the heart of this work are the task team managers, who have 'the principal operational role of the Bank, the role that does the work that justifies the existence of the organisation: preparing loans or making studies' (Wade 1997: 29).

As noted above, issues which concern the actual quality of the Bank's work are located in the less powerful Technical Networks, 'which have large staffs and small budgets', in comparison with the country management units in Operations 'which have large budgets and small staffs' (Bread for the World 1997b: 6). Staff in the Technical Networks are meant to supply their expertise to task team managers on demand. These support services are weakly placed in the Bank's incentive system, which centres on pressure on staff to move money, to make and recover loans.[23] There is less pressure to ensure compliance with Bank standards such as environment, resettlement, information disclosure or gender equity. Directives do exist to set out Bank policies on best practice in these and many other areas. However, there are over 150 mandatory actions or procedures spelled out in

---

[23] Late in 1997 the Bank introduced new products which are designed to modify the 'moving money' incentives with new concerns to enhance the quality and success rate of loans. These products include Adaptable Programme Loans and Learning and Innovation Loans. The first is a loan with a phased-in implementation process to enable borrowers to pilot test solutions with small amounts without risking large amounts and exposing the Bank. At the same time, the borrower retains the Bank's commitment to supporting the development sector in question. The Learning and Innovation Loans are a smaller version of the Adaptable Programme Loans and are intended to foster iterative learning and solution testing (Bread for the World 1997b: 9–10).

these directives – it is difficult to comply with all of them.[24] Inclusion of social concerns in project preparation therefore depends upon the commitment of the individual task team manager. Although issues of gender equity and social justice may interest many staff members, they sit uneasily in the Bank's culture as 'value-laden and subjective' concerns (Kardam 1991: 72).

This puts the onus on internal gender equity advocates or 'policy entrepreneurs' to promote the merits of sensitivity to gender issues in the work of their Country departments. Indeed, one account of the considerable progress between 1985 and 1995 in the Bank's response to WID gives most credit to such insiders: 'the available evidence suggests strongly that internal WID entrepreneurs played a critical role in promoting the subject, with varying support from top management' (Razavi and Miller 1995: 47). There are only a few individuals in positions of responsibility for Women in Development concerns within the six regions. They are strongest in the Africa region, where just a few people have made a huge contribution to the Bank's analytical work on gender and adjustment, and in the Asia region, where the WID focus has been among other things on micro-credit. They are also found in the technical support services outside of the gender unit, where they have made important contributions to bringing gender into the Bank's research and policy work on participation, urban poverty and the environment.

Internal gender specialists are in a difficult position. Careers in the Bank are not made by arguing the case for what is seen as a marginal interest. They, and other staff who are feminists or are sympathetic to gender equity positions, are in a minority position both by virtue of their sex (though some are men of course), and by virtue of the fact that whether they are economists or not, their feminist convictions mean they are in a counter-cultural position in relation to the Bank's dominant cognitive framework. The vast majority of the Bank's staff are economists, and they are also mostly men,[25] two facts which are

---

[24] Interview, NGO, Washington DC, 9 September 1997. These directives had been rationalised down from 400 'operational policies', examples of 'best practice' or 'good practice', and they have less force than they had before. This may not make much of a difference for some directives which had previously been respected mostly in the breach. One NGO interviewee suspected that this is the Bank's way of defending itself from charges that it is not respecting its own policies, weakening procedures that should be mandatory like resettlement, indigenous peoples, gender policy.

[25] The composition of Bank staff in terms of professional training and gender has been

not immaterial in terms of creating an organisational culture resistant to feminist concerns.[26]

Moreover, they do not necessarily get the degree of support they ought to from the very institution that should be backing them up: the central gender unit. That unit, in its various guises over the years, is more often engaged in defending Bank policies to the outside world, than in promoting an internal critique or change process. An example of this lack of support is the surprising failure of the central gender unit to mention, in its 1994 gender policy paper, a path-breaking Technical Note produced by the Africa Region Gender Team on gender and economic adjustment in 1993 (Blackden and Morris-Hughes 1993). This Technical Note – *Paradigm Postponed: Gender and Economic Adjustment in Sub-Saharan Africa* – takes on board and advances contemporary feminist critiques of structural adjustment, and was very much welcomed by gender equity activists outside of the Bank as evidence of the Bank's growing openness to the feminist critique. It was the basis for a report on gender and adjustment by donors to the World Bank's Special Programme of Assistance (SPA) for Africa, a consultative forum of donors to the Bank's IDA facility for lending to the most indebted nations, in Oslo in 1994. In another example of the Bank's resistance to the work of its internal gender advocates, the Bank economist who presented this same report at a plenary SPA meeting in Washington in 1994 took pains to undermine its credibility, using the word 'anecdotal' five times to describe the evidence used to demonstrate the differential impact of structural adjustment on women and men, and the word 'controversial' nine times to describe the report as a whole.[27]

Committed insiders ought to be a resource for women's move-

changing gradually, with growing numbers of sociologists and anthropologists being hired, and with more women being appointed (Razavi and Miller 1995: 31).

[26] A growing body of feminist organisational analysis is demonstrating that the balance of genders in an organisation's staff, and a range of other features of organisations such as the tolerance of justice and equity concerns in intellectual and ideological frameworks, the openness of decision making, the rigidity of calibrations in status hierarchies, and so on, can create gendered organisational cultures which profoundly affect the impact of an organisation's work on women and men, as well as the experience of women and men within organisations (Kardam 1991; Razavi and Miller 1995). For general expositions of approaches to feminist analyses of development bureaucracies see Goetz (1997) and Staudt (1997).

[27] Notes made by the author during SPA plenary meeting to discuss gender and macroeconomic planning, Washington DC, World Bank, 20 March 1994.

ments, yet these staff members say they have relatively few contacts with women's movements, and have even at times been criticised by outside feminist activists. In spite of a commonality of aims, there is mutual ambivalence between gender equity advocates on either side of the institutional divide. Outsiders are suspicious of insiders, even though insiders could use their support. At the same time, excessive contact with outside feminists could undermine the credibility and perceived professionalism of insiders.

Gender issues in Bank–NGO interactions

It might be expected that the involvement of NGOs in the Bank's work has been an entry point for dialogue on gender equity issues and, indeed, for enhancing women's participation as policy-making partners and as policy beneficiaries. This has not been the case. This is somewhat counter-intuitive, as assumptions are commonly made about the comparative advantage of NGOs in representing the interests not just of the poor, but also of women. Certainly the Bank appears to be making this assumption; for example, the 1997 World Bank progress report: *Implementing the World Bank's Gender Policies* claims that 'involving NGOs helps to promote attention to gender' (World Bank 1997c: 3). In fact, this is a relatively unproven proposition. A growing number of studies of NGOs demonstrate that they have few inherent features of organisational structure or culture which favour the representation of women's interests. Although they may be more effective at including women as clients of development programmes than some state development bureaucracies are, their flatter hierarchies, decentralised structures and egalitarian ideologies do not, in fact, necessarily enable more women to control these organisations, and indeed, NGOs can be particularly masculine environments (Mayoux 1998; Rao and Kelleher 1997; Siddarth 1995).

Bank studies show that although NGO involvement in project implementation improves the degree and quality of local-level participation, there is no automatic inclusion of women as participants. Only half of Bank operations which involve NGOs have had a component addressing gender equity, and that has been at the initiative of the Bank (in particular its gender specialists), not the NGOs (Siddarth 1995).

There is also a certain amount of conceptual muddiness in attitudes which assume that development NGOs can represent 'civil society' in general, or women's movements in particular. This assumption is made frequently, for instance at the May 1997 External Gender Consultative Group meeting, Lyn Squire, Director of the Policy Research Department and the head of the SAPRI project on the Bank side, said that the Bank was 'counting on NGOs to ensure a broad representation of civil society' (World Bank 1997a: 28). Yet development NGOs are just a small part of civil society, and represent just one associational form. In legal status, purpose, and organisational structure they differ greatly from trade unions, business associations and many kinds of social movements. Confusing NGOs with 'civil society' is convenient for the Bank; development NGOs are much more appealing interlocutors than trade unions or social movements, which tend to be more overtly political and with whom it is much more difficult to establish common institutional procedures and norms on which to base interactions.

This confusion also explains why NGOs have not been effective at representing women's movements; women may favour less visible and formalised associations with loose networks, flat hierarchies, diffused authority and responsibility. Many women's associations – particularly grass-roots self-help and urban community networks, explicitly avoid formal organisational status (i.e. registering with the state) in order to preserve organisational autonomy. Engaging NGOs to engineer 'participation' by these kinds of associations can be unrealistic. In Chile, for example, NGOs are organising community improvement projects in low income areas on a World Bank-funded Social Investment and Solidarity Fund (FOSIS). These NGOs were operating in the urban areas from which the women-dominated *poblador* movement had organised protests against the Pinochet regime in the mid-1980s. Channelling funds only through officially registered organisations requires the amorphous *poblador* groups to become more formal and institutionalised. According to a recent study, this actually sidelines many of the women's groups who wish to avoid registering themselves as statutory bodies in order to continue evading the potentially exploitative interests of the state: 'The poblador movement, already in decline, has been successfully marginalised by structures into which it doesn't fit and a discourse which brands its approach as immature and obsolete' (Taylor 1996: 784). In addition, the formalisation of community self-help has the effect of depoliticising local social movements; the FOSIS funds are for specific tasks: self-help projects or skills training, not public protests demanding employment. As Lucy Taylor (1996) suggests, NGO–state–Bank engagement in this case has the effect of demobilising civil society, shifting the protest energies of the *poblador* movement away from challenging the state towards colluding in the state's withdrawal from direct responsibility for reconstruction and poverty reduction.

Throughout the 1980s the NGOs formally involved in dialogue with or monitoring the Bank apparently did not see it as their role to promote gender equity in the Bank's work, although gender issues were sometimes raised in relation to other concerns, in particular poverty and structural adjustment. However, since the late 1980s, large international NGOs have been changing as their own internal gender equity advocates push for a greater commitment to gender issues in development. These internal gender advocates are working across organisational boundaries with other feminists in NGOs and governmental development agencies, linking into women's movements internationally and nationally.[28] The work of gender equity advocates both within their own NGOs and through feminist advocacy networks has meant that gradually, the main Washington DC-based international NGOs in dialogue with the Bank have been promoting gender equity concerns with more energy. These include Bread for the World Institute, Oxfam International, the Bank Information Centre, Center of Concern and Development GAP's 'Fifty Years Is Enough' campaign.

Still, the extent to which the gender equity interest is represented by NGOs remains patchy, contingent on the presence of committed feminist activists. There has been difficulty already in ensuring adequate participation of women's associations in the Bank–NGO Structural Adjustment and Participatory Research Initiative (SAPRI) mentioned at the beginning of this chapter. In spite of wide NGO participation in this initiative, the SAPRI global steering committee lacks a feminist economist,[29] and some of the SAPRI Bank–NGO consultations which have already taken place have neglected gender

---

[28] Examples of the networks through which feminists are supporting each other's work in development institutions include, in the USA, the Washington DC-based WID Coalition, Alt-WID, and AWID (the Association of Women in Development), and Women's EDGE (The Coalition for Women's Economic Development and Global Equality).

[29] This is not entirely its fault, as feminist economists are rare, and extremely busy.

issues. The issue of women's participation has raised another problem between NGOs which is taking on a North–South dimension. Washington DC-based NGOs have claimed that their efforts to encourage Southern NGOs to take on gender issues and to involve women's associations have been resented and rejected by Southern NGOs as a form of cultural interference.[30]

However, as one NGO activist involved with SAPRI in Washington DC said, 'it is not as simple as the men excluding women. The women themselves are unskilled in economic analysis and self-isolate from NGO movements.'[31] Women's NGOs dropped out of SAPRI meetings in El Salvador because they were unfamiliar with the technical language of the discussions and the speed with which the initiative was developing. They also protested that the quality of participation was artificial. This differential in levels of technical skills in economic analysis and negotiations is only to be expected given women's associations' characteristic lack of resources and exposure to power, discussed earlier. It speaks to the need for both the Bank and NGOs to take a gender-sensitive approach to the mechanics of 'participation' in order to accommodate and compensate for women's lack of experience of engaging with the formal policy arena.

Generating genuine participation with women requires more than just providing openings for women to come to meetings. The mechanics of participation – the venues, the technical languages, the duration of exchanges – must be adjusted to account for the constraints on women's power and public effectiveness which are caused by relations of gender, class, nationality, and race. Access to participatory fora is not the same as the capacity to express voice effectively or to exercise any kind of leverage in participatory processes, especially when massive power differences are involved. An example of the disjunction between the knowledge and time frameworks of the Bank and women's associations was provided by Hellen Wangusa, of the African Women's Policy Network, in her report to the May 1997 External Gender Consultative Group meeting about Bank–NGO 'participation' over the content of the Country Assistance Strategy in Uganda. She pointed out that women had been unable to make much of an impact, saying that women in Uganda had no idea what a CAS is. She argued that the time-frame for involving them in 'participation'

---

[30] Interview, NGO, Washington DC, 28 August 1997.
[31] Interview, NGO, Washington DC, 9 September 1997.

or 'consultation' has to be much longer than currently provided by the Bank's tight economic planning and project preparation framework (in this case nine months), in order to compensate for their lesser preparation in terms of policy knowledge and bargaining skills (let alone literacy or economic literacy) (World Bank 1997a: 18).

Women's Eyes on the Bank: lobbying the Bank and 'leap-frogging' the state

This chapter finishes with another look at the Women's Eyes on the Bank campaign to draw out both advantages and tensions in North–South partnerships in women's movements, and also to suggest some implications for global governance in the Bank–NGO lobbying relationship. Initially, the campaign was intended to strengthen the knowledge of Southern women's organisations about economic policy and to shift the locus of lobbying from Washington to borrowing countries themselves (Siddarth 1996: 18). The campaign was structured around regional 'chapters' consisting of groups of women's organisations which would maintain pressure on the Bank to respond to the campaign's demands. Eight women agreed to act as focal points for these chapters. However, just over one year into the campaign only two chapters – the US and Latin American ones – were still functioning actively. It is far too early to judge that the campaign has fizzled out in the more dormant chapters. Nevertheless, the evolution of the campaign to date is illustrative of the power differences between women's movements North and South, of the importance of geographical location, and also of delays in the spread of communication technologies to marginalised social movements.

This is precisely why Washington-based NGOs tend to take such a prominent role in campaigns to influence the Bank. They tend to be highly skilled in information collection and in lobbying and are close to the legislative process in the USA which has a disproportionately strong influence on the work of the World Bank. For women's movements, this provides the opportunity to 'leap-frog' the legislative dynamic in their own countries where they may be either too weak to have an impact, or prevented from participating by a repressive state. Northern NGOs can try to influence the Bank, and if they succeed, policy changes are imposed on Southern governments by the Bank, in what has become known as the 'boomerang pattern' (Keck and Sikkink 1998: 12–13).

A positive example of this dynamic has occurred through the Women's Eyes campaign. In 1996 the Mexico chapter of the campaign investigated the Bank's claims to have addressed gender issues in its economic and sector work in Mexico. It exposed the lack of attention to gender equity in three areas: the Bank's 'Second Basic Health Project', the Mexican Country Assistance Strategy, and the labour law reform which the Bank is promoting for Mexico (Women's Environment and Development Organization 1997: 15). The Mexican chapter wrote a letter to the Bank's US Executive Director – not the Mexican Executive Director, from whom it expected little sympathy – objecting to the lack of women's participation in the Country Assistance Strategy. The US chapter of the Women's Eyes campaign helped to mobilise a representation from the US women's movement behind this letter, getting its member organisations to sign it before it went to Jan Piercy, the US Executive Director. This had a huge impact. Within the Bank, the country director for Mexico called the US chapter of the campaign to ask for help in setting up a meeting with gender specialists in the USA. The US chapter of the campaign refused to do this, and insisted instead that he should meet with women's groups in Mexico, which he did, along with a handful of his task team managers in the spring of 1997. The Latin American chapter of the campaign has also worked with the US chapter to arrange direct meetings in Washington between a ten-person delegation from Latin American women's groups and the top management of the Latin America region at the Bank. This resulted in commitments from senior managers to improve the quality of gender analysis and design in projects.

This is an excellent example of the benefits of 'leap-frogging' the state in order to bring back stronger policy commitments from the Bank. Its success owes greatly to the fact that the Southern-based actor in this case is itself very strong in its own analytical and lobbying skills, and in its relations with the US-based actor. Also important is the commitment of the US-based actor to 'repatriate' policy discussions as quickly as possible so as to enhance local ownership. But the global and national governance implications of this are ambiguous. It can undermine democratic or potentially democratic dynamics locally, if social movements voice their interests beyond national boundaries rather than investing in improving the quality of domestic government–civil society relations. And the impact of 'leap-frogging' can be disappointing. If policy 'fed back' through the Bank to

Southern governments is perceived as externally devised and derived, not as a legitimate product of national debates and political struggles, it can be resented and resisted, undercutting the legitimacy of local social movements (Abugre and Alexander 1997).

It is therefore important for Southern women's movements to develop good relations with their own governments, something which is very difficult even in full democracies, where women have few channels of access to the political arena, and where their struggles for gender equity are still not seen as legitimate concerns for politics. Alliances and coalitions on an international level can prove extremely fruitful in building the leverage of domestic women's movements and in enhancing their knowledge base and analytical skills. The Women's Eyes on the Bank campaign has shown a capacity to do this so far, but primarily this has been with a Southern women's movement which is already very familiar with the politics and tactics of leverage and lobbying.

Conclusion

Over the last thirty years, women's movements have developed increasingly sophisticated and politically credible critiques of economic development, and have targeted their concerns at multilateral economic institutions, most particularly the World Bank. This chapter has investigated the relationship between women's movements, the feminist critique of neoliberal economics and the World Bank.

How has this MEI modified?

In the second half of the 1990s the Bank has embarked upon an important restructuring process – a new 'strategic compact' – to augment its impact on important new development areas, with a particular focus on social development, participation, and partnerships. Although it can be expected that gender equity concerns will be better addressed in these new policy approaches, the women's movement cannot take the credit for these changes. They are the results of a much broader process of critique and pressure on the Bank coming from a range of development actors, from borrower country governments, a wide range of development NGOs, and many Northern governments.

The Bank's attitude to gender issues has definitely become less dismissive than when these issues first came up in the 1970s. The Bank has installed an internal machinery to promote gender equity in its work, setting up standards of best practice in this area, and expanding the resources it targets to women, such as lending programmes for girls' education and women's reproductive health, and grants to institutions providing micro-credit to poor women borrowers. It has been much slower to review its structural adjustment policies from the point of view of their impact on women, and has made little serious effort to entertain feminist critiques of macroeconomics in its economic and sectoral work.

What are the motivations driving MEI–GSM engagement?

The World Bank's response to the women's movement is motivated by several factors. The first is the indirect effect of women's movements on the Bank through the Executive Directors. Some of these Directors have taken their domestic women's movements seriously and have sought to represent their concerns to the Bank. They have done so by questioning the Bank's commitment to the gender equity issue, and by challenging Bank assumptions as to the gender-neutral impact of its macroeconomic policies. The second factor prompting the Bank's response to women's movements is a growing perception of the size and importance of these movements globally, a perception which Wolfensohn took away with him from the 1995 Beijing conference. Finally, engagement with women's movements is a part of the Bank's efforts to promote the social sustainability of its work through improved partnerships with civil society groups.

From the point of view of women's movements, engagement with the Bank is an imperative created by the growing immiseration of women as a perceived result of neoliberal economic policies such as structural adjustment in the South and economic austerity in the North. The majority of the world's poor (70 per cent) and of the world's illiterates (60 per cent) are female (UNDP 1995: 5), and women's weak market positions and inadequate rights to physical and social assets leaves them vulnerable in contexts of social and economic change. Economic austerity policies promoted by institutions like the World Bank and the IMF are seen to have exacerbated these problems by obliging women to extend their domestic and community caring functions to compensate for state withdrawal from social service provisioning. Engagement with the Bank is therefore seen as critical to a project of developing more gender-equitable and humane development policies.

What is the significance of the MEI–GSM relationship?

This chapter has shown that global women's movements have put the Bank on the defensive, at least in terms of its public relations, and this should be seen as a real achievement for a social movement which is probably more diffuse, diverse, and less well resourced than others. Triggered by the challenges posed by women at Beijing, the Bank has stepped up its efforts to enhance women's experience of development, and is gingerly beginning to entertain the feminist critique of economics.

Nevertheless, women's movements have had less of an impact on the Bank than the environmental movement or than the NGOs promoting the participation agenda. This chapter has suggested several reasons for this. The first is that until recently, there has not been a concerted global civil society coalition demanding gender equity in the Bank's work. This has to do with a range of constraints facing women's movements, including their lack of resources and lack of lobbying expertise, as well as the technical barrier of economic planning languages, and the fact that women's economic interests can clash, particularly across differences of class and nation.

A second reason has to do with the centrality of the US women's movement to the success of any campaign directed at a US-based institution. The US women's movement has not thrown its weight behind gender and development issues. Nor, in spite of its enormous size and great successes, can it command the same quantum of domestic support as the environmental movement was able to do. Gender equity issues are still seen as more controversial, and more 'culturally specific' than are concerns with the environment or even human rights.

A powerful way of influencing the Bank is still through national governments, which means that for women's movements, a persistent obstacle remains their poor representation in their own governments, and the sexism within state structures which makes governments such poor representatives of women's economic interests. Although the Bank's governance structure still privileges states as representatives of their societies, the successes of global social movements in by-passing individual governments and tackling the Bank directly is contributing to a considerable openness towards civil society groups. This has been of particular importance for women's movements given their generally low level of influence over individual governments.

3 The World Trade Organization and labour

This chapter examines the relationship between the World Trade Organization (WTO) and labour. The analysis proceeds in the following manner. Firstly, an overview is provided of the WTO and its significance. Secondly, the global labour movement is profiled and some preliminary points are made about its status in the social movement and NGO community. Thirdly, labour's engagement with international economic institutions other than the WTO is surveyed. Fourthly, labour's particular concern with the WTO is explained. Fifthly, labour participation in the first ministerial meeting of the WTO is examined for what it reveals about both the WTO and labour. Sixthly, the general relationship between NGOs and the WTO is surveyed. Finally, the implications of the WTO–labour engagement for the International Labour Organisation is considered.

The primary argument of the chapter is that labour's inability to advance its concerns in the WTO framework risks losing a potentially significant constituency. Organised labour is more supportive of the WTO's trade liberalisation project than other elements of the social movement community. Disagreement with various NGOs over the social clause issue highlights organised labour's desire to work within dominant institutions. However, the meagre results of the WTO Singapore Ministerial meeting, continued resistance at the WTO and increased opposition to reform of the ILO put continued cooperation in doubt. For a multilateral institution seeking to sink roots in national societies such a development should be a cause for concern.

The World Trade Organization

The WTO came into being on 1 January 1995. The Contracting Parties of the General Agreement on Tariffs and Trade (GATT) created it through the final agreements which ended the Uruguay Round multilateral negotiations. Its establishment provides a sister institution for the Bretton Woods pairing of the IMF and World Bank some fifty years after their creation. The WTO takes its place in an environment of multilateral trade rules dating back to 1945. A significant characteristic of this post-war trading regime has been the need to balance liberalisation with the desire for policy autonomy by many states and communities. Two key features of the WTO which shift this balance away from policy autonomy are the strengthening of its dispute settlement system and the innovation of biannual ministerial meetings. These changes increase the importance of the WTO and invite further scrutiny by concerned publics world-wide.

The roots of the WTO can be traced back to December 1945 when the USA invited fourteen countries to begin negotiations on liberalising international trade.[1] The negotiations followed two paths. The first was the attempt to create an International Trade Organisation (ITO) that would facilitate trading relations as Bretton Woods facilitated monetary relations. The other path was an initiative to implement quickly an agreement to reduce tariff levels. The tariff cutting exercise resulted in the GATT which was signed on 30 October 1947. It was thought that once the ITO was complete the GATT would be subsumed in the larger organisation.

The draft charter for the ITO, known as the Havana Charter, was drawn up in March 1948.[2] In addition to addressing tariff policy it contained sections on employment and economic activity, economic development and reconstruction, restrictive business practices, intergovernmental commodity arrangements and subsidies. It was more wide ranging than the GATT, which focused on tariffs in manufactured goods. In negotiating the Havana Charter the USA push for a pure free trade system was limited by its own internal commitment to agricultural protection. With echoes of the Senate's refusal to endorse

---

[1] The countries were Australia, Brazil, Canada, China, Cuba, Czechoslovakia, Luxembourg, France, India, the Netherlands, New Zealand, South Africa, the Soviet Union and the United Kingdom.

[2] For details see Wilcox (1949). A detailed account of the US position and activity during the creation of the ITO and GATT can be found in Brown (1950).

Woodrow Wilson's effort to have the US join the League of Nations following the First World War, the US Congress refused to give its agreement to the ITO. More influential than isolationists in rejecting the agreement were liberal forces which heartily condemned concessions the US negotiators made to other countries. The US branch of the International Chamber of Commerce opposed the ITO because they thought it was based on economic nationalism and jeopardised the free enterprise system (Kock 1969: 59). Congressional opinion was so set against the ITO that in December 1950 the US administration dropped the initiative and asked Congress to continue giving its support to GATT.

Following this failure the international trade regime was forced to fall back upon the GATT. While GATT strove for the lofty goal of free trade, it implemented what was most feasible. Although the Agreement aimed for liberalisation on a non-discriminatory and multilateral basis, major exceptions to these principles were permitted to accommodate diverse concerns.[3] There were exceptions from GATT rules for textiles, agriculture, regional trading groups, developing countries and safeguards to prevent serious injury to domestic producers. GATT did not demand the politically impossible – that all nations liberalise immediately and unconditionally. GATT members, or Contracting Parties, were not coerced into accepting complete liberalisation. States balanced domestic interests and made whatever concessions they deemed feasible. One observer has described it as a disarmament treaty for mercantilists (Wolf 1990). Small steps were gradually taken over a long time period to reduce trade barriers and liberalise trade flows among countries.

The compromise between wanting to provide clear rules and allowing for domestic autonomy can be seen in the mechanisms developed for settling disputes between Contracting Parties. When Contracting Parties had a disagreement, they could utilise GATT's dispute settlement procedure which was covered by Articles XXII and XXIII (Pescatore 1993). Article XXII provided for consultation if Parties believed that they were not receiving GATT benefits while Article XXIII allowed the matter to be brought before the GATT Council. After 1962 it became GATT practice that disputes which

---

[3] Finlayson and Zacher (1981) have identified seven key GATT norms. Ruggie (1982) refers to the accommodation of domestic social purpose in international regimes as embedded liberalism.

could not be resolved through consultation (Article XXII) were handed over to a panel which examined the issue. Once the panel had considered the issue a report was presented to the Parties. If they could not work out an agreement based on this report within two weeks, it was transmitted to the GATT Council. At the GATT Council (assembly of all GATT Contracting Parties) a decision could be taken to accept a report, but only if it was unanimous. The party which lost the case would have to agree. Reports usually demanded that a country terminated an offending practice or authorised the aggrieved party to undertake counter-measures or retaliation.

Although the GATT dispute settlement process enjoyed some success it has also had two major weaknesses. The first was the ability of a Contracting Party (prior to completion of the Uruguay Round) to veto the process at numerous stages. A dissatisfied party could block the creation of a panel, block adoption of the report by the Council or fail to undertake the obligations outlined in the report. Contracting Parties had to agree that their activities violated the rules and should be changed. A strong domestic interest often mitigated against such a position. The second problem was that even if the country accepted a panel report in question, it could choose to keep the offending policy, leaving the injured party to suspend benefits in kind. The dispute then fell back on to unilateral action by the aggrieved party. The party which had its complaint supported by a panel would have to undertake retaliation through its own domestic legislation. This could take the form of tariffs or suspension of trade benefits to the offender. Offenders were not sanctioned; they just had benefits of equal value withdrawn by the complainant.

The unilateral nature of the process raised serious problems for the whole system. The countries able to take unilateral measures tended to be the economically powerful such as the USA, Japan and the EU. Smaller states were less likely to take action against the giants because they feared a trade war that would cost them dearly. One of the purposes of having an international legal framework for trade is to facilitate relations based on rules rather than power. Law should restrain powerful states from abusing their economic power to the cost of smaller states. Since the GATT process relied so heavily on unanimity, this goal was difficult to achieve.

The WTO dispute settlement procedure reversed the unanimity principle which had hindered acceptance of reports (Petersmann 1997). Panel reports are now automatically adopted sixty days after being issued unless there is a consensus that it be rejected. Since the side benefiting from the report would be unlikely to agree to reject, it seems most probable that a consensus to reject would very rarely be achieved. Such a procedure would result in almost every panel report being adopted, even if it went against the interests of the larger states. Thus, a major step was taken to turn a system from one which encouraged delay by favouring unanimity of acceptance to a speedier process which could override the wishes of particular states. This is a move away from a system of negotiation traditionally the preferred option of the Europeans, to one of adjudication, the aim of the USA.

The result of this change in dispute settlement is to make the WTO a prominent international organisation in terms of having a developed enforcement mechanism. It allows for the possibility of greater implementation of agreements and the gradual accumulation of a body of case law on trade issues. This should greatly strengthen the rules-based nature of the trading system. An implication of this increased ability to ensure compliance is increased attention to the WTO's operation. A stronger international legal system means reduced domestic autonomy. It violates what some have seen as 'the policy tolerance which had been a central, if largely implicit element of the international consensus that had created and maintained GATT' (Destler 1986: 34).

This violation of policy tolerance means that more political attention is focused upon the rules that will be enforced in the WTO. Contra-dictory pressures are put on the WTO both to prevent and to assist its power being extended into new issues. Those states and social interests that feel the international trading regime was and is biased against their interests will resist expansion of the WTO's remit. For example, in a country such as India where the GATT's movement into intellectual property rights caused widespread social backlash on the part of poor farmers, there is no appetite to see the WTO move into issues such as competition and investment.[4] Alternatively, those groups seeking a strong international legal forum capable of enforcing rights are attracted by the WTO's dispute settlement procedures. Advocates of integrating competition concerns at the WTO see it as a means of restraining the practices of offending states and firms. Labour sees the WTO as adding muscle to the decisions of the ILO.

[4] For a critique of the WTO which stresses the biases against developing countries see Das (1998a; 1998b).

One WTO official likened the institution's role to that of being a sheriff in a world of weaker international institutions.[5] Numerous interests seeing the arrival of the new sheriff want it to adjudicate in their area of particular concern.

One of the key tasks of the first WTO ministerial meeting in Singapore in December 1996 was to begin to clarify the relationship between the WTO and other international institutions. The USA and the EU favoured a policy of moving issues into the WTO because it was both an effective and multilateral institution. They pushed for the WTO to take on investment, competition and labour issues. Many developing countries resisted such an initiative claiming that other existing institutions were the appropriate place to deal with such issues. They argued that investment and competition issues were better dealt with at the United Nations Conference on Trade and Development (UNCTAD) while labour issues should be confined to the ILO. In general, developing countries view UNCTAD as being more sympathetic to their concerns than the IMF, World Bank and GATT which were created for and are controlled by developed states (Williams 1994).

Just as the dispute settlement mechanism procedures raise the stakes of developments at the WTO, the commitment to holding biannual ministerial meetings is sure to maintain the issues and politics of trade liberalisation high on the public agenda. Whereas GATT members were called together to start or conclude negotiating rounds at well spaced intervals, the WTO will play host to high profile intergovernmental meetings every two years. This provides a focus for both media coverage and political organisation at regular and short intervals. Social movements have added another event to their lobbying calendar. Time between meetings can be spent focusing on preparation for the next ministerial.

These meetings may keep the momentum for liberalisation going, but they also provide a rallying point for people with conflicting views. For example, during the second ministerial meeting in Geneva in May 1998 protesters marched through the city overturning cars and vandalising McDonald's restaurants and the exteriors of expensive hotels. In addition to facilitating the lobbying of civil society actors, the regular convening of trade ministers from around the world provides more opportunities for open conflict between states. With one

[5] WTO official briefing NGOs at the 1996 Singapore WTO meeting.

group of states continually seeking to expand the agenda and many others trying to cope with the existing arrangements and obligations it appears there is a recipe for continued disagreement and perhaps even breakdown.

Global labour

We have selected labour as one of the three global social movements for examination. Similar to women's movements and environmentalists, it poses it's own distinct challenges for study and analysis. This section will highlight several difficulties that will become apparent during the subsequent analysis.

The global labour movement is composed of several parts. At the highest level are the international organisations which bring national union confederations together. The largest and most active of these is the International Confederation of Free Trade Unions (ICFTU), which in 1996 represented 127 million people from 136 countries (ICFTU 1996c: 5). In 1948 the ICFTU split from the existing World Federation of Trade Unions (WFTU) because of Cold War tensions between capitalist and communist states, as well as between communist and non-communist unions.[6] Since the collapse of the Soviet Union, the WFTU is no longer a major player. An alternative international confederation to the ICFTU is the World Confederation of Labour (WCL). The WCL is much smaller in membership (23.7 million members in 1996) and financial resources than the ICFTU and represents workers primarily in Belgium, Holland and Latin America. Its distinction is that it was originally a confederation of Christian unions and continues to stress a spiritual or humanistic dimension to its policies (WCL 1995). The majority of its members are in developing countries.

A second element of the global labour movement are the International Trade Secretariats (ITSs) which bring together unions in a particular economic sector. Prominent examples include the International Textile, Garment and Leather Workers' Federation (ITGLWF), the International Metalworkers Federation and the International Federation of Chemical, Energy, Mine and General Workers' Unions (ICEM). The ITSs engage in day-to-day relations with firms and tend

---

[6] On the conflict between communist and non-communist labour unions at the WFTU and in Europe see Busch (1983: 42–72); Lorwin (1973: 219–82); Radosh (1969: 304–47).

to be on the front line of labour–capital conflict (Lipow 1996). They are responsible for organising workers on the ground and mounting industry-specific campaigns.

A third part is the international and transnational activity of national unions or confederations. For example, the US-based United Electrical, Radio and Machine Workers of America (UE) have entered into a Strategic Organizing Alliance with the independent Mexican labour federation, the Authentic Labour Front (FAT). FAT has agreed to target TNCs in the Mexican maquiladora zone that have a bargaining relationship with the UE in the United States, while UE has set up a solidarity fund to help finance FAT organising (Alexander 1994). A fourth element is the transnational organising of local union affiliates. This involves the initiative of grass-roots coordinators to link up with their counterparts in other countries.

A fifth, and significant, element of the global labour movement involves the numerous civic groups not affiliated to the above mentioned structures. These groups share an interest in improving labour issues, but may or may not be working in conjunction with the established union structure. These groups range from research institutes with a labour focus to NGOs involved in labour issues to unions not yet recognised by their governments or the international trade union structures. These groups share much in common with the women's movements and environmental movements examined in other parts of this book.

Since the ICFTU is the largest umbrella organisation of international labour, much of this chapter will focus on its engagement with international organisations and the WTO in particular. However, the relationship between the ICFTU and other elements of the labour movement is a central part of the analysis. For example, the debate over core labour standards at the WTO revealed the limits of the ICFTU speaking on behalf of the whole labour movement, especially unions in developing countries. In addition, some grass-roots activists see the ICFTU as being distant from the concerns of workers and biased to conservative policies (Moody 1997: 227–48). Thus, the reader should keep in mind that the focus of this study is on a relatively established but by no means universal aspect of the labour movement.

In the distinction sometimes found in the literature between 'new' and 'old' social movements, labour is in the latter category. It is old in two senses. Chronologically, the labour movement and its international activities date back to the middle of the nineteenth century

(Busch 1983: 6–30; Lorwin 1973: 3–196; Price 1945; Van Holthoon and Van der Linden 1988). As early as 1818 Robert Owen had called upon governments to institute an international programme of labour legislation. One of the first calls to form an international labour movement dates back to William Lovett and the London Working Men's Association in 1838. By 1864 the First International was formed, bringing together a wide variety of workers' organisations from across Europe. This was followed by the Second International (1889–1914), the founding of International Trade Secretariats and the creation of international union confederations.

Labour is also 'old' in the sense that it is based upon class divisions and antagonisms while the new social movements centre around issues such as the environment, gender or peace. New social movements are often portrayed as being located in civil society, intending to change values and lifestyles, organised at the grass-roots level and participating in direct action or cultural innovation. In contrast, the workers' movement is characterised as being located closer to the polity, intending to integrate itself with the political system, organised upon the basis of hierarchy and acting through political mobilisation (Scott 1990: 19). While it is helpful to note that labour is a distinctive social movement the differences can be overdone. Labour also operates in civil society, seeks to change values and lifestyle, has grass-roots organisation and participates in direct action. Alternatively, new social movements are engaged in influencing the state, political action and political mobilisation. The differences may be a question of degree rather than kind. The two most notable differences are in organisational structure and the history of some labour groups in corporatist structures of the state.

Labour is often not included in literature about social movements transforming society because of these distinctions. An interesting example of how labour is sometimes segregated from other social movements in analysis is provided in a typology of NGOs at the World Trade Organization utilised by Bellmann and Gerster (1996: 35). They divide NGOs engaged with the WTO into three categories – umbrella professional associations; research institutions and universities; and non-profit organisations. Workers' organisations are classified as professional and lumped together with chambers of commerce, importers and exporters, and chemical, agricultural and pharmaceutical associations. Environmentalists, consumers, development and women's organisations are located in the non-profit sector. From this perspective workers' organisations appear to be more of an interest group than part of a social movement.

This higher degree of institutionalisation and formal structures for decision making and accountability in the labour movement can sometimes give it a privileged position vis-à-vis other social movements and can lead to conflict with them. Some institutions such as the IMF may regard labour as a key and reliable social partner. Within the social-movement community itself labour may be seen as a leading element. For example, during the ICFTU 16th World Congress the Chilean ambassador to the UN and coordinator of the UN Social Summit, Juan Somavia, called upon labour to be the core of a broad-ranging social alliance influencing the direction of globalisation.[7] His vision was of labour leading a world social movement to exert pressure upon governments to live up to recommendations of the Summit. Labour was identified as the key actor because of its long history of fighting oppression, existing organisational structure and a degree of representativeness and democracy greater than that of other social movements.

The mechanics of cooperation between labour and other social movements is sometimes difficult to envision. The labour movement does have a clear organisation structure, but the environmental and women's movements do not. The insistence by labour that it is the largest and most democratic non-governmental organisation may restrict its desire to compromise and cooperate. At the World Congress, the general secretary of Education International (EI) made the point that while the ICFTU should make more use of the Conference of NGOs at ECOSOC 'we insist that the UN recognise that representative, democratic organisations like the ICFTU and the ITSs are not the same as the thousands of NGOs and "one person think tanks" swarming like honey bees around UN summits' (Van Leeuwen 1996).[8] Cooperation with environmentalists may be particularly problematic. Although some Congress delegates mentioned concern about clean working environments, it often seems that this is a health and safety issue. ICFTU members seem willing to consider cooperation with

[7] The ICFTU World Congress is held every four years and is the primary policy-making body of the Confederation. The 16th World Congress was held in Brussels on 24–29 June 1996. References to events or statements at the Congress in this chapter are based upon the author's notes.

[8] A similar stress on the importance of representativeness and accountability in distinguishing between NGOs can be found in Harris (1996).

other social movements, but this may be based on a clear hierarchy or on a case by case basis. The possibility of forging a long-lasting, broad-based coalition is more problematic.

Labour and international organisations

The labour movement is actively engaged with numerous international organisations. In addition to the WTO three key relationships have been with the ILO, the Bretton Woods institutions and UN World Summits. All of these relationships are characterised by the labour movement seeking to influence institutional policy to improve the social protection of workers.

The labour movement has a long-standing relationship with the oldest UN affiliated international organisation, the ILO. The spectre of communism following the Russian Revolution convinced the victors of the First World War that some heed must be paid to workers' interests in post-war reconstruction and the creation of a new, stable international order. The result was the founding of the ILO as part of the Treaty of Versailles. It is a unique international organisation because its tripartite organisation gives workers a direct input into decision making. Representation is distributed between government, employer and worker representatives on a 2 : 1 : 1 ratio.

Although organised labour has better access to the ILO than other international organisations, there is considerable unhappiness with its operation. The ILO's Conventions protecting against unacceptable working conditions are voluntary. Even when governments accept particular Conventions, there is no sanction to guarantee adherence. It keeps the profile of workers' issues on the agenda, but has no teeth to protect workers. We will return to the ILO later in this chapter.

A second institution with which the ICFTU is becoming more engaged is the IMF.[9] Indeed, one of the highlights of the ICFTU's 16th World Congress was the unusual decision of the director of the IMF, Michel Camdessus, to address union delegates. The IMF is of central concern to many union members in developing countries because its policies of privatisation, deregulation and liberalisation are seen to be the cause of enormous suffering, savage decreases in living standards, and a justification for anti-union campaigns (Harrod 1992). In his introduction of Camdessus to the World Congress the ICFTU's

---

[9] See also chapter 5 on the IMF.

President Trotman relayed how Barbadian trade unions had conferred with the IMF and World Bank about their structural adjustment programme (SAP). In the negotiations unions were able to scuttle devaluation proposals, reduce the number of required layoffs and participate in a wages policy. This was cited as the first example of a tripartite approach to SAPs and suggested as a precedent for union–IMF relations.

Camdessus' speech was straightforward and revealing (IMF 1996i). He emphasised that countries approaching the IMF for assistance are in a state of near ruin and require emergency action. The financial restructuring was painful, but postponement of adjustment was even more disastrous. He praised unions for their long struggle to create new opportunities for their members and called upon them to assist in making globalisation opportunities available to all. He foresaw a dual role for unions – to facilitate training of their members and to hold the state accountable for its financial misspending. While the IMF could set guidelines for state expenditure, it could not ensure that this expenditure went into productive programmes. It was up to unions and other social organisations to pressure states to reorient their spending policies with regard to social infrastructure projects. The IMF and unions could be partners on the road to financial stability.

While the ICFTU leadership viewed the IMF's mere presence as an indication of the growing trend of international organisations' acknowledgement of the key social role of the ICFTU, many delegates were unimpressed by the director's speech. The general secretary of ICFTU's Inter-American Regional Organisation for Workers (ORIT), Luis Anderson, expressed outrage at the idea that workers were responsible for their own poverty because of lack of training. He was reluctant to offer a hand of cooperation when IMF policies promoted exclusion. Antonio Lettieri, representing the Italian union confederation CGIL, also indicated that it was unlikely the IMF would win workers' assistance in implementing SAPs that attacked their livelihood and means of survival. Delegates from the Colombian and Ecuadorian union confederations saw SAPs as the cause of increased poverty, unemployment and marginalisation rather than the cure.

A similar division of opinion over whether to work with the IMF was in evidence among US unions as the institution's funding came up for review in the US Congress in 1998. The umbrella confederation for US unions, the AFL–CIO, offered a critique of IMF policies but supported continued Congressional funding (AFL–CIO 1998). In contrast, the United Auto Workers opposed more funding for the IMF because of the institution's austerity measures and their effects on workers in the developed and developing countries (UAW 1998).

The views of many union members are probably accurately reflected in an educational cartoon book published by the ITS Public Services International (PSI) (Dubro and Konopacki 1995). In the booklet the leadership of the IMF's sister institution, the World Bank, is portrayed as power hungry, black suited bureaucrats unable to see reality through their institutional glasses. Humble union leaders, women's groups, idealistic youth and a former World Bank consultant confront them. The African trade union official notes that for many of his people, SAP stands for 'Suffering for the African People'. The policies of the Bretton Woods institutions are seen to be contributing to greater poverty and hardship rather than offering an alleviation of these conditions.

Potential interaction between the IMF and the ICFTU is limited by widely conflicting goals. The IMF is seeking the help of unions to limit government corruption and contribute to good governance, whereas the unions desire a rethinking of the core assumptions underlying structural adjustment programmes. The IMF wants the unions to contribute to the success of their plans while the unions want to change the plans themselves (ICFTU 1995). Many ICFTU World Congress delegates seemed unwilling to accept the severe financial constraints upon states seeking IMF help. For their part, the IMF failed to offer anything other than sympathy for the fact that restructuring hurt the weakest the most, and that those paying the cost were not responsible for accumulating the debt. The significance of the dialogue lay in the fact that it was taking place more than any actual accomplishments of the relationship to date.

Labour's interaction with the World Bank has tended to be of a limited nature, but has recently improved. Traditionally, the World Bank has taken a negative view of organised labour and seen it as an obstacle to development programmes (Deacon, Hulse and Stubbs 1997: 69–70). Organised labour has been viewed as a special interest group which lobbies against reforms designed to help the poorer majority. Labour's opposition to privatisation of government services and its support of tripartite decision making brings it into conflict with Bank structural adjustment loans.

In contrast to gender advocates and environmentalists, there is no section of the Bank devoted to dealing with labour organisations and issues. Labour officials are often directed to the Social Protection Sector of the Human Development Network. This sector has responsibility for labour markets, pensions and social assistance. At other times labour groups have tried to engage with other parts of the Bank such as the privatisation group or teams in assisted countries. The ICFTU has proposed the establishment of a Labour Forum or a dedicated section within the Bank, but this has not been implemented. Despite recent openings, the labour perspective is that the Bank tries to restructure labour markets without dealing with labour representatives.[10] There seems to be little recognition of labour's role as a social force or the significance of fair industrial relations.

Despite the limited and difficult relations between the Bank and labour just highlighted, there is also evidence of recent change and the possibility of improvements. In the 1990s the Bank research programme has taken up a number of issues of concern to the labour movement. For example, the Bank's 1995 *World Development Report* (World Bank 1995b) examined the issue of workers in a global economy while the 1997 report focused on the role of the state in development (World Bank 1997b). While neither report backed a labour line, both had some elements that pleased organised labour and labour organisations were consulted for their views during the research. In addition, some of the studies of the social protection unit have turned to issues of concern to labour such as export processing zones and child labour (Fallon and Tzannatos 1998; Kusago and Tzannatos 1998).

The eruption of the East Asian financial crisis in July 1997 provided the opportunity for labour to have a greater influence in the World Bank. The head of the World Bank NGO section, John Clark facilitated meetings between the ICFTU's Asian regional organisation (APRO) in Singapore and Malaysia as the World Bank president toured the area. This was followed up by an ICFTU visit to Washington in March 1998 where the IMF director and World Bank president met union representatives. As a result of those meetings Bank President Wolfensohn has suggested a point person be appointed at the Bank to deal with labour issues. The financial crisis has forced the Bank, as well as the IMF, to think about labour's role as a social actor and potential partner, rather than an annoying interest group which must be overcome. In January 1999 the ICFTU had their first meeting with

---

[10] Interview, ICFTU official, Washington, DC, May 1998.

Executive Directors of the World Bank in Washington DC. The ICFTU pushed its case for the integration of a social dimension in World Bank policies and stressed the importance of sound industrial relations to good governance and development (ICFTU 1999a).

An example of this change in policy towards organised labour can be seen in the 1998 agreement between the World Bank and South Korea for a structural adjustment loan (World Bank 1998b). Whereas five years earlier, the Bank would probably have advocated the restriction of labour rights, present policy advocates expanding labour rights and providing limited social security for those thrown out of work. This is a belated recognition that social stability will influence the success rate of economic restructuring programmes and that one key element of social stability involves labour organisations. This 'new' approach may not stand the test of time. South Korea's financial crisis threatened wider systemic damage and its union movement was particularly strategic. It is too early to tell whether this is a new pattern or an expedient exception.

Another area of global labour activity has been some of the UN World Summits. Particularly important was labour's contribution to the UN World Social Development Summit in Copenhagen in March 1995. The Summit brought together leaders from 114 countries to focus specifically on social issues. It was one of numerous recent UN summits such as the Rio Conference on the environment, the Cairo Conference on Population and the Beijing Women's Conference. In preparation for the Summit, the ICFTU held a conference with the Danish Labour Organisation to prepare the trade union negotiating position. The ICFTU expressed concern about a range of issues such as employment, democracy, equality, international labour standards, education, training and sustainable development. Labour took a prominent role at the Summit and believes it exercised considerable influence in the content of the Summit's 'Ten Commitments'.[11] Perhaps most important for the labour movement was a promise to support basic labour rights and the ILO conventions which form the basis of their campaign for a social clause at the WTO.

[11] The Declaration of the World Summit for Social Development contained ten commitments which bound governments to strive for a more equitable world. These were broad statements which committed governments to respect for human rights, the eradication of poverty, full employment, social integration, quality education, social dimensions to structural adjustment programmes, international cooperation and development of least developed countries. On the Summit itself see Felice (1997).

As important as participation in the Summit may have been, the real challenge for labour and the other social movements is moving towards implementation of the Summit agenda. The ICFTU sees itself as playing a key role in putting pressure upon governments to abide by their commitments. In the wake of Copenhagen the ICFTU published a Summit *Users' Guide* (ICFTU 1996a). The guide outlines the commitments made by governments and suggests how national and local unions can work towards its implementation. The central task is for unions to press their governments to establish national commissions to monitor progress towards implementation.

In March 1996 the ICFTU sponsored a follow-up seminar to the World Summit in conjunction with the United Nations Development Programme (UNDP) and the ILO. Held on the first anniversary of the Summit, the seminar was meant to reflect upon the degree to which implementation was taking place and what further steps were needed. Representatives from the ICFTU, ILO (including the employers' organisation), UNDP, European Commission and social movements gave their views. The general sense was that a spirit of action had been generated at Copenhagen, but little activity in the following year had taken place (ICFTU 1996d). Again, a key element in the agenda for the future was seen to be lobbying for the establishment of national commissions to monitor national implementation.

There is some overlap between the ICFTU's vision of its role following the Social Summit and that of the IMF director's vision of unions and the IMF. In both cases unions are seen to have the role of making the state live up to earlier commitments. In the case of the IMF, the commitments are financial propriety as agreed through SAPs. For the Social Summit, it is the Ten Commitments made in Copenhagen. In both cases unions are part of a broader civil society coalition pressuring the state. They are seen as being one of the more powerful civil society elements capable of exerting influence. A notable difference is that in the case of SAPs it is hoped that unions will help consolidate the IMF agenda whereas the unions are hoping that the Social Summit goals will bolster their agenda, which includes changing the terms of SAPs!

Labour and the WTO

The international labour movement viewed the establishment of the WTO as one of a number of international regulatory regimes created to protect the interests of capital in the 1980s and 1990s (O'Brien 1998). On the regional level, the North American Free Trade Agreement sought to protect investors' rights while the relaunch of European integration in the early 1980s also followed a liberal strategy. Combined with the deregulation of the financial system and other regional agreements in the developing world, these initiatives allowed international capital either to escape national regulation or to create new forms of regulation to its benefit.

Labour's task was to re-establish protective social regulation at the national, regional and international levels. Nationally, the challenges varied. In developed countries there was the movement of workers from full time secure employment to part time and insecure employment which was often governed by far less strict regulation. For many developing-country labour forces the primary challenge is widespread unemployment. In those developing countries with growing export sectors the challenge is Export Processing Zones or Special Economic Zones where protective national labour legislation was either weakened or abolished. Prominent examples of trying to create favourable regulation at the regional level include the European Social Chapter and the NAFTA labour side accord. In the OECD, labour pressed for inclusion of labour standards in investment agreement negotiations and more academic work on the issue of labour standards.[12]

It was in this context of seeking to advance progressive labour regulation that much of the global labour movement approached the issue of bringing labour concerns into the WTO. The labour movement's goal at the WTO is to have core labour standards (social clause) brought into its purview. The social clause would commit states to respect seven crucial conventions of the ILO (Conventions 87, 98, 29, 105, 100, 111, 138). These conventions provide for: freedom of association, the right to collective bargaining, abolition of forced labour, prevention of discrimination in employment and a minimum age for employment. The key to having the conventions as part of the WTO is that for the first time they would become enforceable and not depend upon the whims of individual states. Labour wanted the WTO sheriff to include core labour standards on its beat.

The case for a social clause at the WTO was constructed to temper, if not eliminate, opposition from its major detractors, liberal free traders and developing states. The ICFTU argues that a social clause

---

[12] One response was OECD (1996).

will help keep markets open by strengthening the political authority of the WTO (ICFTU 1996b). Protectionist arguments in developed countries will be harder to sustain in the face of an established mechanism to deal with labour exploitation. The implicit argument is that workers in developed states will continue to press for labour standards, narrowing the choice for policy makers between national or multinational regulation rather than multinational or no regulation. A failure to address the issue at the WTO may result in developed states taking their own, less liberal measures.

Converting developing country governments to a social clause requires a message which minimises the fear of Northern protectionism. The ICFTU proposals raise the possibility of trade sanctions only for the most obstinate offenders and after years of reports, consultations and multilateral assistance. The ILO conventions set broad principles which can be adjusted to national conditions. There is no attempt to legislate wage rates, so developed states will continue to be subject to cost competition. At the ICFTU's World Congress in June 1996 a delegate from the Malaysian Trade Union Congress (MTUC) emphasised the need to underline that the clause was not a minimum wage. The MTUC committed itself to supporting adoption of the social clause in face of fierce government opposition. The ICFTU is also trying to attract support by claiming that developing countries have the most to gain from their proposals. The biggest competitive threat to low-wage developing countries is from other low-wage developing countries. They should be most interested in preventing a race to the bottom. Evidence of this fear was provided at the Congress when an Indian delegate voiced concerns that China was using oppressive conditions to lure investment away from other developing countries.

The ICFTU maintains an office in Geneva to deal both with the ILO and the WTO. It has access to the WTO Secretariat and to needed documents. The ICFTU enjoys considerable informal access to the WTO and engages with key Secretariat members such as the director-general. The existing system of WTO–NGO relations suits the ICFTU as it is regarded as more legitimate than many of the lobbying NGOs and receives better unofficial treatment by the WTO.[13]

---

[13] Interview with ICFTU official, 13 December 1996, Singapore. Interview with WTO official 2 October 1997, Geneva.

Labour and the Singapore ministerial meeting

For organised labour the first ministerial meeting of the WTO was a crucial event in the furtherance of their global campaign for workers' rights. It would be a test of the degree to which labour issues could be accommodated in the most influential trade organisations. Labour wanted the WTO to set up a working group to consider how 'the rules of the WTO can ensure that the mutually reinforcing relationship between core international labour standards and the multilateral trading system are enhanced' (ICFTU 1996e). The debate about core labour standards revealed a number of significant points about the labour movement, its relationship to other social movements and the WTO.

With regard to the labour movement itself, the drive to integrate core labour standards into the WTO revealed divisions between the ICFTU and other sections of the movement, especially those from developing countries. The policies of the ICFTU are heavily influenced by its largest due paying members. In practice this means the West Europeans and the North Americans. While most affiliates of the ICFTU in developing countries supported the core labour standards initiative, some did not. For example, the Indian Trade Union Congress did not attend the ICFTU's pre-WTO ministerial workshop on labour standards. Moreover, there was some indication that grass-roots labour groups saw the WTO as a source of domination rather than an opportunity for justice.

Whereas opposition to core labour standards from unions tied closely to authoritarian governments in developing countries might be dismissed, it was harder to reject such concerns from more independent groups. For example, the linkage between labour standards and the WTO was rejected in two national conferences of independent Indian unions in March and October 1995. Delegates expressed fears that the social clause initiative was driven by protectionist desires in Northern countries. The Indian union suggestion was that rather than working through the WTO workers should push for a United Nations Labour Rights Convention and the establishment of National Labour Rights Commissions. The issue was not whether all workers should be entitled to basic rights, but whether the WTO was the appropriate institution for such a task. The conclusion amongst many grass-roots Indian activists was that the WTO, along with the IMF and World Bank, were irrevocably tied to exploitative

Northern interests. In their view everything possible should be done to stop the expansion of WTO powers to new areas, including labour standards (ALU 1995).

The distrust voiced by many grass-roots organisations in developing countries over the social clause issue reveals the degree to which Northern unions and the ICFTU must work to repair the damage of their Cold War legacy. Whereas the ICFTU argues that the extension of legal protections to corporate interests over issues of intellectual property rights must be accompanied by regulation in the field of workers' rights, some groups in developing countries see extended regulation in terms of past protectionism generated by US anti-dumping legislation. As for the ICFTU itself, some newly independent unions resent their cosy Cold War relationship with government sponsored unions and fear that they will urge the implementation of business unionism rather than engage in anti-capitalist struggles (ALU 1996; Spooner 1989).

The ICFTU arrived in Singapore with little thought having been given to its relationship with other social movements or with specific NGOs preparatory to or during the ministerial meeting. On the weekend prior to the ministerial meeting the ICFTU held a workshop on labour standards to review and publicise its case for integrating core labour standards into the WTO. Invitations to several NGOs to attend the event were issued only shortly before the workshop and in a seemingly casual manner. During the meeting a number of NGOs urged the ICFTU to form a Workers' Rights Caucus to bring together labour unions and NGOs who supported labour standards. The key NGOs were the International Labor Rights Fund (ILRF) (Washington), the International Centre for Human Rights and Democratic Development (ICHRDD) (Montreal), and Solidar (Brussels). On the trade union side the ICFTU provided support in the form of a representative from the Geneva office, a member of the Trade Union Advisory Committee of the OECD and members of the ITSs. Active ITSs were EI, PSI, and the ITGLWF. Significant aspects of the founding of the caucus were that it was initiated by the NGOs rather than the ICFTU and that it was left to the last minute, depending upon the chance of having some activists attending the workshop.[14]

---

[14] The idea of a Workers' Rights Caucus did not last long after the Singapore meeting. The ICHRDD, ILRF and Canadian Labour Congress hosted a Workers' Rights Forum at the 1997 People's Summit during the Vancouver APEC meetings, but there was no continuity from the WTO meeting.

During the week of the Singapore conference the ICFTU and Workers' Rights Caucus held meetings every morning following the ICFTU's own briefing meetings. They had a great deal of work to do over the week because they soon discovered that a coalition of NGOs coordinated by the Third World Network (TWN) had issued a public statement opposing the extension of the WTO's mandate to new issues, including core labour standards.[15] Their primary concern was that the WTO was an inappropriate institution to defend workers' rights and advance the concerns of the peoples of the developing world. They viewed the WTO, as well as the World Bank and the IMF, as institutions of Northern domination. The TWN and a number of development NGOs argued that 'Countervailing measures imposed unilaterally by powerful countries on weaker nations (and hardly conceivable the other way around) would lack legality, moral authority and effectiveness to lead to any effective improvement in workers' conditions or human rights situations in poor or rich countries' (TWN 1996).

In order to discuss their differences the ICFTU and TWN held a closed-door meeting on the second day of the Conference. The meeting was facilitated by the ICHRDD and the ILRF. The ICFTU and TWN each brought ten people to the meeting. Journalists with links to the organisations and the researcher for this project also attended.[16] The ICFTU ensured that it had trade unionists from Africa, Latin America and South Asia attend the session to counter the notion that it solely represented Northern interests. The TWN was primarily represented by people from Southern research institutes. Although the discussion lasted for a couple of hours the main points can be easily summarised. The TWN claimed that the structure of the WTO was biased to such an extent that the incorporation of core labour standards would only be used as a weapon by developed countries against developing countries. Their main agenda at the Singapore conference was to restrict the WTO's powers, especially its attempts to expand in the area of investment regulation. While sympathetic to protecting labour rights the appropriate institution for such a function was the ILO, not the WTO. The ICFTU argument was that the ILO's monitoring activity needed to be supplemented by the WTO's

[15] The TWN is a coalition of intellectuals from Southern based research institutes which pursue an active research programme.
[16] The following account is based upon the author's notes.

enforcement capability. Capital was using regional trade agreements, as well as the WTO to enshrine its rights. Labour had to do the same. The WTO was not the ideal institution, but it would be far worse to have no link between labour standards and trade. In the same way that one doesn't achieve everything one wants in collective bargaining, the WTO core labour standards relationship was imperfect, but necessary. They agreed to disagree.

Both the ICFTU and the TWN sought to stress their areas of agreement and the fact that on many issues they had no dispute. However, the differences between the two groups were great. The ICFTU advocates achieving gains within the existing structures while the TWN is seeking a new international architecture to give developing states more equality. Whereas the ICFTU saw the prime international cleavage as being between workers and employers, the TWN saw the divide as being North/South. The ICFTU was in favour of international organisations forcing governments to live up to minimum standards, the TWN, because of its view of international organisations, preferred greater state autonomy. In the end, the ICFTU could not answer the TWN's criticism of the structural inequality of international economic institutions and the TWN could not advocate a practical policy proposal to improve workers' rights.

Around the fringes of the debate, but never openly articulated, was a dispute not just about tactics to be adopted to further progressive change, but a contest over legitimacy and representativeness. From the perspective of some TWN members, the ICFTU was a naive Northern dominated institution acting on the behalf of Northern workers to the detriment of Southern workers. It had few links to the poorest of the poor, namely the millions of peasants in developing countries and the informal sector. Its backing of a strengthened WTO was the strategy of a labour aristocracy trying to protect its own. From the perspective of the ICFTU and the ITSs, the TWN was a collection of intellectuals with dubious links to the people they claimed to speak for. They had no mass membership base and no mechanisms of accountability. Their wholesale rejection of working within the WTO offered no hope for improving workers' living conditions.[17]

---

[17] The debate continues after Singapore. One example is a seminar organised by the Organisation of African Trade Union Unity (OATUU) in Tunisia in September 1997 on the issue of labour standards. TWN members joined OATUU and WFTU officials in arguing against a social clause at the WTO while ICFTU representatives including confederations which are part of OATUU argued in favour.

Over the course of the week the Workers' Rights Caucus issued press releases, attended other NGO meetings and hosted an NGO discussion of workers' rights. However, it was noticeable that the unions were an NGO unlike other NGOs. They did not attend the morning NGO briefing because they held their own briefing at the same time. Participation in other workshops on issues such as the environment was limited. They did not take part in the drafting or signing of the NGO statement on WTO accountability. The ICFTU and ITSs were outside the cosy community of environmentalist and development NGOs. They were also better informed on the workers' rights issues than the other NGOs. These differences are partially attributable to the relatively privileged position of the labour organisation compared with other NGOs

The ICFTU was in a distinctive position with regard to the non-profit NGOs at the WTO meeting. One advantage they had was that they were clearly pushing a limited positive agenda. The TWN, similar to many developing countries, was primarily in an oppositional mode, attempting to have issues kept off the agenda. Environmentalists were split with some calling for an end to existing WTO environmental positions, others advocating further engagement. These defensive positions were no match for the expansive agenda of the most powerful states and interest groups.

A second and more important advantage enjoyed by organised labour was its close relationship with several governments. ICFTU affiliates in the USA, Canada, New Zealand, Denmark, Norway, Egypt, Tunisia, Burkina Faso and South Africa were accredited to government delegations. This allowed them access to government briefings and government officials. Since the WTO is dominated by its member states, ability to influence rests upon the ability to lobby key states. On the issue of labour standards, the unions had clear influence in the governments of Norway, the USA and France. The Norwegian government proposed the WTO create a working party to examine labour and trade issues. This was similar to the ICFTU's position. More important was the commitment from the USA and the EU to have some mention of labour included in the Ministerial Declaration. The European Commission, which spoke for the EU, was committed to labour standards, but the British government opposed the initiative and at the last moment the German government declared that labour issues should not derail the conference.

In the USA, the Congress had demanded that the US negotiators address the labour standards issue. John Sweeney, the recently elected AFL–CIO head, worked with the acting United States Trade Representative, Charlene Barshefsky, to push the labour standards issue in a number of arenas. In a pre-ministerial meeting address to the ICFTU's labour standards workshop Barshefsky sent the message that she was 'fighting your fight' (USTR 1996). The US administration was also in the position of needing fasttrack negotiating authority from Congress if a new trade round was to be launched. In light of the bitter debate over NAFTA (Rupert 1995), the rise of the isolationist right, and the renewed activism of the AFL-CIO (Mort 1998), the US government was bound to press the labour standards issue. Significantly, the USA was also the single most important state at the WTO.

The outcome of the labour issue at the Singapore meeting reflected the relative power of developed states to developing states and labour to business. The USA and Western Europe had a very successful week at the WTO meeting. They were able to bring three new issues – investment, competition policy and labour – into the purview of the WTO. On investment and competition policy they secured working groups to begin examination of the issue. On labour they secured a mention of the subject of core labour standards in the declaration and the enshrining of institutional cooperation with the ILO.[18] This was far less than a working party, but allowed developed states to show some progress on the labour issue while not alienating their business constituency.

Although labour and some northern European governments wanted the WTO to create a working party on the issue of trade and labour standards it soon became clear that the contest at Singapore would be about whether there was even any mention of labour in the final ministerial document. A coalition of states which could be

---

[18] The statement on labour standards is the fourth of eighteen paragraphs comprising the Singapore Ministerial Declaration. It reads as follows:

> We renew our commitment to the observance of internationally recognised core labour standards. The International Labour Organisation (ILO) is the competent body to set and deal with these standards, and we affirm our support for its work in promoting them. We believe that economic growth and development fostered by increased trade and further liberalisation contribute to the promotion of these standards. We reject the use of labour standards for protectionist purposes, and agree that the comparative advantage of countries, particularly low-wage developing countries, must in no way be put into question. In this regard, we note that the WTO and ILO Secretariats will continue existing collaboration. (WTO 1996c)

termed anti-imperialist (India), authoritarian (Indonesia)[19] and neoliberal (UK) combined with business organisations and some development groups to oppose any connection between the WTO and labour standards. A number of Southern countries including India and Pakistan demonstrated their opposition to dealing with labour issues when they exploited a WTO technicality to prevent the director general of the ILO from addressing the Singapore meeting. In addition to the government of Britain, Western employers also opposed making any connection between the WTO and labour issues.[20] In last minute negotiations India's adamant opposition was only overcome when the chair of the Singapore meeting agreed to put the following statement in his concluding remarks: 'Some delegations had expressed the concern that this text may lead the WTO to acquire a competence to undertake further work in the relationship between trade and core labour standards. I want to assure this delegation that this text will not permit such a development' (Yeo 1996).

The statement on core labour standards was a classic compromise that was interpreted differently by opposing parties. India, Britain and many Asian states followed Chairman Yeo's interpretation of the Ministerial Declaration and concluded that the issue of trade and labour standards would not reappear at the WTO. At press briefings on the final day the United States Trade Representative stressed that the chairman's remarks reflected his personal view and carried no legal weight. They did not reflect the US understanding of the text. The French representative declared that he was overjoyed with the text because it institutionalised the relationship between the WTO and the ILO and would permit further work on the issue.[21]

The implications of the labour section of the Singapore Ministerial Declaration must await future developments at the WTO. Despite the opposition of many developing countries and most employers,

---

[19] Indonesia's stance against linking trade and labour standards was made more clear by the simultaneous trial of independent union leaders in Jakarta during the WTO meeting. On the trial see *Far Eastern Economic Review* (1996).

[20] The press releases issued by the International Chamber of Commerce, Eurocommerce and the Union of Industrial and Employers' Confederations of Europe at the WTO conference all opposed the linking of labour standards with the trade institution. The declared devotion to the ILO may have more to do with its lack of enforcement mechanisms than its expertise. Employers' support for even a weak ILO was undermined by their boycott of the ILO's negotiations for a new Convention on homeworking in 1996.

[21] Author's notes from the British, US and French Press briefings of 13 December 1996.

reference that leaves some opening to future consideration of labour issues in a WTO framework was inserted into the text. This was some distance from labour's first choice (a working party), but it also avoided the worst case scenario, which was a statement clearly closing off future discussion of labour issues at the WTO.[22] Although labour did not achieve nearly as much as it wanted, the little it did accomplish was due to its ability to influence the leadership of the most powerful states.

NGOs and the WTO Singapore meeting

Since the December 1996 Singapore meeting was the first ministerial meeting of the WTO, it was also the first major occasion that the WTO had to deal with NGOs and, by extension, social movements. Several environmental NGOs arrived in Singapore with developed critiques of the WTO's operation in its first two years (Bellmann and Gerster 1996; Enders 1996; Vander Stichele 1996). In general, the criticism was that the WTO continued the secretive approach of its predecessor the GATT. NGOs complained that despite recent attempts to provide more WTO documents to the public, these were distributed after decisions had already been made. This made it impossible for NGOs to have any policy input. There was also dissatisfaction with the lack of opportunity for NGOs to participate in policy-making fora such as the dispute settlement mechanism. Although the dispute settlement mechanism made provision for consulting outside experts, this was at the discretion of the states involved and the WTO. The week of the Singapore conference reinforced many of these frustrations for the NGOs.

One area where there was no complaint was in the provision of physical facilities by the WTO in cooperation with the Singapore government. An NGO centre was established within walking distance of the main conference centre where the plenary sessions took place. Within the NGO centre, televisions broadcast proceedings live from

[22] At the ICFTU labour standards workshop prior to the WTO meeting Ruggerio's draft statement on labour standards was subject to considerable debate. Representatives from the Workers' Group at the ILO and the head of the Trade Union Advisory Council to the OECD stressed the importance of having some statement which kept the issue alive and allowed them to pursue further work at the ILO and OECD. In their view the worst WTO outcome would be a statement that said the labour standards and trade issue was settled or confined only to one institution.

the Ministerial Meeting. Press conferences of various delegations and WTO officials were also broadcast on a WTO channel. In addition, any interested NGO could record and broadcast a two-minute statement for the channel. NGOs were provided with meeting rooms, computer facilities (including e-mail), WTO public documentation and delegates press releases.

Although the facilities provided by the Singapore government were excellent, the heavy hand of the state was never far away. Prior to arriving in Singapore and upon picking up the registration pack, NGO delegates were informed that no form of public protest would be tolerated.[23] Singapore foreign affairs officials monitored the NGO notice board and copies of every notice were made. Offending notices such as the ICFTU's publicity of Indonesia's simultaneous trial of independent labour leaders were removed. These restrictions did not appear to interfere greatly with NGO activity, but the dynamics of the interaction in a more free society might well have been different.

NGOs which had registered before the meeting were given access to the main hall for plenary sessions and to the press centre. This allowed NGOs to corner national delegates on the fringes of the meeting and to publicise their views among the press corps. There was some unhappiness that NGOs had restricted access to member-states' press conferences. These were held on a different level and an elaborate procedure requiring a delegate from a state to escort the NGO delegate reduced practical access. NGOs felt this to be a problem because they could not publicly press their government officials on particular issues. Some NGOs were able to circumvent this obstacle if they were also accredited to a news agency and had a press credential.

There was some controversy concerning NGO accreditation. In order to secure NGO status at the December meeting NGOs had to register with the WTO by October. The WTO Secretariat made decisions about whether a particular organisation was sufficiently concerned with trade issues to merit accreditation. For example, the ITS EI was refused accreditation because the WTO felt that the activities of a trade union organisation concerned with education 'were not directly related to the trade activities of the WTO'.[24]

---

[23] Joining Instructions, NGO delegate pack.
[24] Letter from Alain Frank, director of WTO External Relations Division to Sheena Hanley, deputy secretary of Education International, 17 October 1996.

Similarly, the ITS PSI was initially refused representation. In PSI's case they persisted, arguing with the WTO in person, and were eventually given accreditation. EI was able to attend by using one of PSI's places. WTO officials claim that very few NGOs were denied accreditation to the Singapore conference, although a few nationally focused human rights organisations were discouraged.[25] This is difficult to verify independently.

The WTO External Relations Department did not consult other multilateral economic organisations, such as the World Bank, about how to handle NGOs during large meetings. Because of the perceived unique nature of the WTO and the sensitivity of some member states to NGO presence, WTO officials felt that they were in a unique situation.[26] In its first attempt to deal with civil society actors on a large scale the WTO determined that everything that was not a state or a member of the press was labelled an NGO. This created an interesting mix of NGOs at the NGO centre. One could overhear a member of the Sierra Club debate with a member of the Enterprise Institute whether there was a greater risk to mortality from the green-house effect or lack of refrigeration in developing countries. Around the corner a member of the Pork Producers Council speculated that the US Intelligence community was backing China's accession to the WTO in spite of the harm it might do to farming interests. Indeed the largest contingent (65 per cent) of NGOs registered for the Singapore conference were business organisations.[27] They attended in order to monitor the conference and lobby when they felt their commercial interests were threatened. They were treated in the same manner as non-profit public interest groups. Since there was no observer status (other than for countries or intergovernmental organisations), some individuals became one-person NGOs. The author of this chapter attended the Singapore meetings as the University of Sussex NGO.

The distribution of non-business NGOs reflected the degree to which various groups had been involved in trade issues. Environmentalist groups had been heavily involved in lobbying during the Uruguay Round and had managed to secure a Committee on Trade and Environment at the WTO. They had a high profile at the NGO centre and organised numerous seminars around trade and environment issues as well as providing developed critiques of WTO account-

---

[25] Interview, WTO officials, 30 September 1997.   [26] Ibid.
[27] Author's calculations from the list of NGOs attending the meeting.

ability. The second high-profile group was the TWN which had held a pre-Singapore seminar with numerous development groups. They published an NGO statement setting out a position for halting the expansion of the WTO agenda. The third significant NGO presence was the labour unions in the form of the ICFTU, the ITSs and the WCL.

The women's movement initially had a relatively low profile at the WTO meeting. There was no preparatory networking for the meeting. A number of women from various NGOs came together early in the week to form a women's caucus. This included women from a range of NGOs such as Oxfam International, Transnational Institute, ICFTU, EI, Catholic Centre for International Relations and Sierra Club, as well as from NGOs specifically dedicated to women's issues such as Women Working Worldwide (WWW), Women's Environment and Development Organisation (WEDO), and Women in Development Europe (WIDE). The women's caucus was able to make contact with WTO officials from the Trade Policy Review Mechanism (TPRM), which reviews the trade policy of member states. They secured an agreement to begin a dialogue concerning gender and the WTO, an issue which officials had not previously considered. A press release was issued which stated that WTO members had ignored their commitments from the Beijing Women's Conference that policy making should be gender sensitive (WWW 1996; 1997).

The formation of the Women's Caucus and initial contacts with the WTO were a small, but significant step in the women's movement's engagement with the WTO. For many working women the WTO is a distant and mysterious institution which appears not to have a direct impact on their lives. For the WTO secretariat gender issues have never been an issue. The women's caucus will now lobby for the analysis of the gender effects of WTO policies and the consideration of gender dimensions in individual countries' trade-policy reviews. It was the first step in getting gender and trade liberalisation on to the WTO agenda.

Subsequent to the Singapore meeting a WTO Gender Caucus met with UN agencies, NGOs and WTO officials in Geneva in March 1997. This group is now known as the Informal Working Group on Gender and Trade. Similar to labour, their evolving strategy entailed having gender issues inserted into the TPRM (discussed in more detail in a following section). Members of the group are also involved in lobbying their home governments to push the WTO to take notice of gender concerns. For example, WIDE has been lobbying the EU to integrate gender into its WTO strategy (Brew 1998). The trade union members of the WTO Women's Caucus are also interested in demonstrating how core labour standards would have a positive gender impact.

The problem of access to information that NGOs identified prior to the Singapore meeting was in evidence. Official WTO briefings of the NGOs at the NGO centre were short and had a surreal element. The director for External Relations appeared every evening and morning to announce that nothing had yet been decided by member states. He would then leave and return either that evening or the next morning and repeat the process. The lack of content in official briefings reflected the degree to which the Secretariat was bound by the desire of some member states for secrecy. The best source of information about what was happening at the meetings came from members of national delegations invited to the NGO centre for morning briefings. These delegates often had close ties to the NGO community and were able to shed some light on developments.

The difficulty in securing timely documentation also persisted for NGOs at the Singapore meeting. Most of the week's discussion focused around a draft Ministerial Declaration that all countries were asked to sign. As the week progressed sections of the declaration, such as the fourth paragraph on labour standards, were subject to intense negotiation. Most NGOs were unable to get a copy of this draft or to amendments that were being proposed by various states. For its part, the WTO Secretariat argued that it was not able to distribute such information unless it was instructed to do so by the member states. This made it difficult to lobby governments because it was not always clear what was under discussion.

In fairness, the information problem was not limited to NGOs. Some national delegations were unaware of the state of negotiations. The government of Singapore had opened the meeting with the intention that business would be conducted in a single Heads of Delegation meeting composed of the trade ministers of each state. However, this arrangement proved unmanageable owing to the large numbers involved and was soon replaced with *ad hoc* meetings of states around key issues. Since these meetings were not arranged beforehand there were times when national delegations, especially from smaller states, were wandering around the meeting site in search of the latest meeting on subject X. The major states were never in doubt about the schedule, but smaller states were not always able to participate.

At the conclusion of the WTO Singapore meeting a number of NGOs gathered to review the progress of the meeting and their relationship to the institution. A statement was issued which urged the WTO to review its process of document circulation and expand NGO participation in policy making. Ideas for expanding the NGO role included the right to make verbal and written statements in policy deliberations, contributing to the TPRM reports and the right for public interest NGOs to participate in public dispute-settlement hearings. The NGOs also raised issues of equal access for developing-country NGOs. This included the need for financial support and the provision of documents in print as well as in electronic form. The WTO was urged to take such measures before the review of their relations with NGOs due in July 1998.[28]

Labour and the WTO post-Singapore

For the labour movement the Singapore conference did not achieve a great deal. Optimistically they could point to states reaffirming their commitment to the ILO and recognition of ILO–WTO cooperation. Whereas at the 1994 Marrakesh GATT meeting labour issues were relegated to a broad chair's statement, they at least made it into the main Singapore Ministerial Declaration. In addition, labour issues had dominated the Singapore meeting, attracting a great deal of attention. The labour movement managed to prevent their worst case scenario which would have been a clear statement rejecting any role for the WTO with regard to labour issues.

Yet, the concrete accomplishments were slim. As mentioned earlier, the Ministerial Declaration included a paragraph on labour standards

---

[28] 'Singapore Statement on NGO–WTO Relations,' Singapore, 13 December 1996. NGOs which signed on were Sierra Club, Focus on the Global South, Humane Society, Eurogroup Animal Welfare, International Institute for Sustainable Development, CIECA, NCDO, Third World Network, International South Group Network, Indigenous Peoples' International Centre for Policy and Research, Center for International Environmental Law, Transnational Institute, Forum Syd, WorldWide Fund for Nature International, Institute for Agriculture and Trade Policy, SEWS, Institute for African Alternatives, Institute del Tercer Mundo, Organisation of African Trade Union Unity, Greenpeace International, International Coalition for Development Action, People's Forum 2001, Oxfam and Friends of the Earth International. The ICFTU, WCL and ITSs did not participate in this exercise.

only because various parties could put their own, often conflicting, interpretation on it. For example, the Declaration confirmed that existing collaboration between the WTO and ILO should continue, but most people had no clue as to what such existing collaboration entailed. The task for the labour movement post-Singapore was to build upon the ambiguous Singapore statement by inserting itself and labour issues into the regular operation of the WTO.

The primary strategy to keep the issue alive has been to insert labour issues into the trade policy review mechanism hearings. The TPRM is a process whereby the WTO regularly reviews the trade policy of individual member states. The ICFTU has published country reports to coincide with country reviews. Its hope is that this will highlight labour issues in each country and that member states will use the policy reviews as an opportunity to raise labour issues. The first instance of such a procedure was the trade policy review of Fiji. The review corresponded with a major dispute between the Fijian government and the Fijian Trade Unions Congress. The ICFTU's report outlined the shortcomings in Fijian practice with regard to the key ILO conventions and the implications for Fiji's export sector (ICFTU 1997). During the review Denmark and the USA raised the labour issue while the chair (Pakistan) tried to rule it out of order. The minutes of the meeting only note that the issue was raised.

The TPRM can be used as a tool to keep labour issues in the headlines, but little more. Hostility to discussing any aspect of labour issues remains intense. An example of this opposition occurred in September 1997 when the Norwegian delegate to the WTO's General Council asked a two-part question of the director-general. The first part sought clarification about the nature of WTO–ILO existing collaboration while the second part asked whether the WTO had received any information on core labour standards that could be shared with WTO members.[29] The first part of the question was straightforward and received a direct answer. The director-general replied that collaboration with the ILO involved three elements. Firstly, the WTO participated in the meetings of some ILO bodies such as the Working Party on the Social Dimensions of the Liberalisation of International Trade. Secondly, the Secretariats exchanged documentation. Thirdly, there was informal cooperation between the Secretariats.

The second part of the question was an attempt to have labour

---

[29] This section is based upon interviews with WTO officials.

issues raised in the WTO's Governing Body by having ILO work reported to it. This would then have opened the door to discussion of the ILO work and the issue of core labour standards in general. The director-general finessed the question by replying that ILO information was publicly available. The representatives of Egypt and Pakistan led a number of other developing countries in condemning the attempt to raise the issue of labour standards in the Governing Body. Many states, especially developing countries, remain opposed to discussing labour issues in any form.

A longer term strategy for bringing discussion of labour issues into the WTO lies in the area of social labelling and company codes of conduct. A number of consumer and labour organisations in developed countries have been putting pressure upon corporations to produce products in a socially responsible manner. Examples include the Rugmark campaign in India, Germany and the USA, and the Clean Clothes Campaign in Europe. Rugmark stamps inform customers that hand knotted carpets from India (and recently Nepal) have not been made with child labour while the Clean Clothes Campaign holds public events to inform consumers about working conditions in the textile and garment industry (ILRF 1996; Shaw 1997). A proliferation of such campaigns may soon start to cause concern about their effect on trade and investment. For example, some states may fear that their products are unjustly being denied access or that investment is shifted to other locations because of consumer and labour campaigns. It may prove advantageous for states to regulate such activity multilaterally.[30] At the moment this remains a possibility, but it is not yet clear that consumer and labour campaigns pose a great enough obstacle for the WTO to become seriously involved in the issue.

One must conclude that very little has been accomplished in the WTO–labour relationship. Labour issues remain a subject of intense controversy. While most states will discuss the environment, many refuse to begin a dialogue about labour issues and trade. What accounts for this vehement opposition to dialogue, much less action? Labour poses a more fundamental challenge to the interests of particular states than environmentalists. Core labour standards are enabling standards which create a space for autonomous labour organisation. They provide for the abolition of the most punishing forms of labour, giving workers the ability to organise independently.

---

[30] Interview, General Secretary, ITGLWF, 24 September 1997, Brussels.

This challenges state elites seeking to keep a tight rein on political power. For example, freedom of association could provide the basis for political opposition to an authoritarian state whereas environmental issues such as using a particular type of net to catch tuna can be accommodated without threatening state power.

Because the WTO remains an interstate body and influence is exerted through the state, labour groups continue to rely on the good will of particular states to advance their cause. This has two major implications for the labour movement. Firstly, no matter how important international activity might be, there is no substitute for exerting political influence within the dominant economic states. Even though the WTO is dedicated to developing a rules based regime, its agenda is driven by the powerful states. These states are primarily the USA and those of the EU, but they are being pursued by Southeast and East Asian states. Labour issues will remain on the WTO agenda to the extent that labour can influence these states. Thus, the strength of US labour is crucial as the US administration tries to tread a fine line between Democrats and Republicans in Congress.[31]

The second implication is that if labour wants to influence WTO policy it must develop allies in developing states. The labour standards issue has often been successfully portrayed as a North–South issue. That division must be broken down in order for progress to be made. The modest support of the South African state is an example to build upon. South Africa was crucial in selling the labour section of the Singapore Declaration to other developing states. The task is formidable as advocates of core labour standards are caught in a vicious circle. Support from some developing countries is needed to advance labour standards, but this support is only likely to be forthcoming from countries with vital and independent labour movements. However, many of these movements would require the respect of core labour standards before they could establish themselves on a solid footing. Many of the governments are opposed to core labour standards and are able to prevent the introduction of steps which would allow this key constituency to mobilise.

In May 1998 the WTO held its second ministerial meeting. This time the meeting was located in Geneva and the emphasis was placed on celebrating the fiftieth anniversary of GATT rather than reaching

---

[31] Interview, USTR official, 1 October 1997, Geneva.

agreement on new initiatives. The ICFTU also attended and tried to persuade ministers and government leaders to make statements indicating that labour standards would have to be part of any future negotiating round. President Bill Clinton indicated his desire to see the WTO and ILO convene a special meeting to address the labour standards issue.[32] In addition, South Africa's President Nelson Mandela urged other developing countries not to rule out the prospect of taking steps to protect working conditions. The ICFTU's goals were limited to reminding decision makers that their issue was not going away. In contrast to the Singapore meeting the ICFTU arrived with a plan to engage other members of the NGO community at the WTO meeting. Working closely with a European NGO, Solidar, the ICFTU provided information to other groups and launched a campaign highlighting child labour issues.

Some of the ICFTU's members with a tradition of social movement unionism such as COSATU in South Africa and CUT in Brazil suggested that the confederation widen its engagement with the WTO.[33] They urged the ICFTU to broaden its concerns from core labour standards to issues such as the role of developing countries, environmental protection and widening participation in the dispute settlement process. The motivation for taking on a broader agenda was to influence other key issues and to demonstrate to other members of society that the labour movement was not simply working at the WTO to further its own narrow interests. Such steps would require the ICFTU to dedicate more staff to its Geneva office and expend greater resources. Although the leadership took note of such concerns, the problem of scarce resources acts against such a strategy. Despite such resource constraints, the ICFTU pulled together a much more comprehensive critique of the WTO by the time of WTO high-level symposia on 'Trade and Environment' and 'Trade and Development' in March 1999 (ICFTU 1999b). This briefing paper highlighted development, environmental, gender and social concerns, as well as labour standards.

The Geneva ministerial meeting was largely insignificant for the labour standards issue because of its ceremonial nature. In addition, its timing in May came just before a scheduled ILO meeting in June where labour standards were to be a key issue. Indeed one of the

---

[32] Address by President Clinton to the WTO, 18 May 1998, Geneva.
[33] Author's notes from an ICFTU pre-ministerial meeting, 15–17 May 1998.

significant aspects of the labour campaign at the WTO has been the spillover effect on the ILO. It is to this issue that we now turn.

Challenging the International Labour Organisation

As we have seen, the labour movement's attempt to have its issue of core labour standards inserted into the WTO was not entirely successful. However, the push for linking the WTO with labour standards resulted in challenging another international organisation to reform and make itself more relevant. This other institution is the ILO.

The ILO presents a significant contrast to the WTO in four ways. Firstly, it is a much older institution, having been founded over seventy-five years earlier in 1919. Secondly, whereas the WTO was founded in the wake of the collapse of the Soviet Union and the apparent triumph of capitalism over communism, the ILO was created in response to the threat of communism and increasing worker militancy after the First World War. Thirdly, the ILO lacks the enforcement powers of the WTO's dispute settlement mechanism and the threat of sanctions. It must rely upon moral persuasion to influence state policy. Fourthly, whereas the WTO membership is restricted to states, the ILO includes representatives of civil society in its membership and integrates them into the decision-making process.

This last aspect deserves some elaboration because the ILO's inclusion of civil society elements in its structure is unique amongst multilateral economic institutions. ILO decisions are taken at a yearly general assembly (International Labour Conference) and in an executive council (Governing Body). Each national delegation to the International Labour Conference contains four delegates. Two represent the government, one represents the country's employers and one represents the country's workers. All four delegates may vote and they can take different positions. Workers or employers (depending upon national controls) may vote against their government's delegates. This tripartite decision-making structure is significant because it acknowledges that a state is not the only legitimate expression of interests within a territory. It encourages the forging of transnational alliances along functional lines among workers or employers. A mixture of government, employer and worker delegate support is usually required to adopt new measures such as an ILO Convention because approval requires a two-thirds majority.

In the ILO we have an international organisation founded twenty-five years before the Bretton Woods institutions and seventy-five years before the WTO, an organisation which has made far more elaborate provision for civil society participation. This casts doubt on a simplistic correlation between recent changes in the global economy and the need for society–institutional linkages. One might argue that the ILO structure is unique because of its subject matter – the condition of labour. An international organisation dealing with labour issues might be thought to require some labour participation.

Such an explanation is not satisfactory for two reasons. Firstly, national labour ministers could deal with labour issues. There is no a priori requirement for labour organisations to participate in decision making through voting. Secondly, a similar argument could be made for civil society participation in the WTO. It is primarily concerned with establishing the rules of trade and commerce, yet the units which engage in these activities have no direct voice. If the WTO is primarily concerned with creating a legal environment for firms to conduct business freely, a case can be made that those firms should have direct representation. Indeed, some prominent business leaders are pressing for a greater role.[34]

This suggests that it may be the political environment rather than the issue area which is most influential in determining the degree to which civil society representatives are integrated into international institutions. More specifically, the degree to which civil society actors are capable of aiding or frustrating the ideal of these organisations is key. The ILO accommodated worker representatives not because it was seen as being more democratic, but because worker militancy was seen to threaten order. The ILO was needed because '... conditions of labour exist involving such injustice, hardship and privation to large numbers of people as to produce unrest so great that the peace and harmony of the world are imperilled ...' (ILO 1994: Preamble).

For all of its history and civil society participation, the ILO has not been a tremendously effective organisation. Many of its Conventions are unratified and many that are ratified are not observed in practice by member states. The USA, in particular, has had a stormy

---

[34] See comments by the chairman of Nestlé (Maucher 1997). The fear that business organisations might dominate the WTO at the expense of other interests is expressed in Vander Stichele 1998.

relationship with the ILO and refused to participate in the Organisation on more than one occasion (Imber 1989: 42–69; Wilson 1934: 325–50). For much of the Cold War, the ILO, as did other UN agencies, served as a battleground between the Soviet Union and the USA (Cox 1977). The core labour standards debate at the WTO offered the ILO an opportunity to reassert itself as an international organisation (Hansenne 1996).

The opportunity for a new ILO initiative gathered force as countries which opposed a WTO–labour standards link reaffirmed their commitment to core labour standards, but argued that the ILO was the appropriate forum. The Singapore WTO meeting passed the issue back to the ILO with the implication that the ILO should make itself more relevant to the debate and the issue area. Since the labour issue was brought to the WTO precisely because key actors felt that the ILO had been ineffective, the challenge was clear. The ILO had to reform or risk increasing irrelevance as actors continued their attempt to pursue labour issues at the WTO.

The post-Singapore response at the ILO took the form of two strategies. The first involved a new Declaration and supervisory mechanism. The second was a proposal for institutionalising social labelling. The employers' group suggested that a new ILO Declaration on core labour standards would provide a legal basis for renewed action covering those states that had not yet signed the key conventions (ILO 1997b). The workers' group felt that such a Declaration was unnecessary. They were much more concerned with creating a new institutional mechanism which would highlight and condemn abuses. Governments from advanced industrialised countries gave muted support to the idea of a new mechanism, but several Asian states including Japan began to push for a review (and weakening) of existing ILO mechanisms.[35]

The second major initiative was a proposal by the director-general for a global social label (ILO 1997a). Noting the proliferation of consumer and corporate initiatives in the field of social labelling and codes of conduct, the director-general suggested multilateral regulation of such activity. The ILO could act to oversee such a system and prevent the misuse or abuse of social labels.

The Ambassador of Colombia on behalf of the Non-Aligned Movement rejected both of these initiatives in a public statement (*South Letter*

---

[35] Interview with Geneva ICFTU official, 1 October 1997.

1997). It rejected the notion that the Singapore WTO meeting had given a new mandate on trade and labour standards. Rather than trying to develop new mechanisms, a Declaration or a global social label, the ILO should be trying to curb Northern protectionism. Indeed, it was ominously suggested that the existing supervisory system should be reviewed for 'objectivity, impartiality and transparency'.

Despite such objections the ILO did adopt a new Declaration on core labour standards in its conference in June 1998 (ILO 1998a). Officially the declaration was titled the 'Declaration on Fundamental Principles and Rights at Work'. It bound all of its members to respect the seven core labour standards and provided for a follow-up mechanism which would highlight abuses. By virtue of their membership of the ILO the Declaration covers countries whether or not they have ratified the relevant Conventions. The follow-up mechanism provides for the compilation of a global report which will cover one of the four categories of rights (freedom of association and collective bargaining, forced labour, child labour, discrimination in employment) each year (ILO 1998b). The report will then be reviewed by the ILO conference. In addition, the follow-up mechanism provides for annual monitoring of the status of ratification of the core labour standards conventions.

A number of developing states such as Egypt, Pakistan, Mexico and Colombia resisted the adoption of a new declaration. During the conference some of these states were represented by their WTO ambassadors who knew little about the ILO, but were determined to resist core labour standards. They were able to have a paragraph inserted in the Declaration which stated that core labour standards should not be used for protectionist trade purposes or to disrupt comparative advantage. In effect, they inserted a WTO trade concern into the ILO after previously arguing at the WTO that labour standards and trade should not be mentioned in the same arena! These hardline states were eventually outmanoeuvred as other developing countries such as India and even China signed on to the non-threatening Declaration.

In ILO terms the new Declaration was another small step in the protection of workers' rights. It was greeted with approval in official trade union circles (ICFTU 1998). The Declaration was a sign that the ILO could respond to demands for increased activity in the face of globalisation. It will allow workers to highlight abuses of core labour standards and to identify consistent offenders. However, the ILO's limits of persuasion are clear. At the same conference that approved the Declaration, the states of Myanmar (Burma) and Sudan were cited for a consistent pattern of abusing workers' rights. There was no sign that such shaming will have any noticeable effect on these states' policy. The same fate is likely to await the work of the new Declaration's follow-up mechanism.

After several years of intense activity it is clear that some limited progress has been made on the issue of institutionalising global core labour standards. In an effort to block WTO consideration of the issue, many states stressed the sole role of the ILO. Efforts to reform the ILO have led to the creation of a new Declaration and follow-up mechanism. The mechanism will serve to highlight continuing abuses of workers' fundamental rights. The lack of an enforcement procedure after the issuing of ILO reports will once again raise the question of using the WTO's institutional power. In addition, one can expect a continued proliferation of initiatives where organised labour can exert some pressure – in the USA and the EU and in the field of company codes of conduct. The limited accommodation of multilateral institutions to the labour movement may not be the blessing that anti-standards forces perceive. Alienating organised labour from the WTO complicates the task of building institutional legitimacy in the civil society of advanced industrial states.

Conclusion

This chapter has investigated the relationship between the WTO and labour, but it has also strayed into labour's relations with other international organisations (especially the ILO) and the WTO's general relations with NGOs. Returning to the key questions raised in the introductory chapter we can provide some answers for this particular case study.

How has this MEI modified?

The WTO is a new institution replacing the GATT. We can see changes between the GATT and the WTO, as well as changes in the brief operation of the WTO. The GATT made virtually no provision for civil society participation in meetings or for the dissemination of publicity material. Beginning with the Singapore ministerial meeting the WTO has gradually opened up to NGOs and other civil society actors. It provides civil society actors with extensive facilities at ministerial meetings and distributes documents on the Internet. In addition, the WTO has held a series of workshops with NGOs on key issues. It has gradually expanded its concerns from engaging with environmentalists to labour organisations, development NGOs and most recently women's movements. In the case of organised labour, ICFTU officials have access to key WTO officials and have been able to put forward their case. From organised labour's perspective the problem is not really with the structure of the WTO, but with the policies that it is bound to enforce.

What are the motivations driving MEI–GSM engagement?

The WTO is concerned about the labour movement for two reasons. Firstly, key states such as the USA and France have put labour issues on the agenda. Secondly, Secretariat officials at the WTO planning for future liberalisation initiatives worry about securing domestic political support in developed states. The disturbance by protesters at the 1998 Geneva ministerial meeting was a visible lesson in why they should be concerned. These gestures of protest served to emphasise the fact that the WTO needed to monitor views in civil society and make alliances with those that are more supportive.

For the labour movement the WTO is one of a number of international organisations and agreements exercising an influence upon their members. They seek to influence it as they seek to influence regional trade agreements, the World Bank, the IMF, the ILO and multinational corporations. To date their concern has not been with the WTO as an institution, but with finding a method to enforce workers' rights on a world-wide scale. If the ILO were up to the task, the WTO campaign would not have been launched. Labour organisations have concentrated on the issue of core labour standards at the WTO and passed over issues of institutional reform or other substantive issues such as environmental protection or the fate of developing countries in the trading order.

What is the significance of the MEI–GSM relationship?

In policy terms neither the WTO nor the ICFTU have accomplished a great deal. The WTO enjoys some support and a sympathetic hearing from the ICFTU leadership, but support at lower levels of the trade union movement is not as obvious. The ICFTU has made its case for core labour standards to WTO officials and has the qualified support of some key states, but opposition amongst the majority of states has prevented any action on labour issues.

The continuing dialogue between organised labour, the WTO and some member states indicates two things. Firstly, labour issues remain on the agenda. Their 'solution' may lie at the WTO or in a revitalised ILO or in unilateral action in developed economies. Whatever the case the concerns of labour will not simply disappear. Secondly, there is an increased recognition that future liberalisation and the stability of the international trading system is partially linked to the degree to which such institutions and initiatives can accommodate social concerns. The fiction of trade agreements being the preserve of states has given way to a grudging consideration of their roots in civil society.

4   The World Bank, the World Trade Organization and the environmental social movement

This chapter examines the evolving relationship between the World Bank, the World Trade Organization (WTO) and the environmental social movement (ESM). Specifically, it explores the demands made by environmentalists on the two multilateral economic institutions (MEIs) and the reaction of the MEIs to this constituency. The interactions between the World Bank, the WTO and the ESM have to be understood in the context of the emergence of a global discourse on environmental issues, the respective institutional histories of the MEIs, increasing attention to the institutions of civil society, and the growth of pluralism and diversity in international society. Although the Bank and the WTO are intergovernmental organisations with a membership comprising sovereign governments, not only are their activities the subject of intense scrutiny by non-state actors, but the membership and administration of these organisations have to varying extents become engaged in dialogue with groups representing diverse interests. This chapter examines the salience of these developments from the perspectives of the MEIs and the ESM.

The argument is divided into three substantive sections. The first section is concerned with the environmental social movement, and provides an introduction to the role of the ESM in international politics. The aim of this section is to outline an introduction to the various actors which comprise the ESM, and to assess the sources of influence possessed by various components of the movement. The second section of the chapter focuses on the troubled history of the World Bank's relationship with environmental activists. This section traces the relationship between the Bank and the ESM, examines the impact of environmentalists on Bank policy and assesses the extent to which the Bank has adapted to the demands of its critics. The environmentalist critique of the world trading system is the subject of the third section of the chapter. The WTO came into existence in 1995, and from the outset it was subject to challenge by environmentalists. This part of the chapter explores the demands made by environmentalists and the WTO's response. In both these sections the relationship between the MEI and other social movements forms an important part of the context in which discussions between the international organisation and the ESM is conducted. The final section attempts to derive some general conclusions about the relationships examined.

The environmental social movement

One of the key strands within contemporary politics can be labelled environmentalism (Pepper 1996). Whilst not easy to classify, environmentalism can be taken to signify a concern with the environment. In other words, the fact that the environment has become a political issue.

Since the 1960s the environment as an issue has moved from the margins to the centre of political debate. Evidence of the increased political salience of the environment is to be found in the eruption of national environmental agencies, and ministries of the environment in the developed and developing worlds. No single event or publication is responsible for this increased attention to the relationship between human activity and the natural world. We can cite environmental accidents, irrefutable evidence of environmental degradation and the growth of a post-materialist culture, but these events do not in themselves constitute a force for change. The development of environmentalism has been accompanied by the growth of an environmental movement; in other words, the material developments have been shaped by human agency. Most commentators agree that an environmental movement consisting of a number of disparate actors exists, and many believe that it has helped shape the agenda, and exercised a significant degree of influence on the efforts of national governments and international organisations to respond to the perceived environmental crisis. In common with other social movements the environmental movement encompasses a variety of organisational forms. These include political parties, non-governmental organisations (NGOs), community based organisations (CBOs), and business organisations. Some organisations are single issue specific whereas others address a wide range of issues. Moreover, the movement consists of organisations whose orientation is wholly environmental and others who merge environmental concerns with other issues, such as peace or women's rights.

Furthermore, no single ideology permeates the environmental movement, and different strands of environmentalism can be discerned within it. It has become commonplace to distinguish between radical and reformist versions of environmentalism. This distinction has given rise to differing terminologies. For example, Andrew Dobson (1990) uses the terms light green and dark green, and Robyn Eckersley (1994) refers to a divide between anthropocentric and ecocentric approaches. The reformist approach broadly accepts the prevailing political and economic structure and attempts to promote technocentric solutions to environmental problems. This managerial approach is concerned to make environmental choices serve human interests. The radical perspective pre-supposes profound changes in humanity's relationship with the environment in order to care for it, and refuses to compromise with existing social and economic structures.

There is thus no single unified global environmental movement or ideology of environmentalism. Nevertheless, despite differences in size, orientation, aims, ideology, resources, organisational forms, organisational culture and range of activities, it has become commonplace to speak of an environmental movement encompassing individuals and groups. For Dalton the various strands of environmentalism are linked by a perception that they represent a challenge to 'the prevailing socio-political forces of advanced industrial societies' (Dalton 1994: 7), and for Lipschutz (1992) it is a common ethic which defines the movement. The notion of an environmental movement articulating and espousing an alternative development paradigm from the conventional socio-economic one and challenging the conventional political systems of Western democracies is widely shared. One should, however, be wary in accepting this standard viewpoint. The existence of an environmental movement need not depend on the existence of a common ethic or alternative paradigm. A number of national and international organisations organise around issues pertaining to environmental degradation and in varying ways attempt to promote greater environmental awareness. The environmental movement which is the sum of these organisations and activities is diverse and heterogeneous. An environmental movement exists because a large number of individuals and groups attach significance to the preservation, conservation and promotion of environmental values. These organisations are based on wide public support, recognise in most cases a commonality of interest, and form alliances on specific projects.

The ESM is widely recognised to be a significant transnational force despite its diversity. It is frequently categorised as a new social movement because it possesses three characteristics shared by new social movements. Its origins lie in post-industrial society, it espouses a new form of politics, one distrustful of orthodox democratic forms, and its ideology challenges the prevailing economic paradigm. This conclusion can be maintained but it should be subject to the following qualifications. First, concern with the environment pre-dates post-industrial society and modern environmentalism arose at the beginning of the twentieth century (Garner 1996; McCormick 1989). The new wave of environmentalism ushered in by developments in the 1960s to some extent builds on the old environmentalism but also is characterised by new features. The first condition mentioned above holds to the extent that the second wave of environmentalism transcends the first. Second, clearly not all groups within the environmental movement espouse a new form of politics. This is evident in the fact that Green political parties have contested elections in a number of countries. But leading environmental NGOs do articulate a citizenship based politics which challenges prevailing practices in democratic societies and world politics (Wapner 1996). Third, while it is possible to envisage accommodating environmental concerns within the prevailing growth-oriented economic paradigm, most environmentalists propose solutions which necessitate a paradigm shift. The concept of sustainable development provides an excellent illustration of the influence of environmentalists on the orthodox development paradigm. Since the 1992 Rio Earth Summit sustainable development has become the dominant approach to development. Opinions vary, however, concerning the merit of sustainable development. For some it represents a paradigm shift but for others it merely accommodates environmental language and fundamental change is not addressed.[1]

In this chapter there is neither the time nor space to engage in

---

[1] See, for example, the different approaches of the Brundtland Commission (World Commission on Environment and Development 1987) and its critics (for a summary of critical responses see de la Court 1990).

extended discussion of the diversity of the environmental movement. Among the many points of difference in the environmental movement in the context of its relationship with the World Bank and WTO three issues merit initial mention. The first concerns the distinction between Northern and Southern environmental groups. This distinction is based not solely on geopolitical and spatial differences but reflects asymmetries in power, and different value systems. Different issues are at stake within societies and cultures at different stages of development. Secondly, the ability of environmental organisations to lobby international organisations is a function of size and command over material and ideational resources. The resources to gain access to governmental officials, and international bureaucracies is unevenly distributed among environmental organisations (Sklair 1994: 210–12; 1997: 514–38). Finally, reformist and radical environmental groups have adopted differing strategies and access the outcome of interactions from opposing standpoints.

Environmental NGOs and global environmental politics

This examination of the relationship between the World Bank, the WTO and the environmental movement will concentrate on the activities of environmental NGOs (ENGOs). This is not because of any decision to privilege ENGOs above other organisations within the environmental movement but in conducting the research the organisational mode represented by NGOs provided a more accessible departure point to the questions posed by the project. Within the new politics of the environment NGOs have emerged as prominent and significant actors. Since the 1980s, ENGOs have grown in size, scaling up their operations in order to influence states and international organisations. Although the vast majority of environmental groups remain rooted in their activities and focus at the local, regional or national levels many ENGOs have organised to take advantage of the opportunities created through engagement with international organisations.

The international politics of the environment with its emphasis on scientific knowledge, erosion of national interest and search for global solutions provides an entry for non-state actors into the global political arena (Princen and Finger 1994). Environmental issues require, 'integrative, interdisciplinary, multilevel approaches – what those schooled in diplomatic protocol, classical European power politics, East–West superpower confrontation or trade negotiations are not used to' (Princen and Finger 1994: 31). It is within such a world that NGOs find their place and carve out their own niche in environmental politics. The impact that NGOs can exert on global environmental politics arises from the fact that they are being increasingly recognised as independent and valuable contributors to international negotiations. The fact that NGOs have been granted observer status by the United Nations and other international organisations enhances the role they play in global politics. The Rio Earth Summit provided a startling display of the prominence of the environmental movement in global deliberations. Over 20,000 participants from 9,000 organisations based in 171 countries were present at the Earth Summit (Meyer 1995). According to Rowlands this demonstrated the importance of civil society since it showed that governments alone cannot address the environmental crisis (Rowlands 1992: 220).

The different types of NGOs sometimes collectively, often individually, address a wide range of environmental issues. Despite a variety of NGOs and projects, NGOs derive the power that ultimately enables them to be influential actors in global environmental politics from one of a combination of three basic sources. One key source of influence derives from the existence of an extensive network linking environmental and other groups. Transnational NGO networks are important in the development of pressure group politics at national and global levels of decision making. Campaigns at both the local and international levels benefit from the creation of coalitions and alliances to pursue specific goals. Transnational NGOs like Friends of the Earth (FOE) and Greenpeace serve as transmitters of information between local and international levels of political activity through their involvement in policy making at national, regional and international levels. Transnational networks across geographical and institutional boundaries are crucial in the effort to monitor and change the policies of states and international organisations. And they also possess the potential to mobilise people to affect domestic politics. Contacts between Northern ENGOs and Southern ENGOs alert Northern NGOs to issues warranting attention, and provide Southern groups with international support. This network connects Northern groups to a wide range of people and places including many that official agencies have difficulty in reaching through traditional means.

A second source of influence for ENGOs arises from their scientific knowledge and expertise. Central to addressing nearly all environmental issues is an understanding of the relevant scientific information pertaining to both the present and the future. Where other actors are unable or unwilling to conduct necessary research or perhaps unaware that studies are necessary NGOs are ready to fill the void. Where scientific data are available these organisations can conduct additional independent research in order to be able to make comparisons and check the validity of both sets of findings. The impact of knowledge structures on environmental issues is not confined to scientific expertise. In so far as NGOs are able to focus on the root of a problem, and can foster community solutions to common problems thus adapting more quickly to local needs and aspirations than governmental structures, they are likely to expand their influence.

A third lever of influence arises from their relationship with the media. NGO activists have developed an extensive network of contacts within the media. The media is used to disseminate information, and embarrass governments and international organisations. Campaigns against particular projects and specific policies are profiled in print and visual media. Different organisations use the media in different ways. The media is an outlet for the publication of research findings, and it is also used to attract attention and publicise a particular issue through reporting on high profile stunts or mass rallies and protests. The media is used to reach both the informed public and the mass public. When elites are the target the attempt is made to provide additional/conflicting information in order to influence policy formulation. Campaigns to heighten awareness or change public perception are part of an effort to mobilise mass opinion. In their attempts to reform the World Bank and the WTO environmentalists have targeted elites and the general public.

The World Bank and the environmental movement

The World Bank's command of material and intellectual resources places it at the forefront of the development assistance regime. In its dialogue with social movements Bank projects and policies have both been the subject of intense scrutiny. Since it first opened its doors for business in June 1946 the World Bank has shown a remarkable adaptability to changes in the global political and economic environments. Initially a single institution – the International Bank for

Reconstruction and Development (IBRD) – the World Bank Group now also includes the International Development Association (IDA), International Finance Corporation (IFC), and the Multilateral Investment Guarantee Agency (MIGA). The operational policies of the Bank and their accompanying intellectual rationale have changed over time in response to changes in the global political economy, the development assistance regime and changes in the internal structure of the Bank. The relationship between the Bank and social movements is the result of the interplay of changes in these three frameworks.

The World Bank: development assistance, organisational structure and changing priorities

Changes in the development assistance regime mirror changes in the global political economy, and here it is the systemic variables which are crucial in determining change. If the 1970s mark the beginning of an increased role for NGOs the real expansion did not take place until the end of the 1980s. The declining role of the state in the developing world, the consequence of economic crisis and neoliberal policies fostered by international financial institutions, and the new political context ushered in by the downfall of the communist project provided the systemic conditions under which NGO activity expanded. Developments in the 1980s and 1990s served to undermine the role of the state. The move to structural adjustment lending at the beginning of the 1980s effectively weakened the state in many developing countries. The growing power of market-related processes led to a decline in state autonomy to control domestic and external politics. The emergence of NGOs (and by extension other social movement organisations) in the 1980s is one result of the triumph of neoliberalism. Adjustment policies affected state–civil-society relations in three ways. First, structural adjustment results in the shrinking of the state especially in terms of the delivery of welfare services. Second, the non-profit sector increases its provision of basic needs such as education and health as a result of diminished state provision. Third, NGOs expand both delivery and advocacy in response to alienation and demand (Quadir and Shaw 1996). The collapse of communism at the beginning of the 1990s further enhanced the visibility of NGOs and provided an opportunity for greater collaboration between multilateral development banks and NGOs. The triumph of liberal capitalism with the collapse of state socialism in Eastern and Central

Europe reinforced the dominance of market-oriented approaches to development. Thus the increased interactions between the World Bank and NGOs in the period since 1988 is in part a response to these external developments.

But the impact of external developments is mediated through the organisational structure of the World Bank in which the largest lenders, and senior members of the bureaucracy play influential roles.[2] Support for increased cooperation between the Bank and NGOs came from the dominant shareholders in the Bank: the United States, Japan, Germany, United Kingdom and France. These countries supported increased cooperation between the Bank and NGOs, effectively internationalising their bilateral development policy. Furthermore, the management and staff of the Bank possess a relative degree of autonomy and exercise an important influence in the shaping of policy (Williams 1994: 107).

The Bank's approach to social movements is conditioned by its organisational ideology, and the relationships which exist among its various departments and professional staff. One can discern both a dominant organisational ideology and changing fashions in World Bank thinking about development.[3] The dominant ideology of the Bank inscribed in its Articles of Agreement, articulated by successive presidents, disseminated in its research output and underpinning its lending priorities, is economic liberalism. Economic liberalism is premised on the efficacy of the market. Liberal economic theory insists that the favoured route to economic growth is through the market mechanism. Another central tenet of liberal economic theory is a commitment to economic growth. The application of certain universally valid economic principles will mobilise domestic resources, savings and investment, and lead to rapid growth resulting in the alleviation of poverty. In this perspective economics is essentially a technocratic enterprise. Economics is a value-free science which can provide universal solutions to the eradication of poverty. Within this liberal paradigm the Bank's approach to the financing of economic development has not remained static and has changed during its history.

Five periods can be distinguished in the Bank's history.[4] The

---

[2] For a detailed discussion on the decision-making structure of the Bank see chapter 2.

[3] On the evolution of the Bank's approach to development see Stern with Ferreira (1993).

[4] See Stern with Ferreira (1993: 111–20) for an analysis of the first four periods.

expansion in the Bank's dialogue with social movements began during the adjustment lending and policy dialogue phase (1980–92) and has been intensified during the current phase which we term participatory development (1993–present). Although adjustment lending initiated at the beginning of the 1980s is still dominant in the Bank's portfolio, since 1993 greater attention has been given to issues such as poverty, participation, gender, environment, governance, capacity building and implementation quality. Moreover, the Bank's portfolio has given greater attention to financing social sectors, conservation programmes, and policy reform. For example, in the period FY 1981 to FY 1983 the Bank's total lending for human capital development averaged 5 per cent of lending. But by FY 1993 to FY 1995 it equalled 16 per cent. The World Bank is now the largest external provider for social investment in the developing world. Furthermore, its environment programme is the world's largest programme of environmental investment, reaching $10.5 billion in 1995. The creation of a Bank-wide Learning Group on Participatory Development in December 1990 (World Bank 1994h: 1) marked the first institutional interest in participatory development. In August 1994 the Bank's management adopted the recommendations proposed by the Learning Group. The Bank's dialogue with NGOs began before the emphasis on participatory development but has subsequently been heavily influenced by the development of participatory approaches because a key element in the participatory paradigm is the emphasis on stakeholders. The stakeholder concept provides a legitimacy to 'NGOs, various intermediary or representative organisations, private sector business and technical and professional bodies' (World Bank 1994h: 2).

The Bank is not a monolithic organisation, and change in the Bank is as much driven by internal considerations as external pressures. Moreover, important constituencies and individuals in the organisation can slow the pace or effectively block reform. Not all sections of the Bank have embraced the increasing contacts between civil society associations and the Bank with the same degree of enthusiasm. The public output of the organisation may often mask internal disagreements, and policy implementation frequently is uneven across sectors because of the absence of consensus. Moreover, the relationship between the Bank and NGOs in any given country is heavily dependent on the head of the resident mission. Some social movement activists perceive the Bank in monolithic terms and develop their strategy on that assumption. However, many of the social movement representatives in Washington recognise the plural nature of the organisation, and therefore attempt to cultivate informal linkages with sympathetic Bank staff. In a similar vein, neither the NGO Liaison Unit nor the Environment Department perceive the environmentalist movement as a single entity, and formal and informal contacts with movement representatives are based on this recognition of difference.

The World Bank and social movements: responding to change

Before examining the changing relationship between the Bank and the environmental movement this section will briefly contextualise this relationship through reference to the development of a dialogue between the World Bank and social movements.[5] The relations between the environmental movement and the Bank are developed in the context of the general increase in the Bank's contacts with social movements given the reciprocal nature of these interactions.

Soon after taking office James Wolfensohn, the current president of the World Bank, embarked on a number of visits to Bank member (borrowing and lending) countries. In his first address to the Board of Governors he set out a new vision for the Bank which included an expanded dialogue with civil society organisations. He told the Board of Governors that '... we can do much more to reach out to NGOs and civil society' (Wolfensohn 1995: 19). This was based on his travel experiences where he '... met with representatives of the NGO community and civil society. We are really interdependent. But we must build mutual trust' (Wolfensohn 1995: 20). And he pledged to '... accelerate and deepen the effort to work with existing and new partners – with specific measures for reaching out to the private sector, NGOs and civil society' (Wolfensohn 1995: 22).

This was not the first time a Bank president had acknowledged the significance of non-state actors for the Bank's agenda.[6] The explicit reference to civil society signalled, to some extent, new thinking but it is not at all clear that Wolfensohn's speech marked a fundamental

[5] For a more detailed examination of the evolution of Bank policy towards NGOs see chapter 2.

[6] Barber Conable had signalled the relevance of NGOs in his address to the Bank's Board of Governors in Berlin in 1988 He stated, 'I have encouraged Bank staff to initiate a broadened dialogue with NGOs ... I hope and fully expect that this collaboration will flourish.' Quoted in Salmen and Eaves (1989: 2; 1991: 94).

shift in Bank priorities. Part of the problem in assessing the relevance of Wolfensohn's intervention is that although one can find references in recent Bank literature to stakeholders and civil society, no clear definition of either term emerges. The Bank's recognition of diverse groups in civil society in practical terms amounts to the development of policies towards NGOs.[7] Thus in examining the evolution of the Bank's policy towards social movements this chapter will concentrate on the relations between the Bank and NGOs.[8]

In the past two decades the World Bank's contact with social movement organisations has expanded considerably. Three reasons can be adduced for this shift: the increasing importance given to NGOs within the development assistance regime (Gordenker and Weiss 1996); the change in development policy and the increased salience of participatory approaches; and the stridency of NGOs. From the perspective of the World Bank, NGOs are defined as, 'groups and institutions that are entirely or largely independent of government and characterised primarily by humanitarian and cooperative rather than commercial activities' (World Bank 1989). Specifically, NGOs refer to private organisations that pursue activities to relieve suffering, promote the interests of the poor, protect the environment or undertake community development. A number of attempts have been made, over time, to develop a typology of NGOs. One Bank document (Salmen and Eaves 1989: 17–25) identified five functional categories of NGO along a public–private continuum approximating the degree to which they represent social (common goal) ends on the public side to economic ends on the private side. Recent thinking in the World Bank has seen a shift away from this fivefold distinction to a simpler distinction between operational NGOs and advocacy NGOs. Operational NGOs are defined as those 'whose primary purpose is running or funding programs designed to contribute to development, environmental management, welfare or emergency relief' (World Bank 1996d: 1). In contrast advocacy NGOs are defined as those whose primary purpose is advocating a specific point of view or concern and which seek to influence the policies and priorities of the Bank, governments and other bodies' (World Bank 1996d: 2). This definition is not one accepted by many NGO activists who see it as inaccurate and divisive.

---

[7] For a history and summary of the various linkages which have been developed see Shihata (1992) and World Bank (1996c).

[8] The Bank produces materials designed to facilitate its contact with NGOs. See, for example, Malena (1996).

The Bank interacts with NGOs in a variety of ways.[9] The linkages between the Bank and NGOs cover a wide spectrum of the organisation's activity.[10] The Bank analyses these interactions according to a threefold categorisation: operational collaboration (Malena 1995), economic and sector work (World Bank 1996c: 14–16), and policy dialogue (World Bank 1996c: 16–19). The World Bank portrays its increasing involvement with NGOs as a cooperative venture with the capacity to improve the efficiency of the Bank's role as a development agency. NGOs, it is argued, possess a comparative advantage in the delivery of development services, especially to the poor. In the context of an expanding development agenda which now includes 'new issues' such as gender, participation, governance and capacity building NGOs have a tremendous potential for enhancing the pursuit of the Bank's goals (World Bank 1996d: 2).

By interacting consistently with NGOs the Bank can tap into NGO know-how and expertise. Operational collaboration between the Bank and NGOs assists the Bank in its pursuit of environmentally sustainable development. At the same time the Bank perceives this as an opportunity to broaden NGOs' awareness of its development work. Secondly, the Bank recognises the important political role played by NGOs in determining the climate for aid (World Bank 1996d: 3). It is not so much that the Bank actively courts NGO involvement but it recognises the effectiveness of NGOs in lobbying donor governments. The Bank's ability to mobilise resources for development is thus to some extent dependent on the activities of NGOs. Bank rhetoric on NGOs stresses collaboration, mutual benefit and enhanced effectiveness. From the perspective of social movement activists the reality is often one of confrontation, conflict and co-option. To some extent it can be argued that what the Bank seeks is not so much partnership as a form of co-optation. Moreover, substantive collaboration between the Bank and NGOs helps to enhance the Bank's reputation. It is generally recognised that the environmental movement has achieved the greatest success of all groups lobbying the Bank. The next section examines the changing history of the Bank's relations with the environmental movement.

---

[9] The Bank has conducted a number of studies to assess the impact of its collaboration with NGOs. See, for example, Bhatnagar (1991) and Hino (1996).

[10] See the annual reports (first issued in 1983) on relations between the Bank and NGOs.

The World Bank and the environmentalists: from confrontation to cooperation?

Among environmental groups with a focus on the lending policies of the World Bank a division is discernible between those groups which seek partnership with the Bank and those which perceive such links as dangerous.[11] No single environmentalist perspective exists on the Bank, which reflects the diversity of the environmental movement. Furthermore, the relationship between the Bank and representatives of the environmental movement is subject to change over time. From the perspective of environmentalists, perception of the Bank is shaped by the evaluation of its responses to the environmentalist critique of its policies. Some NGOs have had a long-standing adversarial relationship with the Bank; others have moved from a position of confrontation to cooperation; and others largely involved in operational activities have only ever enjoyed a close working relationship with the Bank. The response of the Bank to the environmentalist challenge has been shaped by the ability of environmentalists to prevent the Bank from attaining its goals, and internal divisions within the organisation concerning the 'greening' of its portfolio.

The World Bank is currently the largest lender for environmental projects in the developing world, a co-agency for the Global Environmental Facility, and environmental considerations notably in the form of environmental assessments (EAs) have become integrated within its development portfolio. But although the World Bank was the first of the multilateral development banks to express an interest in the environmental consequences of development the foregrounding of an environmental perspective in Bank lending was the result of a struggle between the Bank and its environmental critics. Indeed, many would contend that the Bank's environmental agenda remains largely rhetorical. This chapter argues that the record is neither one of tokenism on the part of the Bank nor a complete victory for the environmental movement but rather a mixed result. There is little doubt that the environmentalists have recorded real gains in the sense that many of their demands have been addressed by the Bank in a positive manner but the organisational ideology of the Bank, and its organisational culture limit its transformation into a Green organisation.

Environmental and development NGOs began to target the policies

---

[11] Interviews, Washington, September 1996.

of the World Bank in the 1970s. Environmentalists were drawn to the Bank because of its pre-eminence in the development assistance regime, and the disastrous environmental consequences of Bank lending. The Bank's traditional development paradigm was blind to the impact of its policies on the environment. Although the first mention of environmental considerations was made by the then president of the Bank Robert McNamara in a speech to ECOSOC in November 1970 (Williams 1994: 130), environmental considerations were not given serious attention in the organisation until 1987. The Bank, until that juncture, appeared unwilling to address the ecological impacts of its lending policies. The pursuit of economic growth at the expense of the environment symbolised an institution confident of its intellectual rationale, policy mandate, and project implementation. Traditional Bank lending often had serious environmental consequences such as acceleration of deforestation and destruction of natural resources and biodiversity. Bank officials were not accountable to the affected populations and neither were they concerned for the environment. The key goals were the promotion of economic development conceived almost solely to mean an increase in GNP, and the maximisation of the rate of return on the loan.

Integrating environmental concerns

In May 1987, Barber Conable, then Bank president, acknowledged serious errors in the organisation's environmental policy. He admitted that the controversial Polonoreste project in Brazil, was 'a sobering example of an environmentally sound effort that went wrong' (World Bank 1991: 22). Furthermore, he announced organisational reforms including the creation of an Environment Department. Since 1987 the Bank has expanded its focus on environmentally sustainable development and has striven to incorporate environmental concerns into policy making. The integration of environmental concerns in the Bank can be assessed along three dimensions: internal organisational restructuring, changing intellectual rationale and new-style lending policies.

One measure of the importance attached to environmental considerations in the Bank's activities concerns the visibility of environmental economists and other professionals on the Bank's staff. The creation of an Environment Department in 1987 raised the profile of environmental issues in the Bank. Between 1970 (when the post of

Environmental Advisor was created) and 1987 environmental issues were relegated to the Office of Environmental and Scientific Affairs, an inadequately staffed section which focused primarily on assessing projects' environmental impact. The creation of the Environment Department brought environmental issues into a more central role in the Bank. The department's role is to conduct policy and research in technical, economic and social areas, to provide conceptual guidance or specialised expertise for staff in regional offices, to establish and maintain information and databases and to train and educate Bank staff on environmental issues. Environmental units were created in each of the Bank's regional units to review Bank-supported projects and liaise with national officials in identifying more general tasks related to resource management. These activities have led to an expansion in environmental staff. Between 1988 and 1991 the regional environment divisions experienced a fourfold increase in staff (Piddington 1992: 219), and between the end of the 1980s and 1994 the number of technical environmental staff increased fivefold (World Bank 1995a: 2). In another internal restructuring the Bank established a vice-presidency for Environmentally Sustainable Development in January 1993 (ESDVP).

The application of environmental economics to development issues gathered momentum with the creation of the Environment Department. But, in its attempt to establish 'maximum convergence between environmental goals and economic policy' (Piddington 1992: 221) the Bank's approach is determined by its organisational ideology. Sustainable development strategies do not challenge the dominant goal of economic growth. Indeed, economic development viewed primarily as growth oriented is seen as a vital component of a sound environmental strategy. In this context it is argued that a symbiotic relationship exists between development and environmental protection. Far from being oppositional development and environmental protection, it is argued, are compatible. This view is succinctly expressed in the Bank's 1992 *World Development Report*, where it is asserted, 'economic development and sound environmental management are complementary aspects of the same agenda. Without adequate environmental protection development will be undermined; without development environmental protection will fail' (World Bank 1992: 25). Sustainable development is therefore both a desirable goal and feasible outcome. Sound environmental protection will only be guaranteed through greater efficiency in the use of resources and technological innovation.

In short, 'rising incomes combined with sound environmental policies and institutions can form the basis for tackling both environmental and development problems. The key to growing sustainably is not to produce less but to produce differently' (World Bank 1992: 36).

Since 1993 ESDVP has attempted to expand the conceptual focus of the Bank's approach to environmentally sustainable development. The new approach to environmentally sustainable development is fundamentally concerned with the promotion of three types of goal: economic goals (growth, equity and efficiency); social goals (empowerment, participation, social mobility, social cohesion, cultural identity, and institutional development); and ecological goals (ecosystem integrity, carrying capacity, biodiversity and global issues) (Serageldin 1996: 2). This approach moves beyond the framework of environmental economics to embrace the concerns of ecologists and sociologists. Central to this project is concern with mapping the conceptual terrain in four key areas. The question of valuation is given prominence with an emphasis on different techniques of valuing the environment, analysis of the manner in which sustainability can be built into national accounts and development of indicators to value the future. Another unresolved issue concerns decision making in the presence of thresholds of uncertainty. Research in this area is concerned with operationalising the precautionary principle and providing the tools to make more informed choices under conditions of uncertainty. The third aspect of this research agenda concerns analysis of the linkages between environmental degradation and macroeconomic policies. Research is being conducted on ways to enhance institutional capacity, and the ordering of priorities. Finally, in keeping with the current paradigm of participatory development, analysis is underway to improve understanding of the human dimension of development (Serageldin and Steers 1996).

The third way in which the Bank has adapted to the environmental challenge is through its lending policies. This involves a number of related initiatives. First, the Bank has increased substantially its lending for projects with primarily environmental objectives. In 1995 the organisation's portfolio of environmental projects stood at $10 billion (World Bank 1995a: 23). This covered 137 projects, and represented a 10 per cent increase since UNCED. Secondly, the Bank has sought to enhance the environment in the process of promoting efficiency through 'an increasing integration of environmental concerns and components in operations with a variety of other primary objectives' (World Bank 1995a: 23). Examples of this integrated environmental approach include efforts to improve energy efficiency, and initiatives to improve the sustainability of agricultural production. A systematic environmental screening of all new projects was introduced in 1989. The Bank claims that 'environmental assessments (EAs) are now firmly rooted as part of the Bank's normal business activity, ... and are now effecting changes in project design as a matter of course ...' (World Bank 1995a: 13). Additionally the Bank has developed sector-specific policies relating to water resource management, energy and forests.

Bank publications on environmentally sustainable development portray a dynamic and adaptable organisation which has successfully incorporated environmental concerns into its lending activities, policy advice and research activities. The environment it is argued has moved from the margins to the centre of Bank concerns.[12] This can be seen as a three stage process. Initially the Bank's aim was to mitigate the unintended consequences of its project lending. Once the mechanisms (e.g., EAs) were in place to achieve this objective the Bank moved to expand its environmental capacity through investing in environmental projects, supporting environmental planning and building the knowledge base. The current focus is on implementation on the ground, scaling-up from project-specific concerns to environmental management at sectoral and national levels and increasing the attention given to establishing appropriate relationships with individuals and organisations in recipient communities.

This record of the evolution of the Bank's environmental policy suggests that the reform process was internally driven. It can be perceived as the successful response of Bank management and member states to a problem in the organisation's task environment. Such a conclusion would be both premature and unwarranted since it fails to assess external pressure on the Bank. It is widely acknowledged that environmental NGOs played a pivotal role in the reform process in the Bank. And it is to the role of environmental NGOs in this process that we now turn. Moreover, consideration of the Bank–ENGO interactions will introduce a critical perspective on the Bank's environmental record.

---

[12] This is inclusive of its private sector activities (World Bank 1995a: part 3).

Environmental NGOs and the reform of the World Bank

The first part of this section will examine the efforts in the 1980s by environmental NGOs to elicit a change in the World Bank's lending policies. It is widely believed in the environmental community that the Bank only became 'Green' as a result of pressure from NGOs. Without NGO pressure, the Bank would never have incorporated environmental considerations into its projects. The evolution of Bank–ENGO relations since the creation of the Environment Department will be discussed in the second part of the section.

The early history of the campaign against the Bank has been told on numerous occasions and will not be replicated in great detail. The standard account of the success of the environmental movement in shifting the Bank's agenda focuses on the role played by NGOs in shaping US policy towards the Bank (Bramble and Porter 1992). The campaign launched in 1983 by a coalition of US environmental organisations (key actors included the National Wildlife Federation, the Environmental Policy Institute and the National Resources Defense Council) against the environmental policies of the multilateral development banks reaped its first success with the creation of the Environment Department in 1987. It is widely acknowledged that environmental NGOs have been the most successful members of the NGO community, and are seen as the model to be followed by other NGOs. The coalition's decision to target the US Congress was eventually successful for a number of reasons. The intensification of the NGO campaign, and the widening of the movement from its largely US base to encompass NGOs from the developing world and other industrialised countries were crucial factors in persuading more members of Congress to support the demands of the environmentalists. The US NGOs were assisted in their campaign by Southern peoples and organisations. A number of civil society associations in the developing world in regions directly affected by Bank projects with adverse environmental consequences provided firsthand information about the local situation (Bramble and Porter 1992: 332–4). But Congressional pressure supplemented by sympathetic media coverage was not sufficient in itself to alter the policies of the Bank. The support of the US Treasury and the replacement of Tom Clausen by Barber Conable as Bank president were key changes in 1986 and 1987. The US Treasury moved from a position of indifference to one of support for reform of the Bank because it needed Congressional approval to expand the Bank's capital base to enable it to increase its role in the debt crisis. And Conable, the new Bank president, not only brought a personal commitment to reform the Bank's approach to its lending (Piddington 1992: 215–16, 219); he also recognised the political importance of the environment issue (Wade 1997: 21–3).

But the 'success' of the environmental movement in 1987, and continued pressure on the Bank, is not solely attributable to the role played by actors in the US political process. Moreover, it is important to note that the alliance between US environmentalists and Republican Congressmen was a temporary rather than permanent feature of the American political system. US environmental NGOs continue to lobby their Congressional representatives but the 'power of the parliamentary purse' so successful with the US Congress in the late 1980s and early 1990s became less relevant in the mid-1990s. Changing Congressional representation and declining American voting power led activists to shift attention post-1994 to Germany and Japan.[13] The relative weakness of German and Japanese NGOs combined with different political cultures has made this approach less successful. Instead the Washington-based ENGOs began a more intensive lobbying of the Executive Directors from Germany and Japan.[14]

We can identify a number of strategies employed by the environmental movement which in conjunction with systemic factors help to shape the ability of environmental groups to influence Bank policy. First, environmental groups mobilised public opinion through campaigns against specific projects. This tactic was especially successful with World Bank lending for the construction of dams. The Big Dam controversies, e.g., Three Gorges in China and Narmada in India, provided not only powerful evidence of the Bank's failure to pursue environmentally sustainable policies but concrete issues around which campaigns could be built. Apart from the Big Dam controversies other notorious failures which were highlighted by environmental critics of Bank policies included the Polonoreste rainforest colonisation scheme in Brazil, a cattle development project in Botswana which accelerated desertification, and a transmigration scheme in Indonesia – a scheme involving massive human resettlement. Second, over the past decade a framework of consultations have developed between

[13] Interviews. September 1995.
[14] Recently Japanese NGOs have taken a greater interest in the activities of the Bank and have begun to lobby their representatives.

certain NGO personnel and Bank staff. NGO activists have sought allies inside the organisation. Recognising the existence of bureaucratic divisions in the organisation advocacy environmental NGOs with a sophisticated view of organisational politics have forged contacts with sympathetic Bank staff (key groups include the Environmental Defense Fund, the Center for International Environmental Law, FOE, and Oxfam International). Ongoing formal and informal contacts between Bank staff and NGO professionals has created a policy community which effectively marginalises outsiders. These contacts range from junior staff right up to management level and are not confined to the Environment Department although the Environment Department has established good working relations with many of the Washington-based NGOs. These contacts provide ENGOs with access to information and also enable them to articulate their views to an official audience. The dominance of ENGOs based in Washington in this process raises questions of equity within the environmental movement since these contacts are limited to Washington insiders, thus effectively marginalising those groups without representation in Washington.[15] In the dialogue with the Bank the NGO community has discovered the importance of maintaining continuity of personnel on specific issues. Contact is often of a personal nature and invitations to meetings are frequently issued to individuals rather than to organisations. The effectiveness of an NGO in lobbying the Bank is as much a function of the personal contacts of particular staff members as of the general standing of the organisation. In the past decade environmental and development NGOs (apart from those already named, key actors include Bread for the World, the Centre of Concern, the Bank Information Centre, and Development GAP) have maintained pressure on the Bank through the network of contacts developed between Bank staff and movement activists.

Third, high level research disseminated to the public, legislators and the Bank in an attempt to create epistemic communities has been instrumental in shifting perceptions. Bank staff are unwilling to waste their time discussing environmental issues with critics they consider ignorant and uninformed.[16] Many Bank staff remain sceptical of the analytical frameworks employed by environmentalists and effective

---

[15] In September 1995 there were no Southern ENGOs permanently based in Washington.

[16] See, for example, the acerbic criticisms of the environmental critique of the Bank made by Piddington (1992: 217–18).

dialogue proves possible only where a mutual respect for the conceptual tools and intellectual rigour of the argument is shared by the protagonists. The dialogue between the Bank and its critics rapidly moved from the level of general considerations to the analysis of specific proposals. The 'greening' of the Bank is based on high-level research and analysis, and the ability of an NGO to influence the Bank depends on the calibre of its staff and quality of its research. Fourth, NGOs utilise national and international alliances in their campaigns to reform the Bank (Wirth 1998). As we saw above it is simplistic to attribute the success of US NGOs solely to their own efforts. US NGOs acting alone are limited in their ability to influence the Bank. The NGO community based in Washington consists of international NGOs such as Greenpeace and FOE as well as US-based environmental organisations. In this context networks refer to linkages between different national associations of an umbrella ENGO as well as coalitions of national groups unaffiliated to a single organisation (Nelson 1996). Environmentalist activists argue that it is essential to have links with international NGOs.[17] Thus efforts are made to create networks linking Northern NGOs, and Northern and Southern partners. Within the advocacy process Northern groups maintain a dominant position. One source alleged that it is difficult to maintain the autonomy of local Southern groups. If the Washington-based partner is not interested then Southern issues are not taken up.[18]

The standard account highlights the success of environmental NGOs in mobilising an effective, credible threat to the Bank's funding. The media campaign and political support of conservative Congressmen for Bank reform took place at a time when the Bank was particularly sensitive to public campaigns. At the beginning of the 1990s the Bank was worried about the level of its funding in an era when the public was jaded with aid and development. The failure of aid and development and the post-Cold War dynamics created doubt concerning the continued relevance of the Bank. Critiques which provided compelling evidence of the failures of Bank policy (Rich 1994; Schartzman 1986) found a willing readership. Environmental groups in Washington were able to establish close links with legislators committed to a reduction in US support to multilateral institutions. Prestige and image consciousness are undervalued in

---

[17] Interviews.
[18] Interview with a Northern NGO September 1995.

international-relations research, particularly in an era when the focus is on structural causation, but governments and international organisations do evince concern about their image.[19] Senior management in the Bank were worried about its negative image and the unfavourable publicity generated by the campaigns mounted by the environmental lobby irrespective of its impact on funding. The Bank's relations with its borrowing governments, and its activities in recipient countries, depend, to some extent, on the views held of the organisation. And in that respect, support for reform of the institution was also internally driven; core members of the Bank (apart from the USA) were committed to change.

There is little doubt that the Bank responded to the pressure exerted by the environmental movement. No agreement, however, exists on the extent to which the Bank has become a Green institution. The official Bank version (World Bank 1995a) presents a picture of an organisation committed to environmentally sustainable development in which environmental considerations have been incorporated into the mainstream of its operations. Critics from academia (Wade 1997) and the environmental community (Horta 1996; Rich 1995) remain unconvinced about the scope and depth of the reforms. Whether convert or agnostic something has changed and at the very least the Bank has been forced to address an issue that it had long ignored. But as one activist put it, 'the Bank only pretends to be Green. It is basically a free market institution which cannot be Green.'[20] In support of the argument that it is not possible to reconcile capitalism and sustainable development my interviewee pointed to the fact that the IFC and MIGA are the fastest growing sections of the Bank. An inherent contradiction existed, it was claimed, between the effort to promote the growth of private capital and support environmental sustainability.

This view is not uncommon among environmentalists. Environment (and development) groups remain unconvinced by the rhetoric of the Bank. Few share the views of one movement activist who asserts that environment is no longer a key issue since the environmentalists have won.[21] To be fair, this Washington insider was referring not only to the

---

[19] The efforts of the 'Fifty Years is Enough' campaign proved more than an irritant to Bank officials who devised strategies to counter what they perceived as ill-informed publicity.

[20] Interview, 10 September 1996.

[21] Interview, 9 September 1996.

stated achievements of the environmentally sustainable policies pursued by the Bank but to the informal network between many working on environmental issues in the Bank and members of the environmental movement. The climate of hostility, suspicion and distrust evident in the early years of the exchange has been replaced by one of cooperation. But, the Environment Department is not the entire Bank, and for many the problems arise from the loan culture of the Bank, and its organisational structure (Wappenhans 1992).

The aims of the ESM can be seen in terms of four broad demands (Horta 1996). The environmental critique of the World Bank focuses on issues pertaining to human rights, democracy, accountability, gender, ideology and power. First, environmentalists demand increased transparency and participation in the operation of the institution. Increased transparency and extended participation will, it is argued, improve the quality of projects by making them environmentally sound and socially beneficial. Representatives of the environmental movement argue that in order to meet these aims the active participation of local communities and their local or regional governmental structures must be ensured. Environmental groups have achieved some success in eroding the Bank's tradition of secrecy and withholding of information concerning its projects from the public. The new information disclosure policy which became effective in January 1994 is evidence of the Bank's response to its critics. The Bank decided to declassify a number of documents, and established a public information centre in Washington with further offices planned in Tokyo, Paris and London. Environmentalists argue that the declassification procedure, although welcome, is too limited (Udall 1998).

The second demand is for social assessment and participation. Civil society representatives campaigned for increased participation of stakeholders in social assessments carried out by the Bank. A key area covered by this demand is the World Bank's dialogue on sustainable development. In September 1994 the World Bank approved a Participation Action Plan based on social assessment guidelines, but few concrete results have to date been forthcoming. In the absence of an internal incentive structure it is likely that the implementation of participatory approaches will be inconsistent at best and non-existent for the most part. Third, the ESM has insisted that the Bank's lending to the environment should be increased. Although the Bank has responded to this in both the brown agenda (projects designed to address pollution in urban areas) and green agenda (projects concerned with natural resource management in mostly rural areas) many environmental groups argue that the focus of Bank lending remains that of mitigating the impact of economic growth on the environment rather than one of promoting sustainability. The focus of Bank lending for the environment tends to be on forestry, fisheries and agriculture. In 1995 the Bank supported more than 100 environmental projects representing a commitment of $5 billion and a total investment of more than $13 billion. The green agenda has formed the central part of the Bank's efforts with issues grouped in this portfolio representing $3.2 billion of the $5 billion commitment. Environmental groups have also campaigned for more widespread use of environmental assessments. Environmental assessments (EAs) are valuable tools for understanding the environmental consequences of proposed new development projects. Since 1989 EAs have become a formal requirement for all World Bank projects that are expected to have significant adverse environmental impacts. However EAs suffer from a number of shortcomings. They are frequently used to legitimise previously established project concepts and, the lack of follow-through, absence of controls and frequent use of foreign consultants serves to diminish the impact of EAs. The appearance suggests tremendous change but the reality of implementation suggests otherwise.

Finally, environmental NGOs have expressed reservations concerning the accountability of the Bank. A major response by the Bank was the creation of an Inspection Panel in September 1994.[22] Community organisations or NGOs representing citizens harmed by World Bank projects can request a full-scale investigation of the situation if there are indications that the Bank is ignoring or violating its own policies and procedures. The first case investigated by the Inspection Panel was the Arun III hydro-electric dam project in Nepal. The investigation began in November 1994 and a report published in December 1994 called for further investigation. When James Wolfensohn cancelled the project in August 1995 he cited the investigations of the Inspection Panel as one of the reasons for his decision.

The story of the World Bank and the environmental movement is one of increasing linkages between the Bank and environmental NGOs, and the appearance that NGO pressure was successful in changing Bank policies and priorities. A note of caution should be entered on both counts. First, while it would be rather narrow and

---

[22] For an NGO critique of the Inspection Panel see Hunter and Udall (1994).

short-sighted to conclude that no change has occurred a quantitative increase tells us very little about the quality of the interactions. On the other hand, the very fact that the Bank has felt the need to address and respond to the demands of this new constituency is a sign of a change in the operation of the organisation. Moreover, increasing integration of environmental NGOs into the Bank's work shifts the relations between the international organisation, governments and civil society. Second, it is very difficult to measure influence. It is not clear to what extent the Bank's approach to the environment after its initial reluctance, and especially in its post-Rio phase, is not heavily influenced by a desire to engage in task expansion. At Rio it became clear that sustainable development had moved from the rhetorical phase to that of implementation. As the leading multilateral development organisation the Bank was unwilling to be by-passed in this new phase. To that end the Bank successfully campaigned to become an implementing agency in the Global Environmental Facility (GEF).

In terms of access to the World Bank a clear difference in resources exists between Northern (especially US) based NGOs and their Southern counterparts. Much of the policy dialogue between the Bank and NGOs is conducted informally (for example, the Tuesday Group meetings) and Southern NGOs are therefore excluded from this process. Representation from the developing world is greater in respect of the more formal channels such as the World Bank–NGO Committee and consultations such as those on forest, water and energy. Participation of Southern NGOs is constrained through lack of finance, and in recognition the World Bank finances the visits of Southern delegates to these meetings.

The World Trade Organization and the environmental movement

The Uruguay Round of trade negotiations (1986–94) redefined the contours of the world trading system, and in so doing transformed the institutional setting of world trade. The conclusion of the multi-lateral trade negotiations resulted in the creation of a new organisation, the WTO, and new rules for world trade. The decision to create a new organisation to oversee world trade rules reflected the dissatisfaction of leading trading states concerning the GATT's inability to provide a sufficiently robust foundation for the global system of world trade. As the successor to the GATT the WTO provides the legal and institutional foundation of the global trading system. The WTO has from its inception been subject to contestation. Opponents of liberal trade challenge the current rules created by the WTO, and fear its liberalising mission. But even among those who accept the tenets of a liberal trade regime dispute arises concerning the development and interpretation of legal standards. The role of the WTO in developing and maintaining international trade law and the world trade system is shaped by changes in the global political economy, the trade regime and the nature of the WTO as an international organisation. The relationship between the WTO and the environmental movement is the result of the interplay of changes in these three frameworks

The WTO and the international trading system

Since the end of the Second World War the multilateral trading system has been based on four key principles: non-discrimination, reciprocity, transparency and multilateral cooperation. From 1947 until the end of 1994 the GATT was the institutional expression of this rule based system. The Uruguay Round of trade negotiations which led to the creation of the WTO transformed the management of world trade in three respects. First, it engineered a shift from trade liberalisation based on tariff concessions (shallow or negative integration) to discussions of domestic policies, institutional practices and regulations (deep or positive integration). Second, it constructed a new agenda expanding the scope (through the inclusion of services, trade-related intellectual property rights, foreign investment, competition policy, and domestic (non-trade) policies) and changing the character of negotiations from a focus on bargaining over products to negotiations over policies that shape the conditions of competition. A third innovation was a movement towards policy harmonisation, for example, in the areas of subsidies, trade related investment measures and services. This transformation of the institutional basis of the world trading system from the negative integration practised under GATT to the positive integration envisaged in the WTO is illustrative of the impact of globalisation on world trade. Globalisation has been accompanied by a growing discourse of multilateralism. The end of the Cold War and increasing liberalisation in national economies gave rise to hopes that the embedded liberalism of the post-war period could finally emerge into a fully fledged liberal order. Trade liberalisation under GATT consisted essentially of tariff cutting exercises. In this sense it can be seen as a negative process of restricting barriers to trade. In this process dispute settlement procedures were weak, and the power of the organisation to discipline errant members severely limited. The WTO not only extends the mandate of the GATT into new areas but also redefines the relationship between national governments and the world trading system through the creation of an effective dispute settlement mechanism, the provision of a trade policy review mechanism (TPRM) and the development of a set of mandatory codes. One measure of the increased competence of the WTO compared with the GATT is reflected in the fact that the organisation's Dispute Settlement Body has received more complaints in its first three years of operation than the GATT did in almost half a century. Moreover, the TPRM which subjects the policies of member governments to periodic surveillance has provided effective scrutiny of deviations from the goal of trade liberalisation. The WTO thus provides a higher and sharper profile for trade issues, and as such attracts the attention of a range of actors. Compared with the GATT, the increased scope, permanence and rule-making authority of the WTO has alarmed environmentalists and other civil society actors who fear that the organisation and control of vital national decisions have been gradually and irretrievably displaced from national control to a supranational organisation shrouded in secrecy. In this vein Bellmann and Gerster (from the Swiss Coalition of Development Organisations) have claimed that, 'The multilateral system ... is gaining ground at the expense of national policy-making' (Bellmann and Gerster 1996: 31). The extension of the WTO beyond trade in goods into intellectual property protection, surveillance over investment issues and the strengthening of the dispute settlement procedures provides a sharper organisational foundation for the world trade system.[23]

The WTO is a complex organisation with a comprehensive scope. It is, first, a legal entity which provides a framework of rules, norms and principles to govern the multilateral trading system. In other words, it is the legal and institutional foundation of the world trading system. It consists of key mandatory provisions, namely, the agreement establishing the WTO; GATT 1994 and other multilateral trade agreements

---

[23] For a discussion of the distinction between blunt and sharp as applied to international organisations see Ogley (1969).

for goods including Sanitary and Phytosanitary Measures (SPS); the agreement on Technical Barriers to Trade (TBT); the agreement on Trade Related Investment Measures (TRIMs); the General Agreement on Trade in Services (GATS); the agreement on Trade Related Intellectual Property measures (TRIPs); the Understanding on Rules and Procedures Governing the Settlement of Disputes, and the Trade Policy Review Mechanism (TPRM). These are supplemented by non-mandatory provisions contained in the plurilateral agreements governing civil aircraft and government procurement.[24] The WTO is a rule-making and rule-supervisory organisation. As a rule-making organisation its main goal is to increase and enhance global policy making. Trade liberalisation is increasingly subjecting domestic policy and regulations to the standards defined by the global trade regime. The WTO's permanent machinery is concerned with ensuring compliance with the rules. Supervision in the WTO covers implementation of agreements, dispute resolution, amendments to the rules and waivers.

Secondly, the WTO provides a permanent forum for the discussion of trade policy, increases direct ministerial involvement in trade issues, and consequently pushes trade concerns higher up the political agenda. Multilateral trade agreements specify the principal contractual obligations determining trade negotiations and trade legislation, and the TPRM facilitates the evolution of trade relations and trade policy.

Thirdly, it acts as a centre for the settlement of disputes. The WTO dispute settlement procedures provide the machinery for settling members' differences on their rights and obligations. Unlike the GATT the findings of panels of experts are binding unless rejected by the Dispute Settlement Body (DSB). Panel reports are adopted in the DSB unless there is a consensus to reject the report (Petersmann 1997). The highest decision-making body is the Ministerial Conference which meets every two years at ministerial level. To date two such meetings have been held (Singapore 1996, Geneva 1998), with a third planned for late 1999 in the United States. In the interval between Ministerial Conferences the work of the organisation is entrusted to a General Council which also acts as the dispute settlement body and the trade policies review body, together with a number of committees.

---

[24] At the conclusion of the Uruguay Round two further plurilateral agreements – on meat and dairy products – were annexed to the WTO agreement but were terminated at the end of 1997.

The WTO and social movements: in defence of the status quo?

The WTO has been in existence since 1 January 1995. Its institutional structure is different from the GATT but in many respects developments in the organisation must be viewed in the light of the history of the GATT. The GATT in its forty-seven-year history failed to establish any formal linkages with NGOs or other civil society organisations. This erasure of NGOs from the governance of the world trading system was not envisaged by the architects of the post-war international economic order. In the context of the post-war reform of the international trading system Article 87(2) of the Havana Charter establishing the International Trade Organisation (ITO) made provision for consultations with NGOs. But the institutional vacuum created by the failure to ratify the ITO was filled by the GATT which evolved into an intergovernmental organisation (Charnovitz and Wickham 1995). Within the world trading system as it evolved in the post-war period the culture of secrecy in multilateral trade negotiations effectively relegated NGOs and other social movement organisations to outsider status.

The WTO is slowly beginning to give greater attention to contact with social movement representatives. The constitutional basis for the engagement with representatives of social movements is provided in the agreement establishing the World Trade Organization. The General Council of the WTO is empowered by Article v.2 to institute review relations between the organisation and NGOs. This article states 'The General Council may make appropriate arrangements for consultation and co-operation with non-governmental organisations concerned with matters related to those of the WTO.' Furthermore, it is possible that NGO access could be provided through the dispute settlement mechanism. Article 13.2 of the Understanding on Rules and Procedures Governing the Settlement of Disputes states, *inter alia*, 'Panels may seek information from any relevant source and may consult experts to obtain their opinion on certain aspects of the matter.'

These constitutional provisions have been extended in three directions since the establishment of the organisation. Two decisions taken in July 1996 provide the framework for current WTO policy towards NGOs. First, the secretariat has been empowered to engage directly with NGOs (WTO 1996b). The guidelines reinforced the intergovernmental nature of WTO deliberations but made some concession to the roles that NGOs can play in the wider public debate on trade and trade-related issues. The Secretariat was given prime responsibility for liaison with NGOs, and was empowered to engage in an expanded dialogue with the non-governmental sector. In the absence of a formal institutional forum informal relations are maintained between the Secretariat and NGOs. The Secretariat provides briefings on its work programme, and receives representations from NGOs. Following the Geneva ministerial meeting the WTO Secretariat increased the frequency of its briefings for NGOs. Apart from these contacts the Secretariat has organised a number of symposia with social movement representatives. The first, held 10–11 June 1994, did little to promote constructive dialogue. It was apparent at this meeting that the intellectual disagreement between representatives from the environmental groups present and the Secretariat could not be easily bridged. The purpose of this symposium on trade, environment and sustainable development was to allow an exchange of views but animosity between the two groups resulted in a dialogue of the deaf. Moreover, tensions within the environmental movement contributed to a meeting regarded by all participants as a failure (GATT 1994). A second attempt was not made until the preparatory phase of the first ministerial meeting when a gathering was convened in September 1996 of thirty-five organisations representing environmental, development and consumer groups. This symposium was felt to be much more constructive by all participants, and its 'success' has since been replicated on a number of occasions.[25] Later high level symposia on Trade and Environment (15–16 March 1999), and Trade and Development (17–18 March 1999) presented opportunities for constructive engagement and demonstrate the changed context of civil society engagement with the WTO since its inception.

Secondly, the General Council agreed to derestrict documents (WTO 1996a). The organisation has increased the public provision of information concerning WTO policy making. Under the procedures most WTO documents will be circulated as unrestricted, some will be

---

[25] Secretariat officials explain the difference between the two meetings in terms of the increased sophistication of environmental groups present concerning trade issues. Environmental (and other) social movement representatives argue that the key difference between the meetings in 1994 and 1996 was a conciliatory process started by the Quaker mission in Geneva which brought together governmental officials, social movement representatives and WTO bureaucrats. (Source: interviews, January/February 1997.)

derestricted automatically after a sixty-day period, others can be derestricted at the request of a member but others, especially those pertaining to important current policy decisions will remain restricted (Van Dyke and Weiner n.d.; Weiner and Van Dyke n.d.). The WTO is currently considering proposals first made at the General Council in December 1998 to liberalise its derestriction regime. The proposals to amend current practices by circulating Secretariat background notes as unrestricted unless an objection is made and to derestrict the minutes of committees after three months have run into objections, principally from India and Mexico, and it proved impossible to make progress when this issue was discussed by the WTO in February 1999. One further innovation of the WTO has been the construction of a website which makes publicly available a wide range of WTO documents including dispute panel reports as soon as they are adopted. The WTO also publishes the *Trade and Environment Bulletin*, which reports on the activities of the Committee on Trade and Environment, and trade policy review reports. Similar publications covering the work of other sectors is not planned but activists have asked for this service to be extended to other areas of the WTO's work programme.

The WTO's failure to provide a mechanism whereby NGOs can be granted some form of consultative status appears reactionary at a moment when most intergovernmental organisations have made such provision. The isolation of the WTO on this issue, and the relevance of non-state actors to the promotion of a liberal trade agenda, is increasingly being recognised by the Secretariat and influential member states. At the Geneva second ministerial meeting, the director-general of the WTO Renato Ruggiero supported the call for increased contact between non-state actors and the WTO, and President Clinton suggested the creation of 'a forum where business, labour, environmental and consumer groups can speak out and help guide the further evolution of the WTO' (*Bridges Weekly Trade News Digest* 1998). This new openness was further confirmed in July 1998 when Ruggiero announced further measures to improve contacts with NGOs (WTO 1998).[26] In pursuit of a new open policy he has intensified his direct contacts with NGO. Since the second ministerial meeting he has met five times with various coalitions of NGOs. He has twice met with US NGOs (November 1998, and March 1999), and once each with

[26] Ruggiero first met with NGOs in December 1997.

international NGOs (July 1998), developing country NGOs (February 1999), and European NGOs (also February 1999).

The WTO and the environmentalists: a dialogue of the deaf?

As previously stated the environmental movement is diverse, and different groups have pursued different objectives in the context of global governance. In what follows attention will be focused on that section of the ESM engaged in lobbying for reform of the rules of the world trading system. These 'reformers' can be differentiated from the 'radical' groups that seek the abolition of the WTO.[27] Reformers believe that the world trading system can be altered to protect the environment whereas radicals reject the rules and institutions of the current system. Of course such a dichotomy is not always easy to sustain since individuals and groups not only shift positions over time but some organisations may well contain a variety of views. The dialogue between the WTO and the environmental movement has to be seen in the context of an evolving discussion begun under the GATT. The response of the WTO to the environmentalist challenge has been shaped by its organisational ideology, organisational character-istics and the ability of ENGOs to threaten its core objective of trade liberalisation.

The WTO is the institutional expression of the commitment to liberal international trade espoused by the leadership of the key advanced industrial countries. Although the rhetoric of the post-war trading system has been one of liberalisation and multilateralism, in reality protectionism and mercantilist sentiments have been ever-present. The creation of the WTO was a conscious attempt to establish a strong global regulatory framework supporting increased trade liberalisation. As such the WTO is principally a legal instrument for the promotion of free trade, and committed to combating protec-tionism. It is therefore not surprising that the WTO has been so resistant to the demands of environmental groups given the fierce controversy surrounding the relationship between trade and environ-mental protection, and the likelihood that efforts to halt environmental degradation may be used as a disguise for protectionist aims.

It is possible to discern a shift in the relations between 'reformist'

---

[27] For example, the loose coalition called the People's Global Action against Free Trade and the World Trade Organisation (PGA). See Ford (1998).

environmentalist groups and the WTO from one of incomprehension to the beginnings of some understanding. Some measure of accommodation is discernible between the trade community and environmental groups with offices in Geneva engaging in lobbying and advocacy activities. At the outset mutual mistrust resulted in limited real dialogue. Both groups are now aware that the existing knowledge on trade–environment linkages is very tentative and in the past two years both the WTO Secretariat and NGOs like World Wide Fund for Nature (WWF), the World Conservation Union (IUCN), the International Centre for Trade and Sustainable Development (ICTSD), the International Institute for Sustainable Development (IISD), and the Center for International Environmental Law (CIEL), have been prepared to examine the evidence in a manner unlikely to maintain the previous degree of polarisation. Broadly speaking the reformers have sought to redirect policies (for example, to inscribe sustainable development concerns on the WTO agenda, and to restrict trade in areas where it contributes to environmental degradation) and alter institutional procedures in the WTO (mainly to 'democratise' the organisation). Other environmental groups such as Greenpeace are less prepared to engage in these discussions.

Reformist ENGOs have developed a two-pronged strategy in their attempts to alter world trade rules. Analysis and research is aimed at changing the way in which the trade and environment nexus is perceived. Policy advocacy requires new information and political support in order to promote the reform agenda. To this end environmental groups like the WWF and IUCN have engaged in analysis of trade and environmental issues with the aim of making policy recommendations. These recommendations are directed at policy makers. In other words, lobbying is concentrated on gaining political support among the informed public rather than the general public. In Geneva, environmentalists have built up contacts with representatives of national governments and WTO staff. At the national level environmentalists have established contacts in various government departments. Within pluralist democracies environmentalists have been trying to affect the composition of national trade negotiating teams in order to increase the participation of environmental ministries in trade talks. Secondly, environmental groups engaged in lobbying the WTO have formed diverse transnational advocacy coalitions. These networks are useful in developing and supporting public campaigns on specific policies.

Integrating environmental concerns

The international trade regime created in 1947 rendered environmental issues invisible. The interaction between trade and the environment was not inscribed on the agenda of multilateral trade negotiations, and played no part in the regulation of world trade. Environmental issues slowly emerged in the 1970s but only gained a definite place on the agenda in the 1990s. Environmental issues were first raised in the GATT in November 1971 immediately preceding the United Nations Conference on the Human Environment (the Stockholm Conference). The GATT Council established a Group on Environmental Measures and International Trade (GEMIT) to examine, 'upon request any specific matters relevant to the trade policy aspects of measures to control pollution and protect the human environment, and report back to the Council' (GATT 1993a). However, GEMIT a political response to the Stockholm Conference, never met because the strength of opposition to merging trade and environment interests was very strong. During the preparatory phase of UNCED new pressures arose for an examination of the trade/ environment nexus. At the Uruguay Round ministerial meeting in Brussels in December 1990 the EFTA countries requested that the GEMIT be convened to examine the relationship between trade and environmental policies. This led to an inconclusive debate in May 1991 at the GATT Council meeting. The opposition of a number of delegations was sufficient to stymie the calls for a GEMIT meeting. Immediately after UNCED, and following the first dolphin–tuna ruling, it was apparent that the trade and environment issue occupied a place on the agenda and that UNCED issues were not adequately covered in GEMIT's remit. GEMIT was reconvened in July 1993 to discuss the results of UNCED. At this time it became clear that both leading advanced industrialised countries and developing countries felt that the time had come for GATT to take up the trade and environment debate. These views were sometimes defensive, for example, the US delegate stated that environmental issues should not be left to environmental experts given the overlap between trade and the environment, and the Indian representative expressed the view that it was imperative for GATT to counter the false propaganda that the organisation was indifferent to environmental concerns. Some delegations adopted a more positive approach, the Brazilian delegate arguing that Agenda 21 should be fully integrated into GATT since poverty is the worst polluter in the developing world.[28]

The standard GATT (and later WTO) position on the environment was adopted at this time. The viewpoint expressed by the majority of member governments was that environmental concerns could be fully accommodated within a flexible interpretation of GATT rules. Moreover, it was stressed that an open non-discriminatory system can facilitate environmental conservation and protection by helping to encourage more efficient resource allocation to generate real income growth. Three key policies were identified – multilateral environmental agreements, transparency and eco-labelling.

The Uruguay Round was launched in Punta del Este, Uruguay, in September 1986 before environmental issues became prominent on the international agenda.[29] During the negotiations environmental issues hovered in the background but were never explicitly part of the negotiations. The dolphin–tuna controversy and the preparatory phase of UNCED raised the political profile of the linkage between trade and the environment. Nevertheless, by the end of the Uruguay Round it had become obvious to governments, trade officials and social movement activists that the new organisation would have to discuss the environment. But concerted opposition remained to the inclusion of environmental issues at the core of the new world trade system. At this stage the campaign to integrate environmental concerns into the structure of the organisation through the creation of a Committee on Trade and Environment was unsuccessful. Opponents of the establishment of an environmental committee based their argument on two considerations. The first argument was based on precedent. It was argued that it had never been GATT practice to create institutional frameworks before matters of a substantive nature had been settled in a particular area. The second argument appealed to political realities. Those opposed to the mainstreaming of environmental issues in the new organisation argued that the issue was so divisive that attempts to resolve it would further delay the ratification of the WTO. They further argued that environment was part of neither the negotiations nor the Final Act. It was therefore decided to consider the institutional structure in consultations prior to Marrakesh.

---

[28] Meeting held on 6 July 1993 (GATT 1993b).

[29] It is interesting to note that John Croome's (1995) official history of the Uruguay Round published by the WTO contains no reference to the environment either in the table of contents or the index.

By the time the Final Act was negotiated it was no longer possible to ignore the concept of sustainable development. Sustainable development was now inscribed in the discourse of the World Bank and United Nations and the negotiators joined the new global consensus. The Preamble of the agreement establishing the WTO states that trade liberalisation policies will be pursued, 'while allowing for the optimal use of the world's resources in accordance with the objective of sustainable development, seeking both to protect and preserve the environment and to enhance the means for doing so ...' The Marrakesh ministerial meeting (April 1994) which led to the creation of the WTO decided to create a Committee on Trade and Environment (CTE). In the interim before the WTO began work on 1 January 1995 a subcommittee of the GATT was created to handle environmental matters.

Environmental issues arise throughout the WTO's organisational structure, but it has been in the CTE that discussions have centred on the interrelationship between trade and the environment. The terms of reference of the CTE are: (i) to identify the relationship between trade measures and sustainable development; (ii) to make appropriate recommendations on whether the multilateral trading system should be modified; (iii) to assess the need for rules to enhance the interaction between trade and environment including avoidance of protectionist measures and surveillance of trade measures used for environmental purposes. The CTE, a deliberative rather than a policy-making body was given two years to fulfil its mandate. Between its first meeting in February 1995 and the Singapore ministerial meeting it concentrated on clarifying the relationship between trade and the environment. By December 1995 the official view was that the activities undertaken by the CTE were unfinished and that the committee should continue to function.

The Singapore conference also provided the environmental movement with its first opportunity to address the achievements of the WTO in a comprehensive manner. Environmental NGOs were strongly critical of the failure of the CTE to make any substantive progress in its deliberations (FOE 1996b; IISD 1996; WWF 1996c). They argued that the CTE instead of addressing the crucial issues on trade and the environment had been side-tracked into discussions on technical issues. Moreover, ENGOs were sharply critical of the manner in which environmental issues had been shifted to the CTE. Sustainable development touches on the WTO's work programme in a number of ways, and environmental NGOs argue that this realisation should influence WTO policy.

Environmental NGOs and the reform of the WTO

Until 1990 trade policy had not captured the attention and hence organisational energies of the environmental movement. Following the decision by the US administration in late 1990 to negotiate a North American Free Trade Agreement (NAFTA), environmentalists in Canada, Mexico and the USA mobilised to exert influence on their respective governments' policies. If opposition to NAFTA brought a serious questioning of the benefits of free trade it was the GATT's ruling in respect of the dolphin–tuna controversy which lit the touch-fuse under a simmering conflict and exploded the trade–environment debate. Concerted pressure on the GATT by environmentalists first surfaced as a result of the 1991 GATT Panel ruling in respect of the dolphin–tuna dispute between the United States and Mexico. The Panel's decision which upheld Mexican sovereignty and rejected the extra-territorial expansion of American law appeared to many environmentalists to be fundamentally flawed. The ensuing debate was frequently portrayed as a clash between free trade economists on one hand and Green protectionists on the other. Differing perceptions of the impact of the liberal trading system on environmental degradation, the potential of market-based solutions for environmental harm and commitment to continued economic growth produced divergent and conflicting policy proposals from liberal economists (and the GATT Secretariat) and the environmental movement.

The attack by environmental activists on the world trading system focuses on substantive and institutional issues. Before looking at proposals for the democratisation of the WTO we will discuss the conflicts over economic policy. The relationship between trade and the environment has given rise to two broadly competing positions (Williams 1993). On one hand, proponents of free trade argue that no inherent incompatibility exists between the goals of environmental sustainability and trade creation and expansion. On the other hand, environmentalists of different persuasions contend that a liberal trade regime automatically creates the conditions conducive to environmental degradation. This conflict between free traders and environmentalists has been labelled a clash of cultures, paradigms and judgements (Esty 1994).

146

The central contention of liberal economists is that trade liberal-isation promotes growth which enables states to tackle environmental degradation. This position is admirably summed up in the *World Development Report 1992* which stated *inter alia* that '... using trade restrictions to address environmental problems is inefficient and usually ineffective. Liberalised trade fosters greater efficiency and higher productivity and may actually reduce pollution by encour-aging the growth of less polluting industries and the adoption and diffusion of cleaner technologies' (World Bank 1992: 67). This view was echoed by the GATT Secretariat's *Trade and Environment Report* (GATT 1992) which argued that (i) GATT was neutral in the formation of policies necessary to promote sustainable development; (ii) the solution lies in assigning prices and values to environmental resources so that the environmental effects of economic activity can be identified and valued; and (iii) if the policies necessary for sustainable develop-ment are in place, trade promotes development that is sustainable. Within the liberal economic paradigm trade liberalisation is not the primary cause of environmental degradation. Unsustainable economic growth arises from market failure and the inability of governments to engage in adequate environmental pricing. The presumption is that restrictions on trade are not only inadequate but also positively dangerous since under the cloak of environmentalism the dangers of protectionism are ever present. Although empirical evidence and developments in trade theory cast strong doubt on the shibboleth of free trade the underlying truth of the law of comparative advantage and the superiority of market-based solutions remain articles of faith for many economists and policy makers.

The environmentalist critique of the world trade system is based on the contention that free trade, unrestricted markets and limited state intervention is inconsistent with efforts to protect the environment. Environmentalists call for trade restrictions to prevent the spread of pollution by trade. Indirectly, unrestricted trade leads to the export of pollution since firms will move production to countries with the lowest pollution standards. A liberal trading regime provides in-centives to expand production and trade whilst disregarding pollu-tion. Environmentalists also argue that trade liberalisation damages the environment by encouraging economic growth. The drive for profit encourages a relaxation of national environmental protection, and a 'race to the bottom' as countries attempt to maintain inter-national competitiveness. In other words, if the costs of environmental protection are significant those countries with low environmental standards will enjoy a comparative advantage. Liberal trade also exacerbates ecological degradation because production for export markets is more environmentally damaging than production for home consumption; in the words of one observer, 'putting agricultural resources at the service of export markets, in countries that are not self-sufficient in food, enormous pressures are created for local peoples to over-exploit other resources simply to eke out the barest existence' (Shrybman 1990: 31). Under such conditions the resultant exploitation of natural resource use is unsustainable.

This conflict between liberal economists and environmentalists has moved from a general debate concerning the trade–environment link to discussion of specific issues in the context of trade and sustainable development (Uimonen and Whalley 1997). These include problems related to trade in products created through environmentally damaging and unsustainable production processes; problems arising from discriminatory trade policies which foster environmentally damaging and unsustainable use of natural resources; problems related to agricultural production; the relationship between the multilateral trading system and multilateral environmental agreements; eco-labelling; and the relationship between the multilateral trading system and transboundary, regional and global environmental problems (WWF 1996b).

Production, process and methods (PPMs) are central to efforts to introduce sustainable development to the global trading system. PPMs refer to the techniques and methods used in the production of a product, and the debate arises because the rules of the liberal trading system regulates products but not the processes used to create them (WWF 1996b: 7). The trade community is opposed to the inclusion of PPMs on grounds of efficiency and the difficulty of ensuring compliance. Given different absorptive capacities and differing environmental values, the attempt to impose global standards will not only shift specialisation away from comparative advantage but will also impose external values on sovereign sates. Moreover, opponents point out the difficulties inherent in devising systems of monitoring and compliance during production processes. On the other hand, environmentalists contend that it is difficult to sustain a distinction between production and products. PPMs are necessary to protect health and the environment. In this view PPMs would assist in the development of more efficient production and stricter environmental standards. A system based on the 'polluter pays' principle would, it is claimed, diminish the necessity for cumbersome monitoring measures.[30]

Environmentalists argue that not only has the CTE failed to make any progress on trade measures relating to multilateral environmental agreements (MEAs) but it has disrupted the existing consensus by apparently extending the WTO's jurisdiction. One interpretation of the CTE's activities suggests that trade measures agreed in MEAs and applied between the parties could still be taken before a WTO Dispute Panel. That is, WTO members could resort to the WTO dispute settlement mechanism to undermine obligations already agreed to in MEAs. Since MEAs are an effective means of addressing trans-boundary global environmental threats the WTO could undermine them. Furthermore, continuing uncertainty over WTO rules could deter parties from the use of trade measures in MEAs (WWF 1996a: 2).

Environmentalists allege that WTO rules on eco-labelling are unclear. For example, it is not certain whether WTO rules included in the Technical Barriers to Trade (TBT) agreement and its annexes cover eco-labels based on non-product related PPMs (IUCN 1996: 36). One aspect of this controversy relates to the fact that it is not clear whether TBT rules apply to standards involving life cycle analysis. Since TBTs refer to product standards and indirectly to PPMs it is not clear whether the rules apply to, for example, the use of pesticides in production even where there is no pesticide residue. They argue that non-product PPMs should be placed on the agenda, and demand the inclusion of eco-labelling practitioners in the negotiations.

Environmental activists have been campaigning for increased participation by NGOs in the WTO. Environmentalists and other groups have portrayed the WTO (and the GATT before it) as a secretive organisation lacking in accountability. It is argued that civil society organisations have a crucial role to play in making the world trading system more transparent and accountable (Enders 1996; Esty 1997). Environmental NGOs with a focus on the deliberations in Geneva argue that access to information and participation in decision making is vital for democracy, and will also improve the policy outputs of the WTO. Reformist environmentalists are aware that the nature of trade negotiations means that an open-access regime for NGOs is not a

---

[30] See Schlagenhof (1996) for an extended discussion of the differing positions of environmentalists and their critics.

feasible proposition (Charnovitz 1996). Thus their demands for participation and transparency are couched in moderate terms. Proposed reforms maintain the intergovernmental character of the organisation whilst enhancing public scrutiny of the multilateral trading system. Environmentalists claim that the WTO can be reformed in ways which do not impinge on the need for secrecy in bodies like the TPRM. They suggest that membership of the CTE should be expanded to include NGOs. The claim is for observer status rather than full membership. Moreover, they argue that the dispute settlement mechanism should make greater usage of independent experts. On the issue of transparency NGOs are very critical of the existing arrangements for the deregistration of documents. They argue that if crucial documents can be kept restricted until six months after being issued the monitoring functions of NGOs will be handicapped.

Until recently, a number of arguments against increased participation by NGOs in the WTO have been advanced by member states. The first argument is based on the politics of trade negotiations. It amounts to a defence of liberal multilateralism based on the principle of state sovereignty. In this view the various groups attempting to lobby the WTO should do so in their home countries. It follows that if trade policy is the result of a domestic political bargain then it is at the national level that environmental, development, business and consumer interests should attempt to influence policy. It has been pointed out in response that participation can be restricted to NGOs with a distinct international focus (Enders 1996: ii). And the presumption that all governments conform to the plural, democratic model is untenable, hence many groups will not gain access to decision makers at the national level (Esty 1997: 5). The second argument rests on the nature of the negotiating process. International trade negotiations demand a high level of secrecy which cannot be guaranteed if participation is granted to non-state actors. In the process of bargaining governments frequently have to trade-off one domestic interest against another. Governments would be unable to make progress in multilateral trade negotiations if other actors were involved. But as Esty points out, 'giving NGOs a voice at the WTO, and, more importantly, the opportunity to observe WTO debates and dispute settlement proceedings does not preclude governments from discussing issues behind closed doors' (Esty 1997: 5). The third argument against greater involvement of NGOs in the WTO's deliberations arises from the belief that the WTO is a forum for negotiations. NGOs may represent various interests and engage in advocacy but they cannot partake in negotiations. Critics point out that the WTO is not solely concerned with negotiations (Enders 1996: ii), and anyway it would not be setting a precedent since civil society organisations have been involved in negotiations in other fora (Bellmann and Gerster 1996). A fourth set of considerations rest on the desire to deny access to special interests in the negotiating process. Advocates of an open trade regime perceive the ever-present threat of protectionist interests. Therefore, the negotiation process in Geneva should not encourage the active involvement of protectionist groups. Moreover, it is feared that any attempt to widen participation in WTO decision making to increase social movement participation will inevitably increase the lobbying activities of the business community. Given the competitive advantage business organisations possess over NGOs any liberalisation in access for NGOs would increase the influence of large corporations. This objection appears to overlook the fact that special interest groups already have access to the WTO through the role of industry (and other sectors) representatives on national delegations. A fifth set of arguments concentrate on the nature of global democracy. A questioning of the representative nature of NGOs is advanced as a reason why the WTO should resist the attempt by NGOs to achieve a formal status within the organisation. It is argued that not only will it be difficult to devise a method of accrediting legitimate NGOs but that many NGOs do not represent a distinct community of interests. Southern governments express the fear that umbrella Northern organisations with resources greater than many Southern governments are likely to exercise more influence in the deliberations than many Third World states. This result would enhance Northern interests at the expense of Southern peoples. Environmentalists and others argue that these objections can be met through careful institutional design (Enders 1996: ii–iii; Esty 1997: 6). It appears that following the Geneva ministerial meeting these objections will become more muted in the near future.

As a political issue the environmentalist demand for increased access to the WTO decision-making machinery is constructed around a campaign for transparency and participation. The ability of NGOs to monitor trade negotiations depends on the transparency and openness of the procedures. The debate on transparency has centred on access to information. Member states of the WTO have varying standards of public disclosure. From the perspective of NGOs the decision to derestrict documents taken in July 1996 marked a welcome improvement on previous policy. Nevertheless, it has been argued that, 'Fundamentally, the procedures do not reflect a desire for the kind of public participation necessary to protect the interests of the many constituencies concerned with the activities of the WTO and affected by these activities' (Van Dyke and Weiner n.d.: 14). The document derestriction policy is inadequate in two respects. First, member states can block derestriction of any document thus ensuring that sensitive issues are likely to remain secret. Second, the timing of derestriction (varying between sixty days and six months) is likely to result in the public availability of documents after decisions have been made.

Working from a liberal belief in the efficacy of pluralism environmentalists argue that governing systems that integrate public input will consistently produce the best outcomes because the wider the range of views the better the decision-making process, and the sounder the outcome (Enders 1996; Esty 1997). Sally Bullen and Brennan Van Dyke, in the context of their trenchant critique of WTO policy, have presented an extended case for public participation (Bullen and Van Dyke 1996).[31] The arguments for increased transparency, participation and accountability are part of a wider campaign by civil society activists to democratise the structures of world politics. In the specific context of the environmental critique of the WTO two key points arise from the nature of the discourse. First, effective public participation will enhance policies designed to promote sustainable development. Given the role of information, science and knowledge issues in environmental policy making an open system will enhance such policy making. Moreover, within the liberal paradigm open economic systems are clearly superior to closed ones. Second, greater public participation in the WTO will garner support for trade liberalisation. It will counter vested (protectionist) interests, and produce increased support for the liberalisation project since the benefits of liberal trade will be more easily understood.

To date the pressure exerted by the environmental movement on the world trading system has met with limited success. A positive achievement is the initiation of discussion of the link between trade and the environment. The contemporary discourse on sustainable development ensures that the issue is now on the agenda of the WTO

---

[31] The following section relies on this paper.

but environmental considerations are still viewed with suspicion. Environmental NGOs can and do intervene in the multilateral trading system at the national and international levels. The WTO is reluctant to admit the participation of NGOs in its deliberations, arguing that NGOs should seek contact with their own governments. It has been argued that advocacy in Geneva will bring limited gains since trade policy is made in national capitals and the WTO secretariat's function is largely that of a service provider.[32] The environmental movement campaigns at the national level but in their opinion, given the internationalisation of trade policy and the impact of globalisation on structural change in the world trading system, campaigning cannot reside solely at the national level.[33] To the extent that trade negotiators and environmentalists inhabit competing and conflicting cognitive frameworks accommodation will be impossible. This has been recognised by the WWF whose initiative in convening an Expert Panel on Trade and the Environment is an important step in trying to bridge the gap between the two intellectual communities.

The impact of the sentiments expressed at the second ministerial meeting by Ruggiero and Clinton have yet to be translated into effective policies. Nevertheless, it is instructive to note that the proposal to engage in a more concerted manner with non-state actors specifically included the business community. From the perspective of social movement activists the inclusion of business groups weakens their potential influence. Given the competitive advantage business organisations possess over NGOs any proposed 'democratisation' measures will increase the influence of large corporations.

Conclusion

This chapter has documented two different case studies. The World Bank has expanded its formal and informal links with the environmental movement. The WTO remains relatively closed to representatives from social movements but a process of increased contacts between the WTO and NGOs is developing. Any conclusions about global democracy must, of necessity, be extremely tentative. A number of points emerge from the narratives developed here. The

---

[32] Interviews with WTO Secretariat officials, January 1997.
[33] One key aim of the environmental movement at the national level concerns the composition of national trade negotiating teams. They seek the increased participation of environmental ministries in trade talks.

contrasting reactions of the World Bank and WTO to the environmental movement suggests caution in drawing conclusions about the
impact of the environmental movement on international organisations. The contrasting experiences arise partly from the fact that the
organisational structure and characteristics are different, and partly
from the ability of environmentalists to identify crucial points of
leverage. Learning curves and the development of a global democratic
politics appear to be specific to the organisation rather than part of a
general trend. Second, it is very difficult to assess influence. We can
certainly trace the linkages which have developed but the importance
of these lines of communication are not easily established. Nevertheless, some change is taking place, and NGOs have been accepted as
legitimate actors (at least as far as the Bank is concerned). Moreover,
NGOs are clearly a permanent feature of the new global politics.

How have these MEIs modified?

This study set out to answer specific questions concerning the
evolving relationships between social movements and MEIs. This case
study of the ESM and the MEIs provides the following tentative
answers. Both the Bank and the WTO have made attempts to
accommodate the desires of the environmental movement for greater
access to the organisation. They have been unwilling to extend
participation to influence on decision making but both have extended
the scope of their interactions with environmental groups. The
member states and management of the Bank and WTO have initiated
greater dialogue with representatives of the environmental movement
for a number of reasons.

It is arguable that underpinning the work programmes of both the
Bank and the WTO is the concept of sustainable development.
Although the concept of sustainable development remains largely
elusive, and arguably is little more than a rhetorical exercise (Williams
1998), both organisations are now committed to promoting it. This
development, on one hand, suggests the influence of civil society
actors in (re)constructing the broad agenda of development and
environment and, on the other, reveals the limitations of such power.
The conclusion reached on the relevance of sustainable development
as global strategy will depend on the underlying framework used to
evaluate the concept. Nevertheless, from the perspective of this
chapter we can document change in the task environment of the

MEIs. Even lip-service to sustainable development changes the orientation of an organisation. Moreover, it presents NGOs with a yardstick by which to measure performance. Of course, both organisations have attempted to capture the concept of sustainable development and to interpret it within their existing paradigms but noticeable change is evident for both organisations. For the Bank the excesses of adjustment lending have been curtailed, as have the consequences of unfettered lending with limited attention to the ravages on the environment. Looking at the WTO we see an organisation that has been forced to place environmental issues on its agenda whereas its predecessor, the GATT, ignored increasing evidence of the linkages between trade and the environment.

What are the motivations driving MEI–GSM engagement?

Clearly, the Bank and WTO have felt threatened and their engagement arises from a desire to protect their interests and activities. In the case of the Bank, environmentalists threatened its core funding. The recent positive overtures to NGOs by the WTO arises from the fear that widespread public opposition could halt plans for a further round of multilateral trade negotiations. Second, the structures of governance have undergone a transformation in response to structural change. Policy making has had to adjust to a changing global economy. The discourse of sustainable development may be inherently problematic but it is not solely rhetorical. In the context of a globalising world economy the complexities of environmental management, and promotion of sustainable development requires partnerships between state and non-state actors. To put this simply, neither the Bank nor the WTO can perform its mandate without attention to environmental groups. This is, of course, more true of the Bank, a service delivery organisation, than the WTO. Moreover, both organisations need legitimacy if they are to perform their functions. In the contemporary political climate legitimacy is not solely conferred by state actors. ENGOs have been effective at highlighting environmentally degrading practices and assigning culpability. The transnational networks of environmental groups have been effective in mobilising international environmental norms and in shaping legitimate sustainable practices.

What is the significance of the MEI–GSM relationship?

Environmental groups have achieved a degree of success in shaping the policy agenda. Even in the context of the WTO they have been successful in making the environment one of the new issues of concern to the organisation. Their influence on both the Bank and WTO is limited, but the fact that they influence policy rather than have control over decision making should not detract from the fact that a new relationship between MEIs and the ESM is emerging. This study has also demonstrated that the dialogue between the MEIs and the ESM is a restricted one in terms of participation. It is mistaken to think that the ESM represents voices from the periphery. This chapter has attempted to demonstrate that the answer is far more complex than any such facile generalisation. At the level of interactions with MEIs the ESM is characterised not only by diversity but also by a highly sophisticated policy elite which shares more than access to modern technology with those who run the institutions. In order to be heard representatives of social movements must of necessity enter into a dialogue with (speak the language of) the holders of power.

As with so many things beauty lies in the eye of the beholder. Those analysts unwilling to relinquish the straitjacket of realism will see in the narratives developed above little to shake their faith in the continuing primacy of the state. The Bank and WTO as interstate organisations will on this reading remain relatively unscathed. The WTO has no formal provision for consultation with NGOs, and recent informal meetings between Renato Ruggiero and NGOs can easily be overturned by his successor. Moreover, state representatives continue effectively to block further derestriction of documents. The Bank, on the other hand, although it has extended dialogue with groups from civil society in practice only has one official consultative forum, the NGO-World Bank Committee. This Committee has never played an important role, and indeed in the context of Bank interaction with NGOs is increasingly by-passed.

Students starting from the premises of pluralist thought will discern the emergence of transnational processes which support an account of world politics in which non-state actors are prominent. The MEI–GSM relationship is thus important from two perspectives. First, it encourages and thus increases the interactions among diverse representatives of civil society in the global system. Politics in this account is not confined to what takes place between official representatives of governments. The activities of the Bank and WTO directly affect the everyday lives of millions around the globe. Although the account given here only focuses on elite representations to these organisations it nevertheless provides sufficient evidence of an emerging global civil society. Transnational advocacy coalitions and the rise of a global civil politics challenges conventional notions of international relations. Second, study of the linkages between the Bank, the WTO and the environmental movement has highlighted the importance of international organisations as actors in international relations, and as legitimising structures within the global system. Within the globalising polity and economy, with increasing attention to standardisation and the creation of global norms multilateral economic institutions are crucial instruments of change. Relatedly, the MEI–GSM relationship is significant because it suggests another nexus of power in the global system. The MEI–GSM relationship examined here at one and the same time extends some aspects of state power and also extends non-state based power. To illustrate one can discuss the pivotal role of the US political process in the campaign for the reform of the World Bank, and the continuing centrality of the Office of the US Trade Representative for discussions on the future of the multilateral trading system as examples of the manner in which the MEI–GSM relationship extends state power. Thus both the US government and American NGOs benefit from US structural power. On the other hand, both the Bank and the IMF represent powerful structures of governance. This is especially the case with respect to their developing country members. The search for environmental standards in development and trade has at times been pursued by environmentalists in opposition to the interests of Third World governments.[34]

In short, engaging with the environmental movement has transformed both the Bank and the WTO. Both organisations now recognise the importance of the environment for their operations. The environment, or to put it more precisely, attention to the environmental consequences of its operations, is now firmly embedded within Bank policy and practice. The fact that the Bank continues to fall below the standards consistent with an environmental approach to development does not lessen the fact of adaptation. The WTO has to date made a weak attempt to accommodate environmental issues

---

[34] For the purposes of the argument it is a moot point whether the governments are truly representative of their peoples.

but limited progress does not signify no progress. If at the Singapore ministerial meeting government representatives could continue to fake action, by the time the second ministerial meeting was held it was apparent that some effort had to be made to mainstream the environment in the WTO's activities. The desire for a further round of multilateral negotiations, and the prospect that the environment could become a contentious political issue, has recently led to efforts to give greater attention to environmental issues in the world trading system.

These changes would not have taken place in the absence of the campaigning by groups within the environmental social movement. Further, a significant part of ESM advocacy has been directed at the MEIs rather than being modified through state structures. Thus the ESM has contributed to change within the processes of global governance. The environmental movement has demonstrated an ability to contribute to agenda setting, and the power to affect the core interest of MEIs. MEIs have recognised that they cannot function effectively if public perception of their activities is resoundingly negative. And they are aware that environmentalists can affect their image. In charting this evolving relationship it is apparent that 'significance' not only depends on the standpoint of the observer but is itself subject to change.

5   The International Monetary Fund and social movements

The growth of the International Monetary Fund (IMF, or 'the Fund') presents one of the most pronounced cases of expanding global economic governance in the late twentieth century. Particularly since the 1970s, accelerated globalisation has propelled the Washington-based Fund into various new areas: training and technical assistance; surveillance of macroeconomic policy; structural adjustment in the South; post-communist transition in the East; and regulation of financial markets, including several major rescue operations. To deal with this enlarged agenda, as well as a much-expanded membership, the IMF has obtained a much larger staff and hugely increased financial resources. To be sure, it would be mistaken to depict the Fund as an omnipotent ruler of the contemporary world economy; however, its voice carries far in global markets, in national economic policies, and – eventually – in local and household budgets.

The IMF's expansion has not been universally welcomed. On the contrary, critics have raised fundamental objections to both the general premises and the specific content of much of the Fund's policy advice. IMF management and staff have on the whole proceeded from neoliberal assumptions that stabilisation, liberalisation, deregulation and privatisation together yield long-term economic health and human betterment in a globalising world. Opponents in social movements have sought to break this neoliberal consensus at the Fund and to move global monetary and financial governance in alternative directions.

This chapter analyses the aims, activities, impacts and difficulties of campaigns to change the IMF. Given its focus on social movements, the discussion of course covers only part of civil society's engagement of the Fund. After all, many influential civic organisations like corporate business associations and mainstream economic research institutes have broadly endorsed the reigning paradigm at the IMF. However, the emphasis in the present examination lies on reformers and radicals who wish to reconstruct global economic governance rather than on conformers who accept the Fund more or less with its existing priorities, policy instruments and *modus operandi*.[1]

Social movements have striven, especially since the 1980s, to alter both the substantive policies and the operating procedures of the Fund. In regard to policy content, campaigns for change have helped to put issues of labour conditions, poverty alleviation, ecological sustainability, gender equity, good governance and debt relief on the IMF agenda in the 1990s. Social movements have also booked some successes in respect of a democratisation of the Fund, as the organisation has in the 1990s moved towards greater transparency and also (albeit to a lesser extent) increased public accountability and participation. The IMF has in general not changed in the ways and with the degree of urgency that social-movement campaigners have wished. Nevertheless, some shifts are discernible.

The reasons why social movements have so far on the whole had a limited impact on the IMF are varied. For one thing, campaigns for change of the Fund have faced a strong neoliberal consensus at the centres of power in the contemporary world political economy. Second, the institutional culture of the IMF has made the organisation relatively closed to a critical dialogue with social movements. Third, the constituents which social movements have supported (workers, poor people, women, etc.) are structurally weak in world politics. Fourth, mobilisation for change of the Fund has usually been thinly resourced in terms of staff, funds, information and coordination. Fifth, social movements have tended to give a low priority to the IMF relative to other institutional targets for change such as the World Bank. Finally, social movements striving for a reconstruction of global monetary and financial regulation have frequently attended insufficiently to their own democratic credentials, thereby giving the Fund added reason not to engage with them.

The elaboration of the argument just summarised proceeds below in the following main steps. The first section details the growth of the IMF in the context of contemporary globalisation. The second section reviews the various aims of social-movement campaigns with regard

---

[1] On wider civil society relations with the IMF see Scholte (1999a, 1999b).

to the Fund. The third section describes the strategies and tactics used by social movements in pursuit of those objectives. The fourth section elaborates on the types and degrees of policy changes at the IMF to which social-movement activities have contributed. The fifth section analyses the circumstances which have prevented campaigns for reform of the Fund from having a greater impact to date. The conclusion draws together general observations in relation to the guiding questions of the comparative research in this book.

Growth of the IMF

Like the World Bank, the IMF emerged from the United Nations Monetary and Financial Conference, held at Bretton Woods, New Hampshire, in July 1944. According to its constitutional instrument, the Articles of Agreement, the Fund exists: (a) to promote international monetary cooperation; (b) to facilitate the expansion and balanced growth of international trade; (c) to promote foreign exchange stability; (d) to create a multilateral system of payments between members; (e) to assist in the correction of maladjustments in members' balance of payments; and (f) to reduce the duration and severity of disequilibria in members' balance of payments (Guitián 1992).

Although these official purposes have remained the same during the half-century of IMF operations, the institutional arrangements and policy instruments of the organisation have substantially changed over time (de Vries 1986; James 1996). During the first quarter-century after it started operations in 1945, the Fund was mainly concerned to establish and manage the international regime of fixed (but adjustable) exchange rates. Its interventions with member governments were relatively infrequent and brief; they were generally limited to countries of the North; and they were mainly restricted to monetary and trade policy measures.

The IMF lost much of its old role with the end of the dollar-centred fixed-rate system in 1971; however, the rapid globalisation of money and finance since the 1960s has prompted the Fund to reinvent itself with an expanded agenda. The 'second-generation' IMF has entered four new general policy areas.

First, the Fund has since the late 1970s exercised comprehensive and detailed surveillance, both of the economic performance of individual member states and of the world economy as a whole. Article IV,

Section 3 of its statutes (as amended with effect from 1978) provides that 'the Fund shall oversee the international monetary system' and that 'the Fund shall exercise firm surveillance over the exchange rate policies of members'. To this end the institution has published the influential *World Economic Outlook* biannually since 1980 and has conducted so-called 'Article IV consultations' with governments – now up to 150 per year (IMF 1997a: 43). Through these discussions the Fund issues authoritative assessments of national policies and economic performance. In the process of surveillance, the IMF has promoted important policy reorientations, partly with a view to accommodating the ongoing globalisation of production and finance.

Second, the Fund has since the 1970s intervened more intensely in many countries by designing for them not only traditional stabilisation measures for short-term corrections of the balance of payments, but also structural adjustment packages for medium- and long-term economic reconstruction. The IMF has supplemented its conventional stand-by arrangements with medium-term credits since 1974 (under the Extended Fund Facility, EFF) and with longer-term concessional loans since 1986–7 (under the Structural Adjustment Facility (SAF) and Extended Structural Adjustment Facility (ESAF)). IMF conditionality (i.e. the policies the Fund expects a state to follow in order to use IMF resources) has substantially strengthened, often placing major constraints upon state autonomy (Denters 1996). The Fund's 'high conditionality' has included requirements for liberalisation, deregulation, privatisation, fiscal reform and (most recently) so-called 'good governance' (IMF 1997b, 1998e). Compared with the Bretton Woods period, the Fund has come to extend loans to many more states: up to sixty per year. Contemporary IMF programmes have often required large credits (sometimes running into billions of dollars) and longer implementation periods (up to fifteen years in consecutive loans). By 1998, eighty-four states had borrowed from the Fund for at least ten years.[2]

Third, the 'second-generation' IMF has undertaken major training and technical assistance activities, largely in order to provide poorly equipped states with staff and tools that can better handle the policy challenges of contemporary globalisation. The IMF Institute has trained more than 10,000 officials in macroeconomic issues, using

[2] Calculation by the Cato Institute, as cited in a circular on the IMF-Strategy listserv, 21 July 1998.

facilities in Washington (since 1964), Vienna (since 1992), and Singapore (since 1998). The Fund's technical assistance missions to governments, also started in 1964, sharply increased in number from the 1980s and now total around 600 per annum (IMF 1989, 1994a).

Fourth, the IMF has pursued various initiatives to restore stability to global financial markets. For example, since the early 1980s the organisation has played a pivotal role in averting defaults on the large transborder debts of many governments in the South and the East. More recently, the Fund has coordinated large-scale rescue operations ('bailouts') in financial crises of so-called 'emerging markets': in Mexico in 1994–5; in Thailand/Korea/Indonesia in 1997–8; in Russia in 1998 and Brazil in 1998–9. In the hope of better anticipating and perhaps preventing such emergencies, the IMF has since 1996 promoted global norms for government publication of economic and financial data (the so-called Special Data Dissemination Standard, SDDS and the General Data Dissemination System, GDDS). To the extent that the Fund has acted as a lender of last resort and addressed questions concerning the supervision of global capital markets, it has moved towards becoming something of a suprastate central bank.

To handle the enlarged agenda just described, the IMF has undergone substantial institutional growth. Its membership has risen from 62 states in 1960 to 182 states in 1998. The IMF Executive Board now meets in at least three (long) sessions each week. Staff numbers have more than tripled, from 750 in 1966 to 2,661 in 1997 (IMF 1966: 133; 1998j: 101). Over recent decades the Fund has developed its own 'diplomatic service' of sorts, with resident representatives ('res reps') stationed in twenty-two countries by the early 1980s, thirty-eight countries in 1991, and sixty-four countries by 1997 (IMF 1990: 3; 1997a: 226). Other external IMF offices have opened in Geneva, Paris, New York and Tokyo.

Since 1970 IMF financial resources have been denominated in the Fund's own money form, the Special Drawing Right (SDR).[3] Over recent decades IMF quota subscriptions have grown from the equivalent of 21 billion SDRs in 1965 to 212 billion SDRs in 1999 (IMF 1995b: 28; 1998d). The Fund also has gold holdings of 103.4 million fine ounces, worth about $32 billion at market prices as of April 1998 (USGAO 1998). Sums available to the IMF from the General Arrangements to Borrow (GAB) have almost tripled from the original

---

[3] As of mid-1998, the SDR was valued at about US $1.34.

6 billion SDRs (in lenders' currencies) in 1962 to 17 billion SDRs since 1983 (IMF 1995b: 45–6). From 1999 up to 34 billion SDRs became available to the Fund through the so-called New Arrangements to Borrow (NAB) (IMF 1997c). Four additional borrowing agreements concluded between 1979 and 1986 have at one time or another given the Fund access to a total of 27.6 billion further SDRs in credit lines (IMF 1995b: 41–9). The Articles of Agreement also permit the IMF to borrow from private sources, although it has never done so to date.

In sum, given this growth in competencies and resources, the IMF has in the last quarter of the twentieth century become a major site of global economic governance. To be sure, the organisation remains under the strong influence of states, especially its larger members. At the same time, however, the Fund has clearly experienced a major growth in responsibilities and authority. It is not only influenced by its members, but also exerts considerable influence over them, weaker states in particular.

Social movement aims

As noted earlier, not everyone has welcomed the expansion of the IMF just described. For example, various circles have rejected the kinds of conditionality that the Fund has attached to governments' use of its facilities. In particular, these challengers have argued that IMF prescriptions have detrimental effects on workers, the poor, the environment, women, and human rights. Other opposition has criticised the IMF's approach to the debt problems of the South, maintaining that the Fund has protected imprudent banks and concentrated the costs of the crisis unfairly on vulnerable social circles. Further critiques have targeted the alleged undemocratic character of IMF operations, highlighting shortfalls with regard to participation, transparency and accountability in Fund policy making. The rest of this section reviews the social movement activities that have pursued corrections to these purported failings of the IMF.

Protection of workers

The labour movement has led efforts to reverse the claimed negative consequences of IMF conditionality on workers. Trade unions and others have argued that the burdens of conventional Fund stabilisation and structural adjustment measures fall disproportionately on working people. For these critics, IMF-supported programmes have increased unemployment and have also tended to downgrade the working conditions of those who remain on the job. Likewise, the social costs of Fund-sponsored restructuring (in terms of cuts in government support to education, health, housing, etc.) have allegedly hit workers especially hard.

The leading voice in the labour movement for reform of the IMF has been the International Confederation of Free Trade Unions (ICFTU). In comparison, the World Confederation of Labour (WCL) and the International Trade Secretariats have done relatively little campaigning on the IMF. Around 1982–3, the ICFTU started to invite representatives of the Fund to its regional meetings. In IMF programme countries, the Confederation has over the years organised twenty-eight national conferences on structural adjustment. Every year since 1988, the ICFTU has submitted a lengthy policy statement to the IMF/World Bank annual meetings. In 1994 the organisation opened a bureau in Washington, largely in order to establish closer liaison with the Bretton Woods institutions. Trade unions in several countries (e.g. Congo and Fiji) have used this office as a channel of communication with the Fund.

At national level, trade unions have tended to mobilise on the IMF only in response to Fund-sponsored programmes in their country. Thus, for example, the Korean Confederation of Trade Unions has campaigned actively on structural adjustment issues since a collapse of the won brought an IMF programme to the Republic of Korea in 1997. Likewise, organised labour in Romania has repeatedly tried to block or slow privatisations mandated in that country under Fund-supported policies. In the USA, however, the AFL–CIO and the United Auto Workers have in 1998 gone beyond immediate national concerns to call for more general reforms of the IMF (AFL–CIO 1998; UAW 1998).

Poverty eradication

Much other mobilisation to change the Fund has focused on questions of development, and in particular on the alleged harmful effects of IMF-supported adjustment on the poor in the South and the East. Certain religious orders, non-governmental organisations (NGOs) and institutes of development studies had already expressed concerns about these issues in the 1970s. In the early 1980s, bodies like the

Overseas Development Institute (ODI) in London, the Overseas Development Council (ODC) in Washington, and the Swiss Coalition of Development Organisations in Berne critically examined the implications of IMF conditionality for poverty in the South (Gerster 1982; Feinberg and Kallab 1985; Killick 1982). In 1983 several witnesses, including a Maryknoll priest working in Peru, testified before the US Congress on the sufferings of poor people under Fund programmes. These criticisms from social movements were reinforced with the publication in the late 1980s of several officially commissioned studies which linked IMF/World Bank-sponsored policies to deteriorating conditions for the poor (Corina, Jolly and Stewart 1987–8; UNCTAD 1989: 153–209). In the first of many such global seminars, representatives of forty-six NGOs from two dozen countries met at Oxford in September 1987 to discuss alternative approaches to macroeconomic adjustment (Nelson 1996: 613).

Calls to protect the poor from the costs of IMF-supported stabilisation and restructuring have continued unabated throughout the 1990s. Prominent actors in this line of advocacy work have included: the Development GAP, the United States branch of Friends of the Earth (FOE-US) and Bread for the World in Washington; the global network of Oxfams; and the Swiss Coalition of Development Organisations (DGAP 1995, 1996a; Watkins *et al.* 1995: ch. 3; Oxfam 1995). Certain development NGOs in the South have also sought to engage the IMF on the issue of poverty eradication: e.g. the Freedom from Debt Coalition in the Philippines; the Forum of African Voluntary Development Organisations (FAVDO) in Senegal; Equipo PUEBLO in Mexico; the Platfòm Ayisyen Pledwaye pou yon Devlopman Altènatif (PAPDA) in Haiti; and Focus on the Global South in Thailand.

Various academic researchers (including in particular those affiliated to institutes of development studies) have in the 1990s also continued to criticise a purported maldevelopment connected to IMF-sponsored policies. These think tanks have included ODI and the Institute of Development Studies in Britain, the Brazilian Institute for Social and Economic Analysis (IBASE), ODC and the Harvard Institute for International Development (HIID) in the USA, the Economic Policy Research Centre in Uganda, the North–South Institute in Canada, the Austrian Foundation for Development Assistance Research (ÖFSE), and so on.

Whereas the development NGOs and academic institutes just named have taken what could be loosely described as socialist and

Keynesian approaches to changing the IMF, other critiques of the Fund's involvement in development issues have come from libertarian quarters. These challengers have argued that 'free markets' provide the optimal formula for poverty eradication and that IMF programmes, like all public-sector interventions in the economy, in the end perpetuate rather than alleviate the problem. On these lines, the Washington-based Cato Institute has continually questioned the *raison d'être* of the IMF, *inter alia* through its annual monetary conferences since 1983 and its Project on Global Economic Liberty since 1990 (Bandow and Vásquez 1994; Cato Institute 1998). Similar free-market critiques of the Fund have emanated in the late 1990s from other Washington think tanks such as the American Enterprise Institute for Public Policy Research, the Heritage Foundation and the Competitive Enterprise Institute.

Ecological sustainability

Next to campaigning on issues of labour and poverty, a few influential NGOs have focused their lobbying of the Fund on countering the allegedly harmful ecological consequences of IMF conditionalities. Environmentalists gave their first Congressional testimony on these matters in 1983, but their advocacy work on the Fund has mainly intensified since 1989. In that year FOE-US launched its IMF Reform Campaign, which has continued to this day. Its activists have argued that Fund-sponsored policies can produce 'wanton destruction of fragile ecosystems [and] depletion of resources at a rate faster than the environment can restore them' (FOE 1996a). Other NGOs pursuing eco-friendly change in Fund conditionality have been the World Resources Institute (WRI) and the World Wide Fund for Nature (WWF) (Cruz and Repetto 1992; Reed 1992, 1996). However, most environmentalist associations have to date ignored the IMF, directing their lobbying of global economic institutions instead at the World Bank and the World Trade Organisation.[4]

Gender equity

Other social-movement initiatives vis-à-vis IMF conditionalities have highlighted gender issues. For example, several women's

[4] See chapter 4 above.

organisations have produced studies of the gendered impact of neoliberal structural adjustment programmes, arguing that the pains of Fund-sponsored policies have fallen disproportionately on women (Antrobus 1988; DGAP 1996b; Sparr 1994; Ssemogerere, Sengendo and Kiggundu 1995; Woestman 1994). On the eve of the United Nations Conference on Women at Beijing in 1995, FOE-US sent the managing director of the Fund a detailed document on gender implications of IMF-supported programmes, to which he gave a generously phrased but otherwise non-committal response. However, on the whole feminist lobbying on structural adjustment has concentrated on the World Bank and the European Union rather than on the IMF.[5]

Improved governance

Finally in respect of conditionalities, several NGOs have pushed the IMF to give greater attention to questions of human rights, corruption and military spending. For example, a few US-based activists have urged the Fund to consider human rights circumstances when providing credits in Latin America. Meanwhile the Berlin-based organisation Transparency International has encouraged the IMF to examine corruption in programme countries (IMF 1998c). Certain NGOs (for example, in Geneva) have argued that IMF-sponsored structural adjustment should incorporate cuts in excessive military expenditure. As with women's groups, however, the scale of these social-movement contacts with the Fund has remained small.

Debt relief

Ever since the debt crisis of the South erupted in the early 1980s, many critics of the IMF have advocated major reductions in the debt burdens of these countries. For instance, a US Debt Crisis Network was active between 1985 and 1990, as were various religious organisations around the world. However, the campaigns of the 1980s concentrated mainly on commercial and bilateral borrowings rather than on loans from multilateral institutions. The IMF was implicated in the debt problem as an important catalyst for rescheduling commercial and bilateral loans, but not as a major creditor itself.

---

[5] See chapter 2 above.

This situation began to change in 1993–4 when the European Network on Debt and Development (EURODAD) launched a campaign with its affiliates in sixteen countries to reduce the burdens in the South of multilateral debt, including sums owing to the IMF (EURODAD 1996a). Prominent partners in the EURODAD effort have included Oxfam, the (British) Debt Crisis Network, the Debt and Development Coalition Ireland, the Nordic Network on Debt and Development, the Swiss Coalition, and the Bonn-based NGO World Economy, Ecology and Development (WEED). EURODAD has also collaborated with campaigns on debt in other regions. Among these ASIADAD, started in 1993, has become rather moribund. However, AFRODAD has shown steady if slow growth since its launch in 1994, and LATINDAD was revived in 1997. In the countries of the South earmarked for action under the IMF/World Bank debt-reduction scheme launched in 1996 (detailed later), NGOs have rallied around coalitions such as the Iniciativa Nicaragua and the Uganda Debt Network in efforts to extend and accelerate this relief. Consultancy firms such as Oxford International Associates and the London-based External Finance for Africa Project have also added to the critiques of the Fund's role in the debt crisis (Martin 1993; Mistry 1994, 1996).

In tandem with the work of the secular development NGOs just mentioned, religious organisations have also provided much impetus behind social-movement lobbying of the IMF to extend debt relief. Behind closed doors, church leaders met with the IMF managing director, Michel Camdessus, in London and Washington in early 1996 to argue for large-scale debt reduction (Vallely 1996). Already the Pope had in 1995 publicly rebuked the Fund on the debt issue (John Paul II 1995). Two years later the Pontifical Council for Justice and Peace convened a meeting at the Vatican with Camdessus and the Presidents of the World Bank and Inter-American Development Bank to discuss debt issues in Latin America (IMF 1997e: 208). At a grass-roots level, the Religious Working Group on the World Bank and the IMF, formed in the USA in 1994, has directed much of its attention to the question of debt relief. Finally, the transborder Jubilee 2000 Campaign, launched in 1996 and covering affiliates in over forty countries by mid-1999, has focused its calls for debt forgiveness substantially on the Fund (Jubilee 2000 Campaign 1999a, 1999b).

Democratisation

In addition to altered conditionalities and debt relief, the third main general goal of social-movement activities in regard to the IMF has concerned democratisation of the institution. In this vein some reformers have argued for changes in the voting system at the Fund in order to reduce the dominant voice of a handful of governments (Gerster 1993). Under the slogan of 'ownership', advocates of increased democracy in IMF operations have also urged greater participation by client governments and civil societies in the formulation and implementation of Fund-supported programmes. With reference to 'transparency', many advocates of change have demanded greater openness about policy-making processes at the IMF: e.g. what decisions have been taken; by whom; from among which options; and on the basis of what information. On the theme of 'accountability', various activists have pressed the Fund to establish comprehensive, systematic and transparent mechanisms of policy evaluation.

A few lobbyists like FOE-US raised issues of democratisation of the IMF already in the late 1980s, but the matter has principally come to the fore since the mid-1990s. Considerable substantive work in this area has come through the Washington-based Center of Concern. Its Rethinking Bretton Woods Project, begun in 1994, has aimed to effect 'genuine institutional reform over the next 10 to 15 years' (Center of Concern 1998; Griesgraber and Gunter 1995, 1996). In 1997–8 the Center coordinated a study group on Transparency and Accountability in the International Monetary Fund. This exercise, which included full participation by current and former IMF staff, focused in particular on increasing the release of Fund documentation and on establishing a mechanism for independent outside evaluation of Fund policies (IMF 1998f). In Britain, meanwhile, two dozen development and environment NGOs set up a Bretton Woods Project in 1995 to further work on reform of the IMF and the World Bank. With broadly similar aims, the Amsterdam-based NGO service organisation BothENDS started a Multilateral Financial Institutions Project in 1994. In North America, the Halifax Initiative has since 1995 grouped eleven advocacy groups in 'A Canadian Coalition for Global Economic Democracy' that has concerned itself *inter alia* with the IMF.

In sum, the greatest social-movement activity for change at the International Monetary Fund has occurred in respect of employment, poverty and debt issues. Since the mid-1990s substantial attention has also focused on purported democratic deficits in IMF operations. More incidental lobbying on the Fund has raised questions of environmental degradation, gender inequity, corruption, human rights abuses and militarisation. Meanwhile other social movements such as consumer unions, indigenous peoples and non-Christian religious groups have ignored the IMF.

Strategies and tactics

Although some noteworthy social-movement initiatives in respect of the IMF unfolded in the 1980s, the main growth in the number, range and sophistication of campaigns for change in the organisation and its policies has transpired in the 1990s. In assessing these activities, the present section first draws a distinction between reformist and radical strategies of pursuing a transformation of global monetary and financial governance. Attention turns thereafter to the various tactics that social movements have employed vis-à-vis the Fund, including direct lobbying of the organisation as well as indirect pressure via governments, other global governance agencies, the mass media, and the general public.

Overall strategies

Regarding strategy, an important broad distinction can be drawn between reformers and radicals in social movements (Jordan 1996). Reformers are those elements who seek change through a reconstructed International Monetary Fund. These circles accept the need for an IMF-type agency in the contemporary world and aim to alter the existing organisation so that it promotes a more secure and equitable global political economy. In contrast, radicals have sought not reorientations in the IMF so much as its contraction or even abolition. In practice, the distinction between reformers and radicals has sometimes blurred. For example, some individuals and groups in social movements have shown a mix of the two tendencies, and some activists have shifted their approach over time or between audiences.

The choice between a reformist and a radical approach of course presents social movements with a key strategic decision. Reformism implies acceptance of the IMF's existence and a relatively long process of patient negotiation for change. Radicalism implies a rejection of the

IMF's existence and in many cases also a refusal to engage in detailed discussions with the organisation. Reformers may regard radicals as 'unrealistic' and 'destructive'. Radicals may regard reformers as 'naive' and 'coopted'. For example, disagreements regarding aims, strategy and tactics sharply divided reformists and radicals in their response to the heavily indebted poor country (HIPC) initiative in 1996–7 (EURODAD 1996b). The balance between reformist and radical approaches within social movements in part reflects the Fund's success or failure in convincing activists of its readiness to hear and respond to their criticisms.

Most of the organisations discussed in the preceding section have pursued a reformist strategy in respect of the IMF. The ICFTU, ODI, ODC, the Swiss Coalition, the WWF, Transparency International, EURODAD, the Vatican, the Center of Concern and others have adopted a policy of 'constructive engagement' with the Fund. Some religious groups like the Maryknoll order and NGOs like Oxfam and FOE-US have shown a mix of reformist and radical tendencies. As a result, their contacts with the IMF have tended to be more confrontational.

Other parts of social movements have taken an unambiguously rejectionist stance in respect of the Fund. For example, many grass-roots associations in programme countries have urged that IMF interventions be removed from their lives. In the USA, several groups affiliated to the Fifty Years Is Enough coalition have likewise called for a major reduction in the Fund's activities. The Fifty Years network was launched in 1994 with thirty-three affiliates. By 1999 it had a US membership of over 205 associations, plus 180 partner organisations in sixty-five countries, and a coordinating office in Washington (Fifty Years Is Enough 1999). Meanwhile, free-marketers associated with organisations like the Cato Institute and the Heritage Foundation have advocated the abolition of the IMF on libertarian grounds (Bandow 1998). During 1997–8, lobbying in Washington saw a tactical coalition of 'rightist' and 'leftist' radicals with the aim of blocking Congressional approval of increased IMF funding.

Campaign tactics

This alliance of convenience is indicative of the growing sophistication of much social-movement activism vis-à-vis the Fund in the 1990s. Quite a few groups have learned how the IMF is organised, how they can acquire direct contacts with its staff, how to obtain and interpret

Fund documentation, and so on. Various associations have produced their own studies of IMF operations. Several campaigns have hired professional lobbyists, consultants and/or information officers. A few organisations based outside the USA have set up representative offices in Washington *inter alia* to monitor the Fund.

Of the various forms of social-movement pressure on the IMF, street protests have been the most visible. For example, banner-waving demonstrators have appeared with some regularity outside Fund headquarters in Washington, particularly in conjunction with the IMF/World Bank annual meetings. Large-scale marches also accompanied the 1988 annual meetings in Berlin and the 1994 annual meetings in Madrid. Trade unions and other grass-roots associations have taken to the streets against the Fund in many programme countries as well, sometimes with violent consequences. Walton and Seddon (1994) have documented 146 austerity protests against multi-laterally supported economic restructuring between 1976 and 1992. In the worst case of 'IMF riots', demonstrations in Venezuela in February 1989 left over 300 dead.

Many social-movement activists have also demanded change in the Fund through correspondence with its senior officials. The managing director alone receives hundreds of letters each year. On a number of occasions a lead NGO has circulated a sign-on letter concerning reform of the IMF. Activists have also submitted petitions in an attempt to draw the Fund's attention to their demands. For example, in early 1989 Save the Rainforest presented Camdessus with a petition critical of Fund policies holding nearly 28,000 signatures from five major member states. Other associations have sent the IMF their position papers and studies of Fund-supported policies.

The 1990s have seen major increases in face-to-face lobbying of IMF officials by social-movement activists. Starting with the Berlin meetings in 1988, delegations of NGO representatives have requested, and increasingly gained, interviews with the Fund's Executive Directors (EDs) at the time of the annual conference. Over half of the twenty-four EDs agreed to such encounters at the 1996 meetings. Various other deputations of trade unionists, religious leaders and NGO activists have called on EDs at other times of the year. Meanwhile representatives of social movements have had occasional discussions with the managing director both in Washington and in several programme countries.

Since around 1992, social-movement activists have also had a number of interviews and briefings with officials in the functional and area departments of the Fund. For example, several delegations of trade unionists have visited Washington and met with some of the IMF staff responsible for their countries: from Zambia in May 1993; from Niger and Mali in January 1994; from Francophone Africa in December 1995; from Central Europe in December 1996; and from Asia in February 1998. In 1993 and 1995, several eco-advocates attended seminars on macroeconomics and the environment organised by the Fund (IMF 1993, 1995d). Since 1995, senior staff in the Policy Development and Review (PDR) department have had several exchanges with development NGOs in relation to the aforementioned IMF/World Bank initiative for debt relief. Finally, representatives of social movements have in the 1990s made various approaches in the field to visiting IMF mission teams and to res reps of the Fund.

On other occasions social movements have invited management and staff of the IMF to their events. For example, the ICFTU has usually included participation from the local res rep of the Fund in its national seminars on structural adjustment. The IMF also despatched a representative to an International Round Table on 'Structural Adjustment and Environment' in Berlin in 1992. The Executive Director for Switzerland accepted invitations from the Swiss Coalition of Development Organisations to undertake joint fact-finding missions to Ghana in 1993 and Bangladesh in 1996.

Considerable political sophistication in social-movement campaigns has also appeared with their employment of indirect pressure on the Fund, for example, via national governments. The most advanced tactics of this kind have developed in the USA, where activists have in 1980, 1983, 1989, 1991–2, 1994 and 1997–8 attempted to block or qualify Congressional approval of increased monies for the IMF. Each of the allocations since 1989 has eventually had conditions attached, e.g., relating to the social and environmental effects of structural adjustment or to increased transparency and evaluation of Fund operations. That said, follow-up mechanisms to ensure the IMF's compliance with these terms have been weak.

In other countries, the Debt and Development Coalition Ireland has successfully lobbied the Dáil and the Ministry of Finance in Dublin to defer contributions from the Irish government to ESAF since 1995 (Hanlon 1997; Somers 1997). Social movements have also engaged representative institutions in those programme countries like Haiti where a structural adjustment programme negotiated with the IMF requires the approval of the legislature. Several UK-based development NGOs have in recent years made submissions concerning the Fund to parliamentary select committees in London. In Switzerland, NGOs have since 1992 used a special extra-parliamentary committee on the Bretton Woods institutions to press the federal government *inter alia* on matters concerning the IMF (Raffer and Singer 1996: 146–9).

Other social-movement lobbying has targeted ministries of finance and central banks, that is, the parts of national governments with which the IMF has maintained its closest contacts. For example, several NGOs in Germany met in early 1996 with the International department of the Bundesbank to discuss reform of the Fund. In 1998 BothENDS coordinated several discussions about the IMF between activists and the Netherlands Ministry of Finance and the Netherlands Bank. Lobbyists in Washington have likewise directed some of their efforts at the US Treasury department. In some countries social-movement campaigners have turned to ministries in the hope of obtaining confidential Fund documents that IMF staff refuse to leak.

In addition, certain campaigns for change have sought indirect influence on the IMF through contacts with other global governance agencies. For example, the ICFTU has joined forces with the International Labour Organisation (ILO) to advocate a larger social dimension in Fund programmes. EURODAD has engaged with the European Commission (especially the Structural Adjustment Unit of DG VIII) in the hope that 'progressive elements in EU policy ... could have some leverage on BWI policies designed in Washington' (EURODAD 1995: 9; see also EURODAD 1996c). Development NGOs have also found substantial sympathy for IMF reform in UNCTAD, UNDP, UNICEF, the Non-Aligned Movement, the Intergovernmental Group of Twenty-Four and the Commonwealth Secretariat. NGO fora running parallel to UN-sponsored global issue conferences in the 1990s have often given prominent attention to questions of debt relief and reform of the prevailing framework of structural adjustment.

At the same time, many activists have hoped that campaigns for change targeted at the World Bank will reverberate on the Fund. For example, since 1996 a network of over 1000 associations from South and North has engaged the World Bank in a Structural Adjustment Policy Review Initiative (SAPRI) to evaluate local experiences of adjustment in programme countries (SAPRIN 1999a, 1999b). The IMF has declined to become an official full participant in SAPRI, but the

NGOs clearly hope that the results of the exercise might nevertheless influence the Fund.

In respect of the general public, a number of advocacy groups have in the 1990s given increased attention to civic education about the IMF: i.e. to make questions of debt, surveillance, structural adjustment and the overall political economy of globalisation more accessible to citizens at large. For example, WEED, Fifty Years Is Enough, and other NGOs have organised symposia and workshops in order to advance public understanding of the Fund. FOE-US has used its longer experience of campaigning on the IMF to produce fact sheets and handbooks about the organisation for use by other groups (Torfs 1996). The Debt and Development Coalition Ireland and the Berne Declaration in Switzerland have each prepared popular information packs concerning the Bretton Woods institutions. Christian Aid and the Maryknoll order have both produced short films on the need for debt relief in the South. Some groups like Oxfam have cultivated links with the mainstream press in the hope of reaching the wider public via the mass media.

Finally, social movements have in the 1990s advanced their campaign tactics with improved communications among the activists themselves. For example, advocacy groups have held meetings concurrently with all IMF/World Bank annual meetings since 1986. Lower telephone charges, faxes, electronic mail and the World Wide Web have enabled those activists with access to these technologies to develop much closer contacts with one another. NGOs have since the mid-1990s maintained half a dozen listservs on the Internet with continually updated information about the IMF.[6]

In sum, then, in the 1990s the International Monetary Fund has encountered many more proponents of change, many of whom have had more specific objectives, a tighter organisation, and greater political skill than their predecessors of the 1980s. Any analysis of Fund policy content and consequences must now take these relationships into account.

---

[6] For example, coc.brettonwds@conf.igc.apc.org (Center of Concern); 50-years@igc.org (Fifty Years Is Enough Network); imf-strategy@essential.org (circulation of information for Washington-based activists); lrp-arg@flacso.wamani.apc.org (FLACSO-Argentina); mdbs-europe-l@ecn.cz (Central and Eastern Europe Bankwatch Network); stop-imf@essential.org (Essential Information).

Impacts

In what ways and to what extent have social movements actually affected policies at the Fund? Needless to say, it is impossible to determine, precisely and definitively, the degree to which reformist and radical campaigns for change have affected IMF behaviour. It is not possible to measure a distinct social-movement influence separately from other forces such as pressure from governments and shifts in the general world political and economic situation.

The present discussion mainly assesses *changes* in the Fund's orientations in the 1990s. However, it is important also to stress the significant positive reinforcement of existing policy lines which the IMF has received from some sectors of civil society. Bankers' associations, chambers of commerce, mainstream think tanks and the like have rarely pushed the Fund to depart from its prevailing fundamental assumptions, modes of analysis and broad prescriptions. Arguably social movements have to date made only a modest overall impact on the IMF, in part because the Fund has received constant countervailing endorsements from other civic circles.

That said, the IMF has also adjusted a number of its policy directions during the 1990s. For one thing, with respect to substantive policy, the Fund has reformulated conditionalities so that they include some explicit attention to social, environmental and governance issues. In addition, as already mentioned, the IMF has, together with the World Bank, developed a modest programme of debt relief for poor countries. On questions of democratisation, the Fund has, with attention to 'consensus' and 'ownership', become more attuned to the political dimensions of its activities. In related veins, the 1990s have seen notable moves at the IMF towards greater transparency (with substantially increased access to information) and accountability (with the expansion of evaluation activities).

These general policy changes have not gone as far as most activists would have liked. However, even vigorous critics concede that the IMF has in the 1990s altered its approach to a number of issues. In each case, social movements have helped to produce the (limited) policy shifts.

The 'social dimension'

Inputs from trade unions, NGOs, development studies institutes and other critics have encouraged the Fund to reconsider its general approach to conditionality in certain respects. Most prominently, IMF-financed programmes have since the mid-1990s given greater attention to the so-called 'social dimension' of structural adjustment. Already in the late 1970s, some commentators were voicing concern about possible harmful effects of Fund-sponsored restructuring on vulnerable groups; however, these issues did not gain real prominence at the IMF until fifteen years later. Camdessus launched the new tone in July 1992 when he declared before the UN Economic and Social Council that 'the essential missing element [in programmes] . . . is a sufficient regard for the short-term human costs involved during adjustment or transition to a market economy' (IMF 1992). Since around 1994, IMF-backed policy packages have regularly included so-called 'social safety nets' to reduce the adverse impacts of adjustment on the poor and weak. These measures have addressed matters including preventive and primary health care, primary and secondary education, and (less often) unemployment benefits and the protection of pensions for the elderly (IMF 1994b, 1995a, 1996l). Also to promote the newly emphasised themes of 'high-quality growth', the Fund's Fiscal Affairs Department (FAD) in 1995 and 1998 hosted high-profile seminars on income distribution and equity, including participation from *inter alia* religious groups, labour organisations and academics (IMF 1995e, 1998h). In 1998 the IMF began a pilot programme of closer collaboration with the World Bank on social aspects of adjustment, and in 1999 two poverty experts from Britain were seconded to the Fund for a two-year period.

That said, the growth of the social dimension in IMF policy should not be overestimated. Although references to safety nets and the like have figured prominently in the Fund's public pronouncements since 1992, practical measures to combat poverty have not moved to the heart of IMF-supported programmes. The relevant policy documents usually discuss 'social issues', 'social needs' and 'social costs' relatively briefly and often in only general terms. (Social consequences have been considerably highlighted in the Asia crisis programmes since 1997.) The director of FAD himself has said that the Fund's work on poverty alleviation remains 'very limited' and 'not a main or explicit objective of the IMF'. Indeed, the purpose of safety nets has 'much to do with strengthening the political sustainability of reform' (IMF 1996c: 102). In sum, 'SAP' in the 1990s has continued in the first place to designate 'structural adjustment programme' rather than 'social action programme'; however, the two have overlapped more in recent IMF packages than they did in the 1970s and 1980s.

Ecological sustainability

Next to questions of poverty alleviation, Fund-supported policy programmes have since the mid-1990s begun to include occasional passing attention to issues of environmental degradation. In early 1991 the Executive Board enjoined IMF staff to develop greater understanding of the interplay between economic policy and environmental change (Osunsade and Gleason 1992: 21). Fund officials have in this spirit produced several studies of macroeconomics and the environment (Gandhi 1996; Gupta, Miranda and Parry 1993; Muzondo *et al.* 1990). However, to date only one or two officials in FAD have worked at length on these questions, and then amongst their other duties (IMF 1996c: 103). As far as one can gather from published materials, only a small minority of structural adjustment programmes have made any reference to ecological degradation (IMF 1996d, 1996h). Environmental issues have never formed a stumbling block in the Fund's negotiations with governments. Executive Directors have shown no inclination – and indeed have often expressed positive reluctance – to expand the IMF's mandate to encompass ecological sustainability. In short, the Fund has responded to pressure from environmental NGOs (and in particular the large environmentalist lobby in Washington) by acknowledging the existence of links between economic policy and ecological change. However, this recognition has not, to date, translated into a major reformulation of IMF prescriptions.

Gender sensitivity

Another area where the Fund has marginally adjusted its approach to conditionality concerns gender. The chief IMF representative at the Beijing Conference on Women made comments unknown to the Fund of earlier days, noting that 'policies that seem to be gender blind may be far from gender neutral in their impact' (IMF 1995f: 287). However, her further statement that 'gender analysis is ... already being used to improve economic adjustment programs' seems rather strong (IMF 1995f: 288). Although the Fund has published one working paper on gender aspects of macroeconomic policy (Stotsky 1996), its officials appear to have made little use of the previously cited research on the gendered consequences of structural reform (page 168 above). Available documents concerning IMF-sponsored stabilisation and structural adjustment programmes have only rarely made explicit reference to women's circumstances, and then have mainly done so as a footnote (Government of Kenya 1996: 38–9; IMF 1996f). The Fund has hired no economists with a specialisation in gender analysis; nor have any staff in FAD explored gender issues in the way that certain officials have studied poverty alleviation and environmental problems. On a more positive note the IMF has in the late 1990s begun to look critically at the gender profile of its staff (IMF 1998j: 101). Part of the reason for this neglect of gender may be that social movements have not given related questions much emphasis in their contacts with the Fund. In particular, as noted earlier, women's organisations have done little campaigning on the IMF.

'Good governance'

Most recently, to the pleasure of groups like Transparency International, the IMF has expanded the scope of conditionality with explicit attention to governance issues. At the 1996 annual meetings, the Interim Committee adopted a Declaration on Partnership for Sustainable Global Growth which called *inter alia* for 'promoting good governance in all its aspects, including by ensuring the rule of law, improving the efficiency and accountability of the public sector, and tackling corruption' (IMF 1997a: 209). Subsequently several Fund publications have addressed these topics (Dhonte and Kapur 1997; Kopits and Craig 1998; Mauro 1997; Tanzi 1998). In 1997 the Executive Board adopted a guidance note regarding governance issues which referred among other things to corruption, enhanced transparency in national decision-making and budgetary processes, improved accounting and control mechanisms, better dissemination of statistics, and civil service reform (IMF 1997f). At the 1998 spring meetings, the Interim Committee encouraged IMF member governments to implement a Code of Good Practices on Fiscal Transparency (IMF 1998g: 122–4).

In concrete terms, however, good governance conditionality has not as yet affected IMF programmes much beyond the already existent pursuit of civil service reform. The Fund has halted disbursement of certain credits (e.g. to Kenya and to Cambodia in 1996) until corruption issues were addressed. IMF management and staff have also urged several governments (e.g. those of India and Pakistan) to reduce 'unproductive' military expenditure. Governance issues have furthermore figured prominently in discussions surrounding the

Fund's interventions in the Asian crisis of 1997–8. On the whole, however, the IMF has not yet developed clear and consistent operational practices in regard to governance matters.

Indeed, some critics in social movements have viewed the Fund's interest in 'good governance' with suspicion as a neoimperialist intervention. Moreover, to the disappointment of some campaigners for change, the IMF has not interpreted the concept of 'good governance' to encompass guarantees of human rights. In handling governance issues, the Fund has insisted on separating the 'economic' from the 'political' and on restricting its concerns to the former.

Debt relief

Debt relief is a fifth area where, partly owing to pressure from social movements, IMF policy has shifted in the 1990s. As mentioned earlier, the Fund became actively involved in the external debt problems of the South and the East in the early 1980s, when the organisation played an important catalytic role in the rescheduling of transborder loans. In the late 1990s, the IMF continues periodically to provide advisory support to commercial banks in their renegotiation of repayment terms for a given country. In addition, the rescheduling of official bilateral debts through the so-called Paris Club has since the 1980s often been linked to the implementation of IMF-sponsored structural adjustment policies.

However, until the mid-1990s the IMF did not regard external debt burdens as a major impediment to the development prospects of the countries concerned. Broadly speaking, Fund officials assumed that standard rescheduling linked to neoliberal structural adjustment would in time resolve the debt problem. Nor did the IMF consider providing relief on the repayment of debts that governments of the South owed to the Fund itself.

The IMF's stance on these issues changed in 1996. Early that year a joint IMF/World Bank staff paper concluded that, even with existing debt-relief mechanisms, eight HIPCs could not achieve sustainable debt burdens in less than ten years (*Financial Times*, 4 March 1996: 10). At the 1996 annual meetings in September, the Interim and Development Committees of the IMF and the World Bank endorsed the so-called HIPC initiative of exceptional debt relief for eligible countries (Boote and Thugge 1997). This plan for the first time included an element of relief on debt payments owed to the Fund. By early 1999, the Executive Boards of the IMF and the World Bank had confirmed the eligibility of six countries for the HIPC scheme, and one country (Uganda, in April 1998) had begun to receive this relief.

The various social-movement campaigns for debt relief described earlier have figured importantly in effecting these policy shifts at the IMF. Persistent pressure on this issue from many religious organisations and development NGOs helped to establish the principle of concessionary debt relief at the Paris Club in the late 1980s and then in the mid-1990s to extend that principle to loans owed to multilateral agencies, including the IMF. In addition, lobbying by a number of groups has had some effect in relaxing the eligibility criteria for HIPC relief and in increasing the degree of concessionality included in HIPC agreements for individual countries. Reform campaigners have also helped to shape the HIPC initiative so that it makes an explicit link between debt relief and safeguards to government expenditure on basic social services.

That said, many social-movement activists remain dissatisfied with the HIPC initiative and prevailing general approaches to debt relief for the South. In their eyes, HIPC arrangements should reach more countries more quickly and should cover a larger proportion of external debts with more generous provisions (EURODAD 1998a; Gordon and Gwin 1998; Oxfam 1998). Critics have also complained that the IMF's contribution to the scheme is modest and involves refinancing loans through ESAF rather than outright debt cancellation. Some campaigners have argued that the Fund has been motivated as much by the opportunity to replenish ESAF and place that credit facility on a permanent footing as by the objective to alleviate the debt burdens of poor countries. For proponents of comprehensive debt write-offs like the Jubilee 2000 Campaign, Paris Club concessionality and the HIPC initiative are wholly inadequate.

Yet the IMF's position on debt relief has clearly shifted between the 1980s and the 1990s. In the words of one Executive Director, 'The Fund has internalised the idea that debt is a problem for long-term development in the South'.[7] Moreover, the IMF has accepted the principle of relief for poor countries on multilateral debts. It remains to be seen how much further social movements might push the Fund on debt relief; however, there is, it would seem, no turning back to standard rescheduling for poor countries.

---

[7] NGO meeting with an ED, observed by the author, October 1996.

Transparency

The five impacts discussed thus far have related to policy content; however, pressure from social movements has also helped to effect several shifts in the institutional operations of the IMF. In particular, the Fund has begun to answer demands for greater transparency in its procedures, more systematic and public evaluation of its policies, and increased participation by client governments and civil societies in the formulation of IMF-supported macroeconomic programmes. In these three ways the Fund has responded (at least partly) to social-movement campaigns for a democratisation of global monetary and financial governance.

The most notable moves towards a more open, participatory, accountable IMF have come in the area of transparency. Calls from FOE-US, the Center of Concern, the Bretton Woods Project and others to make the Fund's operations more visible and comprehensible have obtained a response in the 1990s that was previously unimaginable. The IMF has not only massively increased its production of 'public relations' material, but the institution has also made available substantial numbers of policy documents. The Executive Board has taken a number of steps since 1994 to increase disclosure, particularly after (thanks in part to social-movement lobbying) the US Congress withheld three-quarters of a requested $100 million appropriation for replenishment of ESAF, subject to greater information disclosure by the Fund (*Congressional Quarterly Almanac* 1994).

For one thing, more information has become publicly available regarding the conditions attached to IMF loans. Since 1994, the Fund's press releases concerning the approval of stand-by credits, Extended Fund Facility programmes and ESAF loans have specified some headline economic indicators and target figures. IMF management have also since the mid-1990s urged governments to publish their letter of intent (i.e., the detailed economic programme behind a stand-by credit) or their policy framework paper (PFP, the detailed programme behind a three-year ESAF loan). In response, starting with Kenya in early 1996, eleven governments had published their PFPs by mid-1998.[8] The government of Argentina has disclosed all of its letters of

---

[8] Armenia, Azerbaijan, Georgia, Ghana, Guinea, Kenya, Kyrgyz Republic, Former Yugoslav Republic of Macedonia, Rwanda, Senegal and Uganda.

intent since 1990, and details of each IMF-supported programme in the Asian crisis of 1997–8 have appeared on the Fund's website.

Considerable information has also become publicly available on IMF surveillance of national policies. In July 1994 the Executive Board decided to publish Fund documents that serve as background to Article IV consultations, provided that the government concerned did not object. Over a hundred such papers have been released each year since 1995. In April 1997 the Executive Board took the further decision to publish (subject to the consent of the government concerned) a summary of its deliberations of a country's economic policies in the context of Article IV consultations (IMF 1997d: 148). The IMF issued over thirty such of these press information notes (PINs) during the first year of this disclosure policy.

When the Fund took the initiative in 1996 to establish the Special Data Dissemination Standard, it immediately made the statistics supplied publicly available. With language quite alien to the IMF of earlier times, the Fund argued that official data was 'a public good' to which there should be 'ready and equal access' (IMF 1996f, 1996k). SDDS materials became publicly accessible on the World Wide Web in September 1996 (see http://dsbb.imf.org/). By early 1999, forty-seven governments had subscribed to the scheme.

The shift to greater transparency has also prompted the IMF to 'open up' in several other ways. For example, the Executive Board decided in January 1996 to declassify most files in the IMF archives, albeit under a strictly applied thirty-year rule, with the result that the released documents are unlikely to have immediate policy significance (IMF 1996a: 201, 1996b). In recent years the Executive Board has also issued public summaries of many of its decisions, through both press releases and the columns of *IMF Survey*. A basic organigram of the Fund was published for the first time in the 1996 *Annual Report* and was subsequently also incorporated into the IMF website (IMF 1996a: 220). Since 1997 visitors to IMF headquarters have been allowed to consult a staff list. The Fund has also published the results of several retrospective policy evaluations (see below).

To be sure, transparency at the IMF remains limited in important respects. Most letters of intent, PFPs, and Article IV documents are not published. Nor are minutes of Executive Board meetings available until thirty years have lapsed. Most governments have not (yet) subscribed to the SDDS or the more modest GDDS. The IMF has thus far not followed the World Bank example of establishing public information centres in Washington and a number of programme countries.

Nevertheless, steps towards greater openness at the IMF (and, through it, at national economic and finance ministries) have gained considerable momentum in the 1990s. For example, the full Executive Board turned out in July 1998 for a two-hour discussion of the aforementioned study group report on transparency and evaluation at the Fund. The pace of change remains slower than many social-movement activists would like, but transparency is definitely on the IMF agenda.

Evaluation

Along with its attention to issues of transparency, the IMF has also answered calls for greater accountability in its operations with moves to develop an evaluation programme (Wood and Welch 1998). The Fund has in the 1990s increased internal policy reviews, started external policy assessments, and upgraded its institutional mechanisms for evaluation activities. Critics have complained that the steps taken to date are far from adequate; however, persistent pressure from social movements has been instrumental in effecting a gradual integration of evaluation into IMF operations.

Most of the expansion of evaluation activities at the Fund has taken the form of in-house policy reviews. For example, PDR has performed biennial assessments of IMF surveillance, investigating both the process of formulating advice to governments and the quality of that advice. Since 1992 PDR has also undertaken two reviews of ESAF programmes, an evaluation of IMF conditionality under stand-by and extended arrangements, and an assessment of the Fund's technical assistance. The results of the ESAF and conditionality reviews have been published (Schadler 1995; Schadler *et al.* 1993; Schadler *et al.* 1995; Schadler, Bredenkamp *et al.* 1997). Meanwhile the IMF's Office of Internal Audit and Inspection has undertaken in-house evaluations of technical assistance programmes and the functioning of resident representative offices. The results of these reviews have not been published.

In the late 1990s, following pressure from NGOs and the Group of Seven governments, the IMF has begun to supplement these internal evaluations with policy reviews by external assessors. The Executive Board endorsed the principle of external evaluation in June 1996. The

first outside review, undertaken in 1997–8, examined ESAF programmes, with particular reference to issues that campaigners for
change have long emphasised such as social provisions and ownership (IMF 1998b). In line with urgings from a number of groups
including FOE-US and EURODAD (EURODAD 1998b; FOE-US 1998),
the Executive Board decided to release the IMF staff paper which
responded to the external evaluation and to invite reactions from the
public before taking decisions on the future of ESAF (IMF 1998a). In
July 1998 the Executive Board furthermore announced a second
external evaluation, this time of IMF surveillance activities under
Article IV (IMF 1998i).

To oversee this increased evaluation activity, the Executive Board in
1996 created an Evaluation Committee comprising five EDs. In the
same year the IMF's Office of Internal Audit and Inspection was
upgraded to permit it to conduct more reviews of all aspects of the
Fund's organisational structure and work practices (IMF 1996j).
However, the IMF has as yet not answered repeated urgings for the
establishment of a permanent evaluation unit, independent of management and the Executive Board. Hence the Fund has created no
organ comparable to the Operations Evaluation department and the
Inspection Panel at the World Bank.

On the whole, then, evaluation remains a relative novelty at the
IMF. Not many policy reviews have thus far been undertaken. Some
areas of activity have not yet been assessed at all: for example, the
Fund's involvement in so-called transition economies and its efforts at
financial sector reform. Critics have queried the 'independence' of
external evaluations in so far as the Executive Board has set the terms
of reference and selected the evaluators for these exercises. Meanwhile
the IMF staff who conduct internal assessments have not had training
in evaluation techniques. Reluctance persists in some quarters of the
staff to submit Fund activities to systematic review.

That said, evaluation has gained a place in IMF operations in the
1990s. It seems likely that, with continued pressure from social movements and other quarters, the programme of policy reviews will
expand and be further refined in the years to come.

Ownership

Finally, opposition from social movements has helped to put the
question of ownership on the IMF agenda in the 1990s. Critics have

long charged that the Fund imposes its prescriptions on borrowing governments. That is, it determines the methodology, it analyses the data, and it specifies the policy measures, according to a fairly standard formula. In so far as any 'consultation' takes place, Fund staff tend to talk only with a small circle of officials of the ministry of finance and the central bank. Yet most of these civil servants hold the same general outlooks as their colleagues from Washington; indeed, many have been trained by the IMF. Meanwhile other ministries, the national legislature, local authorities and civil society usually have minimal if any say in policy making. As a result, it is concluded, the country concerned does not 'own' the Fund-sponsored programme. In effect, so the critics charge, the policy process is undemocratic.

As the 1990s have progressed, management and staff at the IMF have gone some way to accepting the importance of ownership, at least in so far as it may be an indispensable ingredient for successful policy implementation. The Executive Board has come firmly to the view that, in the words of one ED, 'if governments don't have a solid base of support for an IMF-sponsored programme, it won't work'.[9] Many Fund officials today likewise declare that 'a broad-based social consensus is needed to sustain an IMF programme' or even that 'by making sure that all voices are heard we increase the success of a programme'.[10] The ethos in the Fund has clearly shifted towards a greater appreciation of questions concerning the political viability of policies.

That said, the change in rhetoric has not to date always translated into substantially different behaviour at the Fund. To be sure, IMF management have taken many more outreach initiatives in the 1990s than before. An expanded External Relations department has given Fund activities much more publicity. In the field, many IMF missions and res reps have become considerably more visible. However, the principle of ownership has not yet thoroughly infused the process of formulating and implementing Fund-supported policies. For the IMF, 'ownership' has tended to mean acceptance by the borrowing government and its citizens of Fund prescriptions. As one official has typically put it, 'we have to persuade the population that an adjustment package is legitimate'.[11] In general, the IMF has continued to

[9] Interview with the author, November 1996.
[10] Interviews with the author, October–November 1996.
[11] Interview with the author, April 1997.

accord client states and local civil societies only limited initiative in the construction of stabilisation and structural adjustment policies. The 1997–8 external evaluation of ESAF concluded that, with respect to ownership, 'it has been difficult ... to reconcile the declared intentions with practice' (IMF 1998b: 18, also 38–42). It does seem that, on the whole, achieving 'consensus' has, for the Fund, not meant building new understandings out of different points of view, but bringing the notional 'owners' round to an unaltered IMF position.

Change and continuity

Considering all of the developments discussed in this section together, how much change have social movements effected in IMF policy in the 1990s? As noted at the outset, it is not possible to measure these impacts with precision or in isolation from other forces. However, trade unions, religious groups, NGOs and certain think tanks have contributed to some shifts both in the IMF's substantive policies and in its operating procedures. Radicals have clearly not achieved their goal of rolling back or eliminating the Fund. Nevertheless, social movements have encouraged the IMF to amend its conditionalities, to accept the principle of concessionary debt relief for poor countries, to take steps towards greater transparency and accountability, and to recognise the importance of policy ownership.

Yet, in relation to the aims of social movements specified earlier, the changes just described constitute fairly modest alterations. Labour protection, poverty eradication, ecological sustainability, gender equity and human rights have not become central planks of IMF activity. The Fund has not come close to endorsing debt write-offs. Some IMF operations continue to be cloaked in secrecy. Evaluation mechanisms for Fund policies remain underdeveloped. 'Ownership' of IMF-sponsored programmes has thus far included fairly few elements of consultation and participation.

From the inside of the organisation, most management and staff at the Fund feel that the institution and its policies have greatly changed in the 1990s. However, from the outside, advocates of fundamental change tend to be more impressed by the persistent predominance of neoliberal convictions at the IMF. The Fund continues in the first place to promote low inflation rates, low balance-of-payments deficits, low government budget deficits, liberalisation of cross-border resource flows, deregulation of markets, privatisation, and a relative shift in the provision of social security from the state to the market and the voluntary sector. Concerns about employment, poverty, ecology, gender, debt and democracy have at most been added on as secondary issues; they have not displaced stabilisation, liberalisation, dereg- ulation and privatisation as the primary IMF objectives.

Counter-forces

What has kept social movements from going further to realise their aims in relation to the International Monetary Fund? Why have they, on the whole, tended to achieve change within continuity rather than a full-scale transformation of Fund practices? The present section discusses several important forces that have worked against social- movement strivings for a thoroughgoing reconstruction of the IMF in the late twentieth century: namely, the power of neoliberalism; the institutional culture of the Fund; social hierarchies; limited resources for social-movement campaigns; the relatively low priority that social movements have accorded to the IMF; and inadequate democratic legitimation of many social-movement activities.

Predominance of neoliberalism

One important reason why social movements have had difficulty effecting change away from the neoliberal paradigm in the IMF relates to the powerful hold which that knowledge structure has had on the contemporary world political economy as a whole. Neoliberalism refers here broadly to the worldview according to which globalised market relations will in time create maximal liberty, democracy, prosperity and peace for humankind as a whole. Contrary to alter- native perspectives such as mercantilism, Keynesianism, socialism, environmentalism and more, neoliberalism prescribes policies of thoroughgoing liberalisation, deregulation and privatisation within a context of accelerated globalisation. In a word, neoliberalism has taken the classical liberal formula for the good society and given it a global twist.

Following the stagnation of post-colonial socialism in the South, the collapse of central planning in the East, and the retreat of corporatist welfarism in the North, neoliberal visions have come to reign supreme across the world. In the 1980s and 1990s, most states – and in particular the strongest governments – have to some substantial degree embraced market-centred solutions coupled with multiparty representative democracy as a universal formula for optimal human development. This neoliberal consensus has also encompassed the most influential global governance agencies, including the Bretton Woods institutions, the WTO, and the Organisation for Economic Cooperation and Development (OECD). Even UNCTAD has largely abandoned its earlier structuralist analysis of the world economy for a more market-oriented approach. Neoliberal views have also held sway in corporate business, the financial markets, the mainstream mass media, various influential think tanks, and many key institutions of higher learning.

Indeed, the majority of the Fund's contacts with civil society at large (as opposed to social movements more particularly) have broadly reinforced the institution's commitment to neoliberalism. On the whole, business associations and economic research institutes have championed the vision of global free markets. In the words of several IMF officials, these circles 'know what we are doing' and 'have a similar view to us'.[12] The managing director of the Fund has delivered most of his speeches to non-official audiences at business conferences and academic gatherings. At the IMF/World Bank annual meetings, representatives of commercial concerns have carried badges as 'visitors' and 'special guests' and have been included in the published list of participants. In contrast, representatives of social movements have worn 'NGO' labels and have been excluded from the published list of participants. Corporate managers and academic economists have had regular exchanges of views with the operational staff of the Fund. However, the IMF has channelled most of its contacts with trade unions, religious groups, NGOs and the like through the External Relations department, thus away from the heart of policy making.

Being on the side of the prevailing neoliberal 'commonsense', the Fund has found it fairly easy to reject unorthodox talk of the kind that social movements have propounded. Thus, for example, the Fund declined invitations in 1992–3 to participate in a WWF project to explore environmentally sensitive alternatives to the prevailing paradigm of structural adjustment. Likewise, the IMF has taken a lukewarm approach to the previously mentioned SAPRI exercise, probably largely on account of the unorthodox character of some of its

[12] Interviews with the author, November 1996 and March 1997.

methodologies. In contrast, the Fund has entrusted its previously mentioned external reviews of ESAF and surveillance entirely to professional macroeconomists. As critical as these evaluators might be, their views have developed from broadly the same methodology as has informed Fund policy making.

Thus, in challenging neoliberalism at the IMF, social movements have confronted a knowledge structure that extends well beyond the institution itself. The Fund's alignment with the prevailing ideology has given the institution far greater power in the contemporary world political economy than its modest staff and operational budget would suggest. Indeed, some campaigners for IMF reform have – deliberately or unconsciously – shifted their language in the direction of neoliberal discourse in order to get a greater hearing from the Fund.

Institutional culture

The structural power of neoliberal discourse has of course militated against major transformation in the World Bank and the WTO as well as in the IMF. Hence the dominance of neoliberalism in the late twentieth century does not explain the generally greater resistance to change in the Fund as compared with the other two global economic institutions examined in the present study. This difference has resulted at least partly from certain distinctive institutional features of the IMF.

As an organisation, the Fund has been highly monolithic: more so than most global governance agencies, or indeed most formal institutions in general. It has also had an interventionist and hierarchical management style. When combined with the power of neoliberal orthodoxy, such institutional characteristics have arguably made IMF staff even more reluctant to engage with the sorts of alternative perspectives expounded by social movements.

Several contrasts between the Fund and the World Bank are striking in this respect. For one thing, the IMF's Bretton Woods twin has housed a greater diversity of approaches to 'development' amongst its personnel, including some pockets of major internal dissent. Certain Bank officials have even tried to use connections with social movements to promote alternative viewpoints within the organisation. The World Bank has also had considerable staff turnover – *inter alia* through frequent use of contract personnel who move in and out of the organisation. In this way, too, the Bank has gained greater exposure to a diversity of perspectives. Indeed, there has been some two-way flow of personnel between the World Bank and reformist organisations such as development studies institutes and development NGOs.

In contrast to the Bank, the Fund has had little division on the inside and porosity toward the outside. The institution has sooner resembled a 'family business'. Traditionally, most officials have joined the IMF relatively early in their careers and have then often stayed with the organisation until retirement. The agency has tended as a result to be rather insular. No staff mobility has transpired between the Fund and social movements.

In management style, the Fund has maintained tight central direction and rigorous internal discipline. Before leaving the door, any IMF programme proposal must have the approval of the Policy Development and Review department, jokingly – but also evocatively – described within the organisation as 'the thought police' and 'the keepers of the theology'.[13] Fund officials have pursued many frank discussions with one another, but always within the walls of the building and invariably within narrow boundaries of 'acceptable' debate. Only once or twice has an official resigned from the IMF out of a fundamental disagreement on policy. In these various ways, then, the monolithic character of the institution has discouraged Fund officials from developing an open dialogue with their outside critics in social movements.

Social hierarchies

Along with the ideological and institutional forces already discussed, hierarchical social structures have also made it difficult for social movements to effect a fundamental reconstruction of the IMF in the late twentieth century. Campaigners for change in the Fund have generally pursued the interests of weaker and marginalised circles in society: e.g. countries of the South and the East, workers, the poor, and women. However, these constituencies have suffered structural disadvantages in politics relative to countries of the North, investors and managers, and men.

Needless to say, it is difficult to promote the interests of the South and the East in respect of an institution that is dominated by the North. (Although distinctions between North, South and East are to

---

[13] Interviews with the author, October–November 1996.

some extent artificial and simplistic, a general structural bias against the South and East is plain.) IMF recommendations have made their deepest impacts in the South and the East, but a large majority of the votes, money, staff and ideas in the Fund have come from the North. Likewise, most social-movement organisations that maintain direct contacts with the IMF have had their base in the North.

Advocacy groups in the South and the East have faced considerably greater hurdles in lobbying the IMF than campaigners in the North. For instance, given the expenses involved, many activists in the South and the East (particularly at the grass roots) have had limited if any access to fax and Internet connections. Fund information pamphlets have appeared in at most five languages – all European – and have had minimal circulation in the East and the South. A huge majority of social-movement representatives at the annual meetings have come from the North. Indeed, campaigners who have travelled from the South and the East have often lacked accreditation and have as a result been locked out of the conference hall. Even on the ground in programme countries, the IMF resident representative has often met more with staff from North-based organisations (e.g., development cooperation agencies or associations of foreign investors) than with indigenous groups (especially NGOs and community based groups). Indeed, in certain countries, local activists have complained that they can only access the res rep through the mediation of North-based organisations.

Even within social movements, activists in the North have often given limited attention to securing a voice in debates about the IMF for colleagues in the South and the East. True, in the 1990s several North-based NGOs have taken persons from the South on to their staff, either permanently or as interns. In a similar spirit, certain North-based associations have in recent years hosted delegations from the South for discussions of debt problems and structural adjustment. For instance, the Debt Crisis Network in February 1996 brought five prominent Africans to Britain for a seminar, also attended by several IMF officials, entitled 'Africa Needs a Fresh Start'.

Nevertheless, these consultations between North and South/East could be taken much further. Indeed, one leading campaigner in Washington for IMF reform has declared dismissively that 'there is so much lipservice about consulting the South – it's a figleaf'.[14] Moreover,

[14] Interview with the author, November 1996.

most South-based groups who communicate with North-based associations have done so in circumstances of substantial dependency, financial and otherwise. The representatives of the South have thereby easily been inhibited from speaking fully and frankly to their own agenda. Although colonial times have passed, Northern solidarity with Southern and Eastern partners in social movements can sometimes still be delivered with patronising tone and paternalistic gesture. Indeed, North-based NGOs have tended to make contacts in the South and the East with people who 'speak their language', for example, owing to university studies in the North.

Along with an inbuilt disadvantage for the South and the East, underclasses have also had far less opportunity directly to engage the IMF. The great majority of contacts between activists and the Fund have involved middle-class professionals, whether they be from North, South or East. Likewise, South–North collaboration within social movements has almost invariably involved urban-based, university-educated, computer-literate (relatively) high-earning English speakers *on both sides*. No joint mobilisation against the IMF has developed between grass-root groups in the South and underclasses in the North.

Nor have elite-based associations (whether from North, South or East) fully exploited their connections with the Fund to put carefully gathered views of marginalised groups on the table. A few church groups and development NGOs have stood out as exceptions with their efforts to incorporate 'voices from the base' into their advocacy work. However, for the rest underclasses have been locked out of indirect as well as direct dialogue with the IMF.

The Fund itself has rarely sought direct contacts with rural groups, the urban poor, and so on. In the words of one leading official, 'We do not meet the people themselves, but we ask [aid organisations] what they want the IMF to do.'[15] The most surprising omission in the Fund's contacts with the grass roots has been peasant associations. Large-scale commercial farmers have periodically lobbied the IMF (e.g., in Zimbabwe), but organisations of smallholders – who represent a substantial proportion of the population in many programme countries – have had little opportunity to engage the institution.

That said, the IMF has taken numerous initiatives in the 1990s to, in

---

[15] Minutes of a meeting in Washington between civic activists and Fund officials, June 1996.

the words of one official, 'groom' labour.[16] From various previous experiences, the Fund has learned that opposition from organised labour can substantially frustrate the implementation of stabilisation measures and structural adjustment policies. In addition, Camdessus has brought from France a corporatist recognition of labour as a leading social partner with government and business. IMF officials have also tended to perceive trade unions as 'representative' bodies in a way that they have presumed NGOs not to be.

'Opening up' to labour, IMF management in 1995 issued special instructions that res reps should, in collaboration with the ILO, nurture contacts with local trade unions in programme countries. In early 1998, Camdessus took several initiatives to meet labour leaders from Indonesia, Korea and Thailand against the backdrop of recently initiated IMF programmes in those countries. The Fund has also co-sponsored four major seminars for labour leaders between 1992 and 1998. The managing director addressed the congresses of the ICFTU in 1996 and the WCL in 1997. However, these overtures fit the pattern noted earlier whereby the Fund has mainly attempted to convert its critics rather than to address their grievances with major policy changes.

Meanwhile a structural bias against women has hampered progress on the social-movement objective of gender equity. True, the IMF has of late adopted an explicit policy to recruit more women to its professional staff, and the managing director has declared that 'never again will we be a "men's club"' (IMF 1996g: 192). However, at the time of writing, very few women have been appointed as Fund officials. The top management of the organisation has never included a woman, no more than three women have served concurrently among the twenty-four EDs, and women have headed only two of the twenty IMF departments. The overwhelming predominance of men among Fund officials has of course reflected a prevailing pattern of patriarchy in global finance more generally (McDowell and Court 1994).

On the whole, women have had notably greater participation and leadership in NGOs and grass-roots associations. However, as noted earlier, the women's movement more particularly has taken few initiatives to engage the IMF. Even the business-oriented organisation, Women's World Banking, has not knocked at 19th Street. Meanwhile,

---

[16] Interview with the author, April 1997.

the marginalisation of feminist economics within the academic profession makes it unlikely that Fund staff will acquire significant sensitivity to gender aspects of macroeconomic policy.

Resource constraints

The structural disadvantages noted above for social-movement strivings to transform the IMF have been reflected in, and at the same time also reinforced by, the low level of resources from which these campaigns have generally suffered. Trade unions, NGOs, religious organisations and grass-roots associations have in most cases lacked sufficient staff, funds, information and coordination capacity to mount fully effective pressure on the Fund.

In terms of staff, most social-movement organisations with desires to change the IMF have lacked personnel with expertise regarding the institution. The several dozen exceptions world-wide have usually had only one or two specialists each. Only a handful of persons in social movements have maintained long-term regular contacts with the IMF: e.g. Stephen Pursey of the ICFTU; Marijke Torfs of FOE-US; Nancy Alexander at a succession of development NGOs; and Richard Gerster and Bruno Gurtner of the Swiss Coalition of Development Organisations. To this day, a number of programme countries lack any local campaigner with extensive experience of dealing directly with the IMF.

Most activists in NGOs and at the grass roots have been overextended with other responsibilities that have kept them from becoming adequately educated about the Fund. Few campaigners have acquired a detailed understanding of the institutional workings of the IMF. In addition, few have developed a level of literacy in economics that has enabled them closely to follow Fund reasoning. Monetary and financial regulators would be more willing to give social movements a hearing if they felt that the critics comprehended how IMF policy operated.

Turnover problems have also inhibited the development of a larger, more experienced cadre in social movements. Too many of the would-be professional activists have been young university graduates on short-term contracts with relatively poor remuneration. Most such campaigners have not focused on the IMF long enough to develop effective strategies and tactics towards the organisation.

Intertwined with and exacerbating personnel problems, financial constraints have also contributed significantly to the underdevelopment of social-movement campaigns on the IMF. Most labour organisations and churches with an interest in the Fund have struggled on small budgets. As for development and environmental NGOs, their work on the IMF has largely depended on grants from a few bilateral aid agencies and a handful of private foundations. Indeed, many NGOs have collapsed for want of funds, especially in the South and the East.

Moreover, it has been difficult for NGOs to develop campaigns on the Fund when their grants have usually been small (almost never above $100,000) and short term (lasting at most two or three years). Many activists have complained about the amount of time 'lost' on fund-raising and about the need sometimes to adjust their grant proposals in order to fit a donor's agenda. Worst of all, competition for scarce monies has sometimes discouraged NGOs from collaborating in their IMF work as freely as they ideally would.

On top of shortfalls in staff and funds, shortages of information have constituted a third resource constraint in the development of social-movement activity on the IMF. For example, many groups with concerns to put to the Fund have not known where to call. The published organigram mentioned earlier gives only a bare outline of the IMF's departmental structure, and the staff list is not publicly available outside the headquarters building. As one experienced campaigner from Africa has objected, 'How can we ever influence the IMF if we barely know it?'[17] The Harvard economist Jeffrey Sachs has exclaimed before US Congressional hearings that the Fund is even more secretive than the CIA.

Sachs exaggerates in so far as the IMF has, as noted earlier, since the mid-1990s published increasing numbers of policy documents. Social-movement activists can now access far more information than many of them realise. However, as also mentioned before, the Fund has not to date released many key programme documents. Again and again, the IMF has cited the prerogative of states to keep these materials confidential. Thus, in spite of recent improvements, lack of access to information has remained a substantial constraint on social-movement campaigns.

A fourth resource problem for groups advocating change in the IMF

---

[17] Remark of an NGO activist at an interview with an Executive Director during the 1996 annual meetings.

has concerned poor capacities for coordination. Although new technologies have helped to improve communications among associations in the 1990s, significant shortfalls in coordination remain. Indeed, especially in the South and the East, many social movement actors have been unaware even of each other's existence. Many grass-roots associations, again particularly in the East and the South, have thus far been in early stages of organisational development. In this regard BothENDS has noted, for example, that 'consistent and elaborate communication with and between African NGOs can be difficult to maintain' (BothENDS 1995: 13). For their part, social-movement activists in the South have complained that North-based partners flood them with far more requests for information and comment than their usually poorly staffed and funded operations can handle.

More interorganisational coordination is possible and would presumably increase the effectiveness of social-movement pressure on the IMF. For example, it is curious that labour organisations and development NGOs have – with a few (mostly recent) exceptions – cooperated so little in the pursuit of debt relief and reforms of structural adjustment. All groups would benefit from a central database concerning social-movement activism vis-à-vis the IMF: i.e., a comprehensive and regularly updated catalogue of resource people, documents, publications, popular education materials, existing collaborative relationships between organisations and so on.

In sum, then, with better resourcing social movements might have achieved much more change in the IMF than they have done to date. Of course, more staff, more funds, more information and more coordination would not by themselves allow these campaigns fully to realise their aims. The structural counter-forces described earlier remain formidable even in the face of enormous commitments of resources. However, substantially increased resources are necessary if social movements are to achieve major changes in the IMF.

Low priority

Resource constraints have hampered all social-movement activity; however, these handicaps have been all the more severe in the case of campaigns to transform the IMF, given that advocates of change have directed most of their efforts at other targets. To be sure, critics of the contemporary world political economy have readily pointed to the Fund as a source of major problems. Yet, in terms of deeds, social movements have devoted comparatively few of their already severely limited resources specifically to the IMF. Most mobilisation for change in global economic governance has focused either on development projects (as sponsored by the World Bank Group, regional development banks and bilateral agencies) or on multilateral trade and investment regimes (as pursued through the WTO, NAFTA, the OECD and so on).

Much social-movement pressure on the IMF has been *ad hoc*. Only a few associations have – like the ICFTU, FOE-US and the Cato Institute – pursued sustained, focused, carefully researched campaigns to influence Fund policies. Even fewer agencies have – like the Bretton Woods Project – been created specifically to engage the IMF. Meanwhile the majority of advocacy groups have treated the Fund with only passing curiosity, if they have given the institution any attention at all.

Most activists with an interest in changing global economic governance have preferred to concentrate on more 'tangible' issues related to trade, investment, infrastructure projects, famine, etc. Thanks in good part to the obscurantism of economistic jargon – much of it arguably unnecessary – questions of IMF conditionality and surveillance have caused many a social-movement campaigner's eyes to glaze over.[18] Few associations have shown interest in following the example of Swiss NGOs in obtaining direct participation in their country's Article IV consultations. Not until October 1997 did development NGOs from Europe and North America undertake a focused discussion of the regulation of global financial markets, with a two-day seminar in Paris (EURODAD 1997).

Campaigners who have tried to generate interest in the Fund among a larger public have confronted a difficult task. As one experienced lobbyist has succinctly put it, 'It takes a lot of pushing to get people mobilised on the IMF.'[19] In spite of increased NGO efforts at civic education on the Fund, questions of structural adjustment, debt relief, foreign exchange crises and so on have for the most part not grabbed the popular imagination.

In the same vein, social-movement advocates have also had limited success in drawing press attention to campaigns for IMF reform. The

---

[18] One ED has agreed, in correspondence to the author (dated February 1998), that this obscurantism is unnecessary, adding 'I felt that its purpose was to keep discussion within a small group of those who understand the mysteries.'

[19] Interview with the author, November 1996.

South-centric Inter Press Service and local journalists in many programme countries have been fairly receptive to covering the issues.
However, the principal world press agencies, major newspapers and
global broadcasters have usually – except during a crisis – given little
space to a debate of Fund policies. At other times campaigners have
considered it cause for celebration when their lobbying has prompted
an article in the *Financial Times* or an editorial in the *Washington Post*.

Insufficient legitimation

A final reason inhibiting greater impact by social movements on the
IMF in the late twentieth century has related to the often shaky
democratic credentials of the campaign organisations. Very often
these associations have attended insufficiently to questions concerning
their representativeness, consultation processes, transparency and
accountability (Bichsel 1996). Ironically, some of the organisations
which have pressed hardest for a democratisation of the Fund have
done little to secure democracy in their own operations. These shortcomings have dented the credibility of many advocacy groups –
especially NGOs – and have allowed the IMF and states to take the
associations less seriously than they might otherwise have done.

On questions of representativeness, for example, the disproportionate weight in social-movement activism of Northerners and
middle-class professionals has been stressed earlier. Many campaigners have had experience neither in the South and the East nor at
the grass roots. Southerners, Easterners and underclasses usually have
had no direct representation in the more powerful North-based
associations; nor have they had formal channels through which to
participate in these organisations. Even an NGO's members in the
North have frequently had no input in policy making beyond the
payment of their annual subscription. In these circumstances NGO
campaigners have often appeared in the eyes of the IMF to represent
only themselves.

In contrast, the Fund has tended more readily to recognise labour
organisations as legitimate partners in dialogue. In general, trade
unions have a substantial dues-paying membership and hold regular
elections of officers. Indeed, labour leaders have often insisted that
their more representative character, compared to NGOs, commands
greater attention from global governance agencies. The emphasis of
this difference has arguably contributed to the previously noted

underdevelopment of collaboration between the labour movement and NGOs.

Many social-movement groups have also attended insufficiently to issues of transparency in their operations. Various organisations have not published annual reports of their activities regarding the IMF. Some have not even prepared a general statement of their objectives for public distribution. Often these associations – again, especially NGOs – have not made clear who they are, where their funds originate, how they reach their policy positions, and so on.

The picture has generally been little better with regard to issues of accountability in social-movement campaigns. Many countries have lacked adequate mechanisms to ensure the public-interest credentials of civic organisations. Too often these associations have been accountable only to a largely self-selected board of trustees, to private funders (some of them anonymous) and/or to foreign official donors. In some cases activists have abused NGO status for tax evasion and other personal gain, thereby feeding worries about all such organisations.

These frequent shortfalls in the legitimacy of advocacy groups have hampered their access to the IMF. Many Fund officials – especially those who have been reluctant in any case to engage in dialogue with reformers and radicals – have seized on poor democratic credentials as a reason to limit contacts with these critics. NGOs in particular are likely to find their influence on the IMF limited so long as they cannot better demonstrate features of consultation, representativeness, transparency and accountability in their relations with their supposed constituents.

In sum, then, a powerful combination of forces has limited the influence of social movements on the International Monetary Fund in the late twentieth century. Several of those forces (resource constraints, social hierarchies, and the strength of neoliberalism) have confronted all contemporary mobilisation for social change, including the activities discussed in chapters 2–4 above. That said, these challenges would seem to have been especially intense for campaigns to change the IMF. In addition, efforts to transform the Fund have faced certain more particular difficulties related to the institutional culture of the IMF and the priorities of social movements. Finally, social-movement organisations have weakened their effectiveness against the IMF by attending insufficiently to their democratic credentials.

Conclusion

This chapter has surveyed a wide range of social-movement activity aimed at transforming the International Monetary Fund. The discussion first covered the various aims, strategies and tactics of these campaigns. It then assessed the impacts of these efforts, finding that social movements have to date tended to affect the margins rather than the heart of IMF policies and operating procedures. This limited influence was explained in terms of both general features of the contemporary world political economy and specific characteristics of the IMF and the social movements that challenge it. How do these findings relate to the primary questions that underpin this book?

How has this MEI modified?

As detailed earlier, developments in IMF conditionality during the 1990s have partly accommodated reformist urgings for change. Fund-sponsored programmes now regularly incorporate 'social safety nets' to guard against excessive pains of adjustment in areas such as education and health care. In the late 1990s the IMF has given high prominence to issues of 'good governance', although this concept has not been formulated in the sort of explicitly political sense that most social-movement activists would wish to see. In addition, the Fund has begun to explore the possible relationships between macro-economic policy and questions such as ecological degradation and gender inequality.

That said, on the whole social, environmental and governance issues have remained secondary concerns at the IMF. The World Bank and UN agencies have generally gone further in incorporating these questions into their programmes. The primary focus of Fund-supported policies has remained stabilisation and the promotion of neoliberal restructuring.

IMF policy has also shifted between the 1980s and the 1990s in respect of debt relief for poor countries. Fund staff have, since the mid-1990s, accepted that external debt burdens can harm the prospects for economic development. On this principle the IMF has agreed, through the HIPC initiative, to extend some relief on repayments of loans owed to itself. On the other hand, the sums of IMF debt relief through the HIPC scheme are projected to be fairly small: around $800 million, of which $271 million had been agreed by April

1998 (IMF 1988k: 4, 7). Moreover, the relief involves refinancing rather than a cancellation of repayments.

In respect of operating procedures, the IMF of the 1990s has become considerably more transparent. Impenetrable drapes have given way to net curtains. An informed analyst can now usually discern the general outlines of IMF prescriptions and practices, although many details remain unclear. The Fund has also accepted the principle of formal policy evaluation, although progress in implementing actual reviews has been slow. Finally, with attention to 'ownership', the IMF of the 1990s has aspired – at least in its rhetoric – to make its policy-making processes more inclusive and consultative. It remains to be seen how far down the road of participation the Fund will in practice prove willing to go.

What are the motivations driving MEI–GSM engagement?

In the case of the IMF, a global economic institution has sought contact with social movements mainly in the hope of building a broad-based consensus behind the policies that it sponsors. Fund management and staff have become convinced that overtures to trade unions, religious groups and NGOs can help construct a – possibly indispensable – popular base for economic restructuring on neoliberal lines. In addition, the IMF has been concerned to counter the threat that social movements can pose to its financial position. In particular, critics have repeatedly complicated the approval of quota increases and other monies for the IMF on Capitol Hill. Given these objectives, the Fund has not engaged with critics in order to give them a proactive role in policy making, that is, out of a belief that inputs from social movements could improve IMF performance.

Yet change is what social movements have pursued in engaging with the Fund. Many activists have advocated fundamental reformu-lations of IMF conditionalities so that they give primary attention to issues such as employment, poverty eradication, ecological integrity, gender equity and the protection of human rights. Large campaigns have demanded that the Fund provide debt relief for countries of the South. Insistent pressure groups have urged that the IMF bring greater participation, representation, transparency and accountability to its operations.

These two sets of objectives show a stark opposition. The IMF has aimed to secure neoliberal restructuring, whereas trade unions, religious groups, NGOs and grass-roots associations have promoted alternative paradigms. Not surprisingly in this light, contacts between the Fund and social movements have often been troubled. Campaigners for change have complained that 'the IMF won't have a frank discussion about the problems of its policies', that 'you cannot critique in a dialogue with the Fund', and that 'if you're too insistent in expressing a different point of view, IMF people tell you to keep quiet'.[20] For their part, Fund officials have frequently objected that '[NGOs] spend the whole time telling us we're wrong', that 'it's hard to get a dialogue going with such people', and that 'some NGOs are just rabid'.[21]

To be sure, the intensity of these confrontations has varied between individuals and between situations. Some of the polarisation has been unnecessary, in so far as many IMF officials have conceded in private that the organisation has made mistakes. Likewise, most reformers and even some radicals have conceded in private that certain Fund interventions may be necessary and can have positive effects. Hence potential exists for a more open, two-way, critical and creative dialogue between the IMF and social movements.

What is the significance of the MEI–GSM relationship?

Although social movements have not influenced the International Monetary Fund as much as the campaigners for change would have liked, their activities have made an impact. As indicated in detail earlier, pressure from social movements has contributed to each of the various shifts in substantive policy and operating procedures. The role of social movements in these developments cannot be precisely measured. Certainly non-official advocates of change have not effected these shifts at the IMF alone, without additional pressures from governments, from other global governance agencies, and from within the Fund itself. However, it seems highly unlikely that the modifications described in this chapter would have occurred in the absence of mobilisation by trade unions, NGOs, churches and grass-roots associations.

Even if social movements have achieved only limited success in changing the IMF, the experience of the past two decades has shown

---

[20] Interviews with the author, October 1996.
[21] Interviews with the author, November 1996 and April 1997.

that these campaigns can also provide other benefits to global monetary and financial regulation. For example, they have supplied not only their members, but also the Fund, governments and the general public with much useful information concerning the nature and consequences of IMF-supported policies. In addition, social movements have offered channels through which stakeholders have been able to voice their views on the Fund and have those opinions relayed to IMF staff.

Most importantly, however, social-movement campaigns for change in the International Monetary Fund have stimulated debate about policies and methodologies at a time when one paradigm, neoliberalism, has made a serious bid for monopoly power in the world political economy. Regardless of the particular merits or otherwise of the neoliberal knowledge structure, any domination by a single perspective sooner or later spells trouble for both policy effectiveness and democracy. Resistance by social movements to IMF sponsorship of neoliberalism has therefore played a vital role in sustaining some elements of diversity and critical debate in global economic governance. Challenges from social movements have pushed the IMF better to clarify, explain and justify its positions. The critics have not so far undermined the general confidence of Fund management and staff in neoliberal policies, but officials have come in the 1990s to apply these prescriptions with some greater discrimination and qualification.

6 Complex multilateralism: MEIs and GSMs

The preceding four cases studies have shown that numerous changes have taken place in the MEI–GSM relationship over the past twenty years. This chapter provides a comparative analysis of these developments and assesses their significance for global governance. We argue that there is a transformation in the nature of governance conducted by MEIs as a result of their encounter with GSMs. This transformation is labelled 'complex multilateralism' in recognition of its movement away from an exclusively state based structure. At present the transformation primarily takes the form of institutional modification, although some policy innovation is occurring. Such changes explicitly acknowledge that actors other than states speak on behalf of the public interest. While signalling an alteration to the method of governance, it is less clear that there is a change either in the content of governing policies or in the broad interests they represent. In the short run the MEI–GSM nexus is unlikely to greatly transform institutional functions. In the longer run, there is the possibility of incremental change in the functioning and ambit of these key institutions depending upon the outcome of continued political conflict.

This chapter begins by outlining the basic characteristics of complex multilateralism and its relationship to other understandings of multilateralism. It then moves on to consider how the five characteristics of complex multilateralism (varied institutional modifications, rival motivations, ambiguous results, differential state implications and socialised agenda) have manifested themselves in our case studies. The chapter concludes by considering the future for MEI–GSM relations and the significance of complex multilateralism.

Complex multilateralism

The nature of governance and authority in the field of public multilateral economic institutions is going through a transitional stage. While it is clear what the transition is from, it is not as obvious where it is going. The changing patterns of MEI operation and the MEI–GSM relationship documented in this study is best captured by the term 'complex multilateralism'. It is a movement away from a multilateralism based primarily on the activity of states. Other groups of actors, whether they be private firms or social movements (as in our study), have an increasingly significant role in multilateralism. However, states remain key actors and it is not yet established to what degree or in what areas they will cede decision-making authority. The practice of multilateralism has become more complicated because of the need to accommodate the demands of GSMs.

The term complex multilateralism might remind readers of Keohane and Nye's (1977) concept of 'complex interdependence'. Indeed, our study may find some resonance with liberal international relations approaches that stress interdependence and transnational relations (Risse-Kappen 1995) However, there are a number of significant differences between our approach and liberal international relations theory. First, the term complex interdependence was used to describe an ideal type rather than the real world (Keohane and Nye 1987: 731). Our concept is meant to capture real world changes. Second, our goal is not to account for state behaviour, but to better understand processes of global governance. State behaviour is only one element of global governance. Our argument is that some attention must be focused upon the interaction of multilateral institutions and civil society groups to understand the form and content of global governance. Finally, our inspiration for this study derives not from the liberal goal of facilitating cooperation between states or increasing efficiency in managing the global economy, but in concern to understand the ways in which non-elites can participate in the process of governing.

Complex multilateralism is a move away from conventional multilateralism understood as 'an institutional form that co-ordinates relations among three or more states on the basis of generalized principles of conduct' (Ruggie 1993: 11). The mobilisation of various elements of civil society in response to increasing globalisation has complicated multilateral governance by bringing new actors into the field. Multilateralism is more complicated because international institutions must take some account of a range of civil society actors. Securing the agreement of government officials is not enough to permit the smooth running of these institutions. Constituencies within and across states must be appeased or, at the very least, their opposition must be diluted and diverted. Multilateralism is changing by providing points of access for these constituencies (including social movements).

Although multilateralism has moved from its state dominated nature, it is a far cry from a society centred multilateralism. The project to build a 'new' or emerging multilateralism which would 'reconstitute civil societies and political authorities on a global scale, building a system of global governance from the bottom up' (Cox 1997: xxvii) is in its infancy. Serious differences divide the broad social movements we examined. Organised labour is challenged by NGOs claiming to speak on behalf of the informal sector. Women's groups in the developing world have an ambivalent and sometimes conflictual relationship with Northern feminist groups. Environmentalists seeking thorough changes to the doctrine of economic growth are in conflict with more conservative conservationist groups. Various NGOs claim to speak on behalf of social movements or constituencies, but the plethora of groups and lack of transparency makes it difficult to determine the legitimacy of their claims.

The institutions we have examined pose a particularly difficult problem for advocates of the 'new multilateralism' because they raise the question of whether popular forces should be attempting to modify existing structures or to build alternative structures. Is it possible to engage with MEIs in the hope that they can be reformed or are they so beholden to exploitative global capitalist interests that they must be dismantled? For example, while organised labour has been trying to integrate its concerns into the WTO, representatives of some of the most disadvantaged peoples have been advocating the WTO's abolition.[1]

Our study suggests that multilateralism as an institutional form is undergoing change. We identify five central characteristics of complex multilateralism. The first characteristic is varied institutional modifi-

---

[1] The Frente Zapatista de Liberación Nacional (FZLN) in Mexico and the Peasant Movement of the Philippines (KMP) have taken a leading role in the People's Global Action against Free Trade and the World Trade Organisation (PGA).

cation in response to civil society actors. Multilateral public institutions are modifying themselves in response to pressure from social movements, NGOs and business actors. Our study concentrated on social movements, but members of the business community have even greater access and are also pressing for greater institutional accountability. Multilateral institutions are going beyond their member states in an attempt to ground their legitimacy within civil societies. Modifications vary across institutions depending upon institutional culture, structure, role of the executive head and vulnerability to civil society pressure.

A second characteristic of this institutional form of world politics is that the major participants are divided by conflicting motivations and goals. The goal of the institutions and their supporters is to maintain existing policy directions and facilitate their smoother operation. The aim is to improve the implementation of policies and management of the institutions. In contrast, the goal of many civil society actors, and certainly of social movements, is to change the policy direction of the institutions. There is even confrontation over the methods institutions should follow to achieve those few goals that are mutually acceptable. For example, there may be agreement to pursue sustainable development, but there is intense conflict over the meaning of sustainable development and whether structural adjustment programmes assist or hinder its achievement.

The clash of rival goals leads to a third characteristic, which is the ambiguous results of this form of organisation to date. If accomplishments are defined in terms of the actors achieving their own goals, both institutions and social movements have enjoyed only limited success. Social movements have found that the institutions' generalised principles of conduct are subject to debate, but relatively immune from revision. Many branches of the social movements we encountered questioned the basic assumptions of the MEIs. However, their influence in changing those assumptions has been limited. Letting new actors into the process does not necessarily translate into dramatic policy changes. The institutions have enjoyed slightly more success by being able to bring elements of social movements into a dialogue and institutionalising some of their concerns, thereby somewhat reducing the level of antagonism directed at the institutions.

If one takes a different measure of success, such as the contribution of complex multilateralism to system maintenance, the verdict is more positive. Indeed, complex multilateralism is an institutional adaptation to the process of globalisation. Its success could be measured in terms of the continued smooth functioning of the institutions themselves. Are the public institutions that form the framework of governance for a liberal global economy capable of establishing roots beyond state and corporate elites? Our study does not provide a definitive answer to that question because this is an ongoing process. Early indications are that they might be able to, but increased policy modification will be required to accompany existing institutional transformation.

A fourth characteristic of complex multilateralism is its differential impact upon the role of the state depending upon the state's pre-existing position in the international system. In general, an increase in MEI–GSM activity undermines the state's claim to be the sole legitimate representative of the public interest within its territory. However, in the case of more powerful states such as the USA, GSM activity has reinforced the importance of the domestic political process for global governance. Thus, the fate of particular policy measures or institutional changes can rest upon the battle between national and transnational forces within the United States and in the Congress. In the case of weaker states, complex multilateralism can highlight their impotence and subject them to increased conditionality from multilateral institutions. It is for this reason that many Southern states oppose the increased participation of social groups in global governance mechanisms. Although there is often pressure by many Southern-based elements of social movements to convince multilateral institutions to takes steps which would support developing countries' state-building capacities, these are usually unsuccessful. In all cases, strong or weak states, Northern or Southern countries, this new organisational form complicates multilateralism and introduces the possibilities of new alliances between governments, institutions and civil society actors.

A fifth aspect of complex multilateralism is a broadening of the policy agenda to include more social issues. Multilateralism is complicated not just because there are more actors, but because some of these actors are pressing for a new agenda. They want their issues integrated into the mandate of the institutions they are trying to influence. GSMs are demanding that the goals of liberalisation and economic efficiency are balanced by aims such as social justice, sustainable development and gender equity. Issues that formerly would have been outside the scope of MEIs are now impinging upon their operation. New issues are often resisted, but the agenda is shifting. The long term implications of a broadening agenda may involve a change in the overall operation and content of the MEIs and global governance.

The following sections illustrate these five characteristics of complex multilateralism with examples from the previous case studies. This is followed by a conclusion where we assess the significance of this institutional form of multilateralism.

1 Varied institutional modification

The IMF, World Bank and WTO have all adapted their institutions to take account of the increasing importance of GSMs. This evolution has been sporadic and uneven, but it is a recognisable trend. It has gone the furthest in the case of the World Bank's relationship with environmentalists, and to a lesser extent, women's groups. The WTO has also created a separate division to deal with environmental issues. However, the environmental area is the exception at the WTO and the IMF has made relatively fewer changes. Yet, even in these two MEIs dialogue has increased and new information channels have been created.

The World Bank has the most extensive contact with social movements and NGOs of the three institutions. It engages NGOs at three levels: operational collaboration, economic and sector work (ESW), and broader policy dialogue. Operational collaboration refers to the inclusion of NGOs in the design and execution of Bank financed projects. ESW comprises a broad range of research and analysis undertaken by the Bank. The broader policy dialogue covers the exchange of information between the World Bank and NGOs regarding the Bank's development policies. This dialogue had formally been conducted through the NGO–World Bank Committee established in 1982. The bank NGO unit is now dispersed through regional departments in an attempt to integrate them into the policy process. There has also been recent discussion about developing a 'development grants facility' to assist in NGO capacity building (Bread for the World 1997a: 5–6).

Our study examined the interaction between women's groups, environmentalists and the Bank. Gender issues at the World Bank have been addressed by the appointment of a Women in Development officer in 1977, the establishment of a Gender Unit in 1987, an External

Gender Consultative Group following the 1995 Beijing Women's Summit and a Gender Sector board in 1997. Other opportunities for contact are provided through the general NGO contact mechanisms. In 1987 the Bank established an Environment Department in response to lobbying of Congress by US environmental groups. Since 1989 environmental assessments (EAs) have been required of projects expected to have significant adverse environmental impacts. By January 1994 the Bank had a new information disclosure policy to declassify documents and established a Public Information Center in Washington. In September 1994 the Bank launched an Inspection Panel to investigate complaints by community organisations that believe the institution is violating its own procedures. In the wake of the East Asian financial crisis the Bank has begun to develop its ties with organised labour through increased meetings with labour officials at all levels of the Bank.

In contrast to the World Bank, the IMF has been a late and more reluctant participant in engaging with GSMs. GSMs come into contact with the IMF through six routes: the External Relations department (EXR), the Executive Directors' office, the management team (including the managing director), certain policy departments, country mission teams and resident representatives. The External Relations department was created in 1981, but maintained a low profile. A fully fledged Public Affairs division was not created until 1989. It was the run up to the 1988 Berlin annual meetings that provided the focus for the publication and dissemination of IMF popular information. The IMF's contacts with GSMs are growing, but they are usually on an informal, non-institutionalised basis. The institution tends to choose its contacts carefully. For example, the IMF has courted organised labour, but neglected women's groups. Behaviour deemed inappropriate by the Fund can lead to a reduction of ties. The purpose of most contacts is to educate the public rather than to revise IMF policy based upon social movement input.

The WTO's relationship with social movements has matured from the days when NGOs had to attend the 1994 Marrakesh meeting disguised as reporters. In its forty-seven-year history the GATT failed to establish any formal linkages with NGOs or social movements.[2] In July 1996 the WTO began to clarify its relationships with NGOs by

---

[2] An exception to this was participation by the International Chambers of Commerce in several GATT working parties in the 1950s (Charnovitz 1997: 255).

Table 6.1. *MEI–GSM Contact*

Institution	World Bank	International Monetary Fund	World Trade Organization
Experience	Early 1980s: relatively broad	Late 1980s: selective and sparse	Mid 1990s: unsure
Structure	Operational collaboration ESW Policy dialogue Gender Sector board EAs Environment department Inspection Panel	External Relations department Executive Directors Management team Country mission teams Policy departments Resident reps	External Relations department Dispute settlement TPRM Workshops

derestricting some documents and allowing its Secretariat to interact with NGOs in an informal manner. The WTO has an External Relations director and publishes material on the Internet. At the December 1996 Singapore WTO ministerial meeting provisions were made for NGO observers, but participation in policy making is restricted to the occasional consultation under procedures of the dispute settlement mechanism.[3] Since the 1996 Singapore meeting the WTO has convened a number of workshops or symposia to bring social movement representatives and Secretariat officials together to discuss a selected issue.[4] Recent attempts have been made by the labour and women's movements to have their concerns highlighted in the country-by-country examinations of the Trade Policy Review Mechanism. Table 6.1 serves as a useful summary of MEI–GSM contact.

Accounting for institutional variation

Although MEIs have adapted to social movement pressure, this has taken different forms. There is no single explanation for the particular form that adaptation has taken, but there are a number of significant influences. The culture of the subject matter in which the institutions

---

[3] NGOs do not have a right to participate, it is at the discretion of the WTO panel.
[4] An example is the September 1997 WTO–NGO symposium on participation of least developed countries in the trading system.

Table 6.2. *MEI transformation variables*

	World Bank	International Monetary Fund	World Trade Organization
Subject-area culture	Development/ participation and economic growth/ efficiency	Finance/secrecy	Trade/rent seeking
Structure	Diverse	Monolithic, SAP country negotiations	Monolithic, negotiating forum
Role of executive head	Dynamic, committed	Dynamic, committed	Limited
Vulnerability to social movement action	Medium	Low	Low

deal, the structure of the institutions themselves, the role of the executive head and the vulnerability of the institution to social movement action all play a role. These are summarised in table 6.2.

The three institutions we examined deal with different subject matter and carry distinct cultures of operation and assumptions about interaction with civil society. These cultures have a role in preconditioning levels of receptiveness to social movement participation and collaboration. The World Bank is concerned with development and has been buffeted by a series of internal and external critiques suggesting that its policies should take the concerns of the target population into account. Before its neoliberal phase, the Bank was concerned with meeting basic human needs. In the face of programme failures it has gradually developed a more participative approach to development policy and planning. However, this 'development/participative' culture is sometimes overshadowed by a 'growth/efficiency' culture. The latter is based on neoclassical economics and favours the business case for policy measures over concern about participation or democracy. Nevertheless, the presence of alternative cultures has created a degree of openness which has carried over into the Bank's dealing with the environmental and women's movements.

The IMF and the WTO, in contrast to the Bank, operate in areas of expertise more sceptical of the value of civil society participation. The

IMF deals with finance, an area which has a tradition of exclusivity and secrecy. Negotiations over debt repayment take place with the elites of countries, not with those who bear the brunt of repayment. In the case of the WTO, civil society participation in trade policy making is more likely to be interpreted as a form of rent seeking than as a democratisation of the political system. Following a tradition of public choice analysis, the practice of free trade is thought to be threatened by protectionist interests mobilising against the general or consumer interest.[5] Interest groups threaten to accrue rents and harm the welfare of society by blocking free trade.

The structure of the three institutions also varies. The World Bank is a larger institution (approximately 7,000 staff members compared with the IMF's 2,600 and WTO's 500) which contains pockets of resistance to the governing ideology. Various social interests find sympathisers within the Bank's elaborate structure and use this space to further their interaction. The IMF and WTO are smaller and more monolithic institutions. There is a much clearer governing ideology and expression of dissent or controversy within the institution is less likely and certainly less visible. A further crucial difference is that the IMF and WTO either engage in or are the forum for sensitive negotiations with or between states. The IMF negotiates stabilisation and structural adjustment policies with states while the WTO serves as a forum for trade negotiations. Both institutions take the task of ensuring government confidentiality very seriously. As a result, both the institutions and the member states are reluctant to open up their operations to outside scrutiny.

The studies on the World Bank and the IMF have highlighted the key role played by the executive head in pushing for increased contact with social movements.[6] The appointment in 1987 of Michel Camdessus as managing director of the IMF led to an increase in the organisation's efforts at public relations. Camdessus has been far more active than his predecessors in making contact with civil society organisations through meetings, speeches and correspondence. In addition, his French background seems to have influenced his familiarity with and openness to bringing organised labour into IMF restructuring plans. At the World Bank, James Wolfensohn has

---

[5] For example, Baldwin (1985).
[6] The key role played by an executive head in international organisations was high-lighted in Cox (1969).

personally taken the gender issue from the Beijing summit and attempted to institutionalise it within the Bank's structures. He has also been responsible for the much stronger platform given to the whole issue of civil society participation in the Bank policy and operation work through the promotion of the 'participation' agenda. With the WTO being such a recent organisation it is unsurprising that its executive head has played a less influential role in light of his struggle to establish the institution itself.

A fourth factor influencing the openness of institutions to social movements is their relative vulnerability to social movement pressure. The World Bank has been the most vulnerable as its budget has come under threat in the US Congress *and* particular development projects have been disrupted by social movement action. The Bank has been forced to respond both to critics in the USA and to potential critics in target countries. The IMF and WTO have been less vulnerable to social movement pressure, but have had to take it into account. US funding for the IMF must go through the Congress and strings have occasionally been attached. For example, 1994 funding was linked to urging that the IMF should publicise its recommendations with greater frequency and detail. Successful pressure on the IMF has focused upon increasing the institution's transparency and account-ability rather than changing the terms of conditionality. The success of structural adjustment policies is also vulnerable to civil unrest in some countries, however this is more difficult for GSMs to target than individual Bank projects. This limited vulnerability may explain the attempt to lure organised labour into supporting IMF policies. The WTO was forced to pay attention to environmental concerns following the US backlash to the tuna–dolphin case. In addition, the WTO must cultivate domestic opinion if it hopes to pursue an agenda of future liberalisation such as a new trade round in the year 2000.

The differences in subject culture, institutional structure and task, role of the executive head and vulnerability to pressure help to explain the varying degrees of MEI engagement with GSMs. Of these four factors the role of the executive is the least crucial as it is constrained by the institutional structure and role. Thus, while Cam-dessus and Wolfensohn may be equally energetic in reaching out to civil society, this is a much easier task at the Bank. Vulnerability to pressure helps to explain much of the motivation behind MEI trans-formation, but the subject culture, institutional structure and role go most of the way to explaining resistance to institutional change.

2 Conflicting motivations and goals

Although there have been accomplishments in the MEI–GSM relationships, the motivations of the various partners are strikingly different and often contradictory. This section outlines the rival motivations behind increased contact. On the face of it there is no obvious reason why MEIs should engage with GSMs. These are interstate institutions which were created to serve the interests of their members, which are states. Why then do they do it? Engagement with GSMs is an explicit recognition by these institutions that governance of the global economy cannot rest solely upon an international – that is, interstate foundation. The institutions have realised that in order for their programmes to succeed and expand, they must sink roots into civil societies around the globe. Institutional practitioners may not like this development, but they have done the political calculus and recognised the emerging reality.

In general, the goal of MEI interaction with GSMs is to neutralise their opposition so that the policy process can function smoothly. This goal is pursued in different forms and to different extents in the three institutions because of their distinct methods of operation and policy functions.

As mentioned earlier, the World Bank has been and remains the most sensitive of the institutions toward social movements. This is for two reasons. First, the World Bank runs particular development projects which are more vulnerable to disruption by social movements. People can organise against, and possibly prevent, the building of a dam more easily than they can affect the decision of the WTO's dispute settlement mechanism, for example. In a more cooperative vein, social movements can assist in reaching the poor and facilitate grass-roots participation. This means that the Bank may want to use particular civil society organisations to deliver its projects. Secondly, the World Bank's budget is particularly vulnerable to US Congressional politics. If social movements can be influential in the US system, the Bank must listen, or at least must seem to listen. As a result of these dual sensitivities, the Bank has taken steps to involve social movements in a wide range of its activities from general consultation to project development. This involvement is meant to safeguard projects by building in social movement support. In some cases, NGOs are used for policy implementation. In addition, the World Bank has acknowledged that social movements may have local knowledge unavailable to Bank staff.

The IMF has opened contact with civil society for two primary reasons. The first is an attempt to counter the criticism of its many opponents. The Fund has been condemned in numerous quarters for the effects of its structural adjustment policies on developing countries. This has included protests in developed countries (street demonstrations during the 1988 annual meetings in Berlin) and food riots in developing countries (Zambia in 1986, Venezuela in 1989), sometimes with loss of life. IMF officials view this storm of criticism as mistaken because the institution only responds to financial crises. The medicine they deliver might be harsh, but failure to take it risks more serious consequences. From an IMF perspective, engagement with civil society can be used to educate the public about its role and the true reasons for structural adjustment. It is an attempt to diffuse opposition through education (propaganda in the view of its critics). In some cases IMF officials might be able to use pressure from civil society to force governments to spend money in productive ways. For example, a strong labour movement might be able to convince a government to switch spending away from consumption to investment in social infrastructure (IMF 1996i). By forging alliances with factions of civil society IMF officials hope to pressure governments into responsible spending policies and facilitate their return to financial health.

Similar to the World Bank, a second reason for IMF concern about civil society groups arises from the need to secure funding from member states. Its opening to civil society can be traced to its need to respond to the demands from funders for increased transparency and responsiveness. Pressure from the US Congress is especially significant for the IMF. Not only must it deal with criticisms from the left (UAW 1998), but it is under constant attack from right-wing think tanks that wish to see an end to state rescue packages (Cato Institute 1998). The IMF must be wary of a left–right coalition restricting its funding in the same way that efforts to expand regional trade have been stalled in the US Congress for the institution.

For the WTO, engagement with GSMs is related to the need to secure the support of key states for further liberalisation. It is particularly aimed at placating the environmental and labour movements in advanced industrialised countries. These movements believe that trade liberalisation in its present form is undermining their interests and that the dispute settlement mechanism threatens to overturn positive regulation. The WTO differs from the IMF and World Bank in that its key challenge is not to discipline the weak, but to tame the strong. In order to extend its authority over advanced industrialised states the WTO must accommodate their civil societies.

The method of accommodation put forward by the WTO is restricted by the fears of some of its members about social movement and NGO involvement. Many developing states reject a role for NGOs either because the states themselves have no history of pluralism or because GSMs are viewed as being Northern dominated and furthering the interests of Northern states. While ready to discuss environmental concerns, their opposition to labour issues is often virulent and their openness to gender concerns almost non-existent. This determined opposition leaves the WTO in a difficult position. It must try to balance the demands by developed states and GSMs for greater participation and transparency with developing states' opposition to moving away from a purely state based institution. As a result, the Secretariat has been reduced to providing information to GSMs.

For GSMs, the motivation for engagement is strikingly different from the institutions'. Whereas the institutions seek to manage a process, the movements generally want to change the direction and content of MEI policy. In most cases they seek to change the underlying assumptions upon which policy decisions are made. However, the movements themselves are diverse, representing a wide range of positions from those who fundamentally disagree with the liberalisation project to those who seek to temper its edges. In general one can say that GSMs seek some form of social protection and a reorientation of policy so that costs are not born primarily by the weakest members of society. In the case of the environmental movement, claims are also made on behalf of the planet and future generations.

In the case of engagement with the World Bank and the IMF, GSMs want the institutions to take account of the effects of their policies on women, the environment and labour. The IMF and the Bank are leaders in establishing the current development orthodoxy. GSMs target the Bank and the Fund because the two institutions also exercise influence on other multilateral institutions, developing states and planning agencies. Until the mid-1980s women's groups were concerned that only a minor segment of the Bank's lending policies had an acknowledged gender dimension. More damaging has been the perceived disproportionately negative impact of economic adjustment measures on women and children. Environmental groups (such as

FOE and WWF) have been concerned about the negative environmental impact of structural adjustment policies. Development NGOs (such as Bread for the World, Development GAP, Oxfam) have been concerned with the implications of these institutions' prescriptions on levels of poverty. More than this, they want the policies themselves to be reformulated so that they cause less violence to their constituencies. Labour groups want the institutions to design policies which enhance employment and bolster the basic rights of workers.

Attempts to influence the WTO are more complicated in that there are several goals. Women's movements have wanted the WTO to consider and publicise the gendered impact of trade liberalisation. Environmentalists have wanted to prevent the WTO's rule making and enforcement system from frustrating national and international efforts at environmental protection. Labour has been trying to have the enforcement mechanisms applied to its issue of core labour standards.

There are elements of each social movement which adopt a more rejectionist agenda for dealing with MEIs. These groups see MEIs almost solely in terms of dominating and destructive Northern capitalist interests attacking the fabric of their societies. For these groups dialogue and attempt at reforming MEIs is not the object. Abolition of the institutions or consigning them to irrelevance is the ultimate goal.

3 Ambiguous results

Although it is too early to come to definitive conclusions about the results of the emerging MEI–GSM relationship, some preliminary observations are in order. First, there are limits to the relationship based upon diverging interests. The core political economy projects of the institutions and those of the movements collide. MEIs are tasked with establishing and overseeing a set of rules and practices which contribute to an ever increasing liberalisation of national economies and the expansion of a global economy. To date, they have not been tasked with balancing this overriding objective with other concerns such as equity or justice, or social or environmental protection. GSMs do take these latter tasks as their briefs and are concerned with the way that MEI activity seems to threaten such goals. GSMs seek to change the basic assumptions of MEIs as they presently operate.

Second, to the degree that one party or the other may be more successful in achieving their objectives, it is more likely that MEIs, rather than GSMs, will achieve short-term success. The MEI project is concerned with blunting opposition and has therefore a more manageable goal. GSMs are concerned with challenging the powers that be and setting new agendas. This is a longer-term task. Indeed, only a limited amount of GSM time is aimed at bringing about institutional reform. Similar to national social movements, a great deal of effort is devoted to shifting public opinion and shaping public values and norms. In addition, GSMs also target other key actors such as environmental or labour campaigns against particular business corporations.

Initially, it appears that interaction with GSMs is a no-win game for MEIs. MEI officials will not gain substantial support from GSMs as long as they follow a neoliberal policy prescription which is seen to attack the interests of these communities. World Bank, IMF and WTO officials are unlikely to persuade GSMs that the wrenching adjustment accompanying liberal globalisation is in their interests. The World Bank has gone the furthest in building bridges and amending policy, but doubts remain about its commitment to balancing neoliberal prescriptions with social protection. The IMF has a hard task in convincing women and trade unionists that the lost decade of the 1980s will not be repeated if its advice is followed. Even more difficult for these groups to accept is the IMF's reluctance to address the issue of how the costs of adjustment are distributed within communities. In the case of the WTO, the environmentalists, labour and women's group are unlikely to accept arguments that trade should be free and other policy concerns should be addressed through other policy instruments.

Closer examination reveals that MEI managers can view the relationship with GSMs as having achieved some positive results. The World Bank has gained some moderate success from its engagement with GSMs. It has been able to institutionalise some of the concerns of women and environmentalists in its structure. While creating mechanisms for dealing with the issues of these two groups, they remain subordinate to the primary policy of the institution and its spending departments. In the case of gender issues, the Bank has seized upon the use of micro-credit both to demonstrate its good intentions in this area and to demonstrate its ability to produce new methods of delivering programmes that show a financial return.[7] Perhaps its

---

[7] The Bank does not directly organise micro-credit operations, but does lend support to NGOs.

greatest gain from taking the gender issue on board has been the rewards for social development coming from recent support for girls' education. The Bank is certainly viewed as the most Green of the three institutions and has created mechanisms to make projects more accountable to target communities.

The IMF has been relatively unconcerned about its relationship with environmentalist or women's groups, but has actively courted organised labour. Labour is viewed as a key social actor which might assist the institution in implementing its adjustment policies and boost much needed political support in target countries. Building political support may be too strong an expression; it would be more accurate to say that the neutralising of opposition from labour groups is an accomplishment. For their part, established labour organisations are tempted into a relationship by the IMF because they require the legitimation of being classified as a social partner and are eager to show some gains to their hard-pressed members. Yet, the relationship is at an early stage of engagement and remains vulnerable to opposition from the grass roots of unionism.

The WTO has put considerable effort into managing its relationship with environmentalists and has recently engaged labour, but is just starting to consider gender issues. The incorporation of environmental issues into the WTO through the Committee on Trade and the Environment (CTE) has been successful in paying lip-service to environmental concerns, but avoided any meaningful action. Indeed the CTE's failure to take action has led to a split within the environmental movement about future strategy. Some groups advocate a policy of continuing to engage with the institution while others advocate a withdrawal from the institution and the creation of alternative mechanisms. This can only be to the WTO's advantage. Relations with labour have been more difficult and are fragile. The failure to go some way to address labour concerns through a social clause suggests that future support is contingent upon some new adjustment.

From the perspective of those social movement elements willing to engage with MEIs a slightly darker mirror image of the MEI results is apparent. The women's movement has made some impact on the World Bank, but none on the IMF and WTO. At the Bank, women's concerns have been institutionalised through developments such as the Gender Sector board and the External Gender Consultative Group. The exercise of listening to women has helped the Bank to make its lending programmes more efficient by pointing out the higher social pay-offs to be gained from investing in women. Yet, women must continue to make a business case for Bank attention and have difficulty influencing the key spending decision makers. They must show that gender initiatives are good for business rather than being good for women. While the Bank has taken the issues of girls' education and micro-credit seriously, it shies away from more controversial issues that might more deeply challenge gender relations in client states. This moderate degree of success has not been matched in the IMF or WTO. Women's groups have few links with IMF personnel. At the WTO women's groups have just begun to meet with officials and are trying to get the WTO to agree to studies of the gendered effects of trade liberalisation. They lag far behind environmentalists and labour in having their agenda taken seriously.

Environmentalists have had some success at the Bank, but made hardly any impact at the IMF and very little substantive change at the WTO. Similar to women's groups, environmentalists have had their concerns institutionalised through the creation of a particular area within the Bank. Moreover, environmental concerns must be addressed though environmental assessments of risky projects. Although there is criticism of the effectiveness of these mechanisms, they do show an improvement from the days when environmental issues were not even considered. Environmentalists initially believed they were making progress at the WTO with the creation of the Committee on Trade and Environment, but this has proved to be disappointing. The CTE has taken so few positive steps towards integrating environmental concerns into the organisation that some prominent groups are now calling for its abolition. Environmentalists have made little headway in influencing the IMF.

The record for organised labour is also mixed. Labour has been slowly brought into closer contact with the IMF. It sees some benefits of engaging with the IMF in terms of increased legitimacy as a social actor, but grass-roots views are more hostile. Labour issues have recently been considered by the World Bank and the East Asian financial crisis has sparked a review of the Bank's dealings with organised labour which may lead to institutional changes. Organised labour made a large effort to have its issue integrated into the WTO, but was largely unsuccessful. The labour movement finds itself being bounced between an intransigent WTO and ineffective ILO. The conclusion labour might draw is that it is best to return to the national arena and pursue unilateral action rather than attempt to reform the WTO.

Despite concerted effort in the recent past, GSMs would generally rank low in an MEI hierarchy of influence. The richest Northern states remain key decision makers. In controversial areas such as gender, environment or labour standards, weaker Southern states are able to block policy initiatives by arguing that cultural difference or economic disadvantage prevent action. Within civil society business organisations and think tanks have enjoyed more access and influence than social movements. For example, the IMF has extensive contacts with business organisations, but not women's groups. Northern based transnational corporations succeeded in having GATT act in the new issue of protection for intellectual property rights, but labour has been unable to advance the core standards issue. GSMs face an uphill struggle to influence MEIs and temper the power of the richest states and private enterprises.

Despite these limited achievements, one can discern the emergence of a distinct section of the GSM community with the inclination and the ability to engage MEIs on an ongoing basis. This suggests that with some flexibility MEIs could cultivate a social movement constituency and that the GSM community is likely to show increasing signs of fragmentation and polarisation. The lines of division between sections of GSMs within the MEI loop and those outside it are becoming increasingly clear. The factors that determine who is in and who is out can vary according to ideology, location, expertise and influence.

Ideology is significant because 'in' groups must at least accept the general goal of liberalisation, even if there is disagreement about its scope, speed and intensity. Location is crucial as those groups able to operate in Washington and Geneva have better access and opportunity to engage with MEI officials. In addition, those groups capable of exercising influence within the US or European domestic political system stand a greater chance of having their views brought into MEI councils. Expertise is important in two senses. MEIs are more likely to listen to groups who have expertise the institutions lack and are unlikely to spend time with groups unfamiliar with liberal economics or an understanding of trade law. Influence upon key state decision makers, whether in the developed or developing world, also increases the chances that sections of a particular GSM will be brought into a dialogue with MEIs.

224

The preceding variables tend to favour mainstream Northern based elements of GSMs. For example, the US section of the women's movement is generally heard more clearly than women from developing countries. The Northern based International Confederation of Free Trade Unions and the AFL–CIO are more likely to be accommodated than trade unionists or unorganised workers in developing countries. Northern semi-professional environmental groups are taken seriously, while the voice of Southern groups tends to be drowned out.

A further factor is required to explain the varying levels of success enjoyed by the women's, environmental and labour movements. The degree to which a movement can put pressure upon key states and the degree to which its concerns can be accommodated without challenging the most powerful interests are key in determining its relationship with MEIs. For example, the environmental movement has had some success in getting its agenda taken seriously at the World Bank and WTO. In both cases pressure on the US political system was decisive. Labour has also been able to use pressure in the USA and Europe to drive its labour standards campaign at the WTO. Its strategic position within national economies has also brought it to the IMF's attention. However, the fact that an independent labour movement threatens both the profits of firms and the political control of authoritarian states makes its concerns a non-starter at the WTO. Environmentalists, on the other hand, pose less of a direct threat to political power and their concerns are discussed at an institution like the WTO. Women have had their concerns integrated into the World Bank in reaction to the shortcoming of developmental policies and vocal protest, but they are less influential than environmentalists. They wield less influence in the US political system and have made little impact on either the IMF or the WTO.

4 Differential state impact

Our study has examined the relationship between MEIs and GSMs in some depth. Although limited, some accommodation has developed between these actors. The question arises as to the implication of these developments for the state and its traditional role as the sole representative of a population within a bounded territory. There is no simple answer to such a question. A blanket generalisation which suggested either that GSM and NGO activity undermines states or strengthens state regulatory capacity (Raustiala 1997) would be misleading. The implication for the state varies considerably depending upon the state in question. Indeed, asymmetric GSM influence upon different states is a source of major contention. In most cases the MEI–GSM relationship weakens state claims to a monopoly of representation, in some cases GSM activity strengthens or highlights the role of particular states, while in others it agitates for a reassertion of sovereignty and greater state building capabilities. Let us take these implications in turn.

MEI accommodation of some role for GSMs acknowledges a reality and effectively legitimises a claim to representation. The reality is that GSMs do have some influence in the conduct of world politics. If MEIs are to continue their role of liberalising the world economy, they must be sensitive to divergent interests and locations of power. GSMs remain subordinate actors in the global political economy, but there are times when they can obstruct or delay the liberalisation project. MEI adaptation is not an exercise in idealistic intentions, but a strategy of realpolitik. MEIs are accommodating a new source of influence in world politics. By providing for increased contact with GSMs the institutions legitimise the movements' claims that they act on behalf of interests not represented by states.

This legitimation of the GSM role is neither unprecedented nor revolutionary, but it is potentially significant. In recent years the UN system has increasingly opened up its activities to non-state actors (Weiss and Gordenker 1996; Willetts 1996) while the ILO was founded on the principle that a society contains divergent interests requiring separate representation (Wilson 1934). The significance lies in the particular nature of the IMF, World Bank, and WTO. Individually, and as a group, they are extremely influential institutions guiding and enforcing the liberalisation process. Their pronouncements, rulings and advice have direct impact upon state policy. Opening up these institutions to non-state influence is more significant than the same steps in other institutions because of the IMF's, World Bank's and WTO's institutional power. It injects another element into governance giving states' decision makers another competitor, ally or adversary in the realm of international public policy making. The implications for particular states varies.

In the case of the United States, the activity of GSMs seems only to underline its central role in world politics. Because of its powerful position, the United States domestic political arena has become the key battleground to influence MEI policy. Environmentalists were able to force the GATT to take environmental issues seriously following a US outcry against a GATT ruling which struck down American measures aimed at protecting dolphins from tuna fishing nets (Skilton 1993). The establishment of a WTO Committee on Trade and the Environment can be traced back to this US controversy. Similarly, attempts to have environmental priorities put on the agenda of the World Bank have been most successful when they attempted to influence US Congressional funding of that institution. For the labour movement, US support on the issue of core labour standards is critical if it is to have the issue considered at the WTO or to reform the ILO. As a lobby, women have less concentrated power in the US political system and have been relatively unsuccessful in channelling their demands through the political system into the MEIs.

For Southern states the picture is more complicated. In some cases GSM activity can demonstrate the weakness of particular Southern states. For example, World Bank or IMF conditionality may coerce states into adopting policies that they would not otherwise implement. In this case national agendas are being influenced not only by stronger states and multilateral institutions, but also by social movements. In other cases, such as with Southern development NGOs, the goal is not to force the Southern state to take particular policy steps, but to strengthen the state by influencing the pattern of development policy of the MEIs. The goal is to increase the ability of poorer states to act. This can take the form of loosening conditionality on IMF/World Bank loans or blocking the expansion of the WTO into new issue areas.

Government officials in stronger and weaker states can both use and be used by GSMs seeking to influence MEIs. For example, it is unclear who was serving whose purposes in the US government's relationship with the international labour movement during the discussion of core labour standards at the WTO. The labour unions relied upon the USA to advance their agenda at the WTO. Only the support of powerful states would get labour issues on to the WTO agenda. The USA used the unions to demonstrate that its advocacy of core labour standards had support among the world's workers. Some have suggested an even more instrumental explanation of US support for core labour standards. Perhaps the US government only used its advocacy of labour standards as a bargaining chip with Asian states to achieve its primary goal in the December 1996 Singapore WTO meeting – an Information Technology agreement reducing barriers to IT trade. This agreement had been discussed at an APEC meeting a month before Singapore, but the USA was unable to secure Asian support. One theory is that at Singapore the US government traded a weak statement on labour standards for an IT agreement. [8]

Weaker or developing states may also forge links with social movements to advance their agendas. To go back to the Singapore meeting, a number of Southern based NGOs echoed the views of particular developing states such as Malaysia and Indonesia that the new issues of investment, competition policy and labour standards should be kept off the agenda of the WTO (TWN 1996). The goal was to portray the attempt of the US and the EU to enlarge the policy competence of the WTO as an exercise in Northern imperialism. This reflected the views of some social movements and served the interests of particular Southern states by strengthening their bargaining position.

5 A more social agenda

Although GSM activists are usually disappointed by their lack of influence upon MEIs, the shift of the MEI agenda is a significant accomplishment. The decade of the 1990s has seen MEIs begin to acknowledge some responsibility for the social impact of their policies. To be sure, GSMs cannot claim sole responsibility for changes in the agenda, but their work in publicising the role of MEIs and issues of concern can take some credit. The institutions in this study have broadened their area of concern to address many of the subjects advanced by GSMs. Undoubtedly, the policy responses are not to the satisfaction of the social movements, but issues need to get on the agenda before they can be addressed. In the longer term a shifting agenda can be a significant factor of change.

All of the institutions have broadened the scope of their activity to include some of the issues of importance to GSMs. The World Bank has taken on notions of gender, although only to the extent that it is financially rewarding. They have also developed mechanisms to evaluate the environmental impact of their programmes. Recent restructuring has committed more resources to social development concerns (Bread for the World 1997c: 2). As a result of the Asian crisis

---

[8] During the course of interviews numerous people have suggested the following possibility, but no hard evidence exists to support such a theory.

they are beginning to look at labour not as an obstacle to development, but as a key strategic actor. The IMF, stung by the recent East Asian financial crisis and earlier criticisms, is taking further steps towards acknowledging that their prescriptions may need to include a social dimension if they are to be successful. In the WTO, provisions have been made for studying the relationship between environment and trade. The issue of labour adjustment and core labour standards has been broached. There are also signs that the lobbying by women's groups is starting to make an impact on Secretariat officials.

The result of this shifting agenda is that it is increasingly obvious that development, financial stability and trade have a social dimension. Despite the head in the sand approach of the 1980s, MEIs have not been able to insulate themselves from broader social concerns about their activity. In each case they have been forced to broaden their agenda to address, if not satisfy, the concerns of GSMs. More Bank money does now go to projects with a gender dimension, the IMF is in discussion with organised labour about structural adjustment programmes in parts of East Asia and the WTO is increasingly engaging with civil society about environmental and labour issues. The functions of the institutions are beginning to change as they attempt to deal with 'new issues'.

The degree to which a shifting agenda leads to new policies remains to be determined by continued political conflict at the global, international, national and local levels. However, it can be noted that a subtle change is underway as institutions adapt to complex multilateralism.

Conclusion

Despite the limits to complex multilateralism our study has revealed that a range of measures have been taken to inform social movements about, and sometimes include them in, MEI decision-making. It is useful to differentiate between short-term accomplishment and long term developments when attempting to determine the significance of this change in the form of governance. In the short term one can see a process of engagement, exchange of information and mutual learning. Members of the institutions and movements are becoming more aware of the roles and concerns of the other party. This contributes to an appreciation, if not acceptance, of each other's goals and possibilities for action. For example, far more members of the GSM

229

community have now gained an understanding of the role and function of the WTO (including its limits for action) than was ever true of the GATT. In the case of the World Bank, there is now some understanding that gender blind development strategies can weaken women's economic position and undermine social development goals. At a minimum, the MEI–GSM relationship signals a move to bridge the gap between the institutions of global economic governance and the mass of non-elite people governed by them.

In the longer term one can envision a range of possibilities for the MEI–GSM relationship from atrophy to effective partnership. The possibility of atrophy must be raised for two reasons. First, it is possible that the institutions or movements conclude that it no longer serves their purpose and give up on the relationship. This could occur if the institutions perceive GSM activity as inevitably hostile and incapable of movement. It could also occur if GSMs sense that openings in the MEI structure are designed only to deflect criticism through co-optation with little possibility of changing policy. Both scenarios are possible, but involve considerable costs for the institutions and movements in terms of heightened conflict.

A second reason for considering the possibility of atrophy is that GSM activity may be reliant upon the nature of the international system itself. It may be the case that the end of the Cold War and recent advances in communication technology have created a unique, rather than permanent, opening in the state system which allows for increased GSM activity and participation. A historical overview has pointed out that NGO participation in international institutions has been cyclical and corresponded with times of peace following events such as the First and Second World Wars (Charnovitz 1997). Perhaps the post-Cold War era is a similar temporary opening for civil society. Renewed interstate conflict between major powers might close off the opportunities for NGO and GSM participation.

There are, however, reasons to be more confident about the ongoing MEI–GSM relationship. The barriers of time and space which have formerly been so effective at separating the mass of people from each other are ever less formidable. The mobilisation of social groups and their connection with like-minded people in other parts of the world show no signs of lessening. This suggests that GSMs will continue to be active, even if they do contain a wide range of prescriptive proposals and strategies. From the institutional side there is also the possibility of development and change. It is gradually being accepted that organisations other than states have an interest in their operation. This includes GSMs. Moreover, organisations adapt and change as interests are redefined and new concerns are incorporated into the structure. Environmental, gender and labour concerns are on the agenda in ways that would have been deemed illegitimate in the 1970s. The possibility remains that they will increase in importance and lead to a transformation in the substance, as well as method, of governance.

Our study raises a number of wider questions which we cannot answer here, but may serve as a basis for further research, investigation and debate. Three questions seem most pressing.

1 What is the appropriate response to complex multilateralism?

This is a question of concern that goes beyond academics to state and multilateral organisation officials, as well as members of civil society. For some, complex multilateralism is a threat because it complicates governing or facilitates the input of groups with undesirable policy programmes. Liberals are concerned about a corruption of their project while many in the South worry about the unequal access of Northern based civil society groups. For those who see moderate social movements as the hope for increasing global democracy, complex multilateralism needs to be strengthened and supported. People with a more radical agenda seeking greater transformation away from the liberal programme may view complex multilateralism as a threat because of its ability to co-opt parts of the social movement community and deradicalise their project.

Policy prescriptions about complex multilateralism will depend upon one's view of the degree to which it is making global governance more democratic and whether or not that is a desirable objective. Our study indicates that the structures of MEI governance are becoming more pluralistic in the sense that they are confronting a wider range of actors. Constituencies previously excluded from the operation of these institutions are increasingly coming into contact with MEI officials and state decision makers involved in their operation. Issues of concern to sectors of civil society are gradually making it on to the MEI agenda. MEIs are becoming more responsive to some sections of public opinion, going beyond the interests of various state elites. In this sense, global governance is inching towards a more democratic form. However, the degree of responsiveness on the part of MEIs is limited. In addition, the composition of the most influential elements of GSMs reflects a narrow base in developed countries. Our conclusion is that there has been a very slight move to democratise MEIs, but the emphasis must be on its incremental and tentative nature.

For MEI supporters, this study should raise concerns about the legitimacy deficits of the IMF and WTO. The IMF and WTO lack solid public support in developed and developing countries. GSMs are key actors in the battle to shape issues and influence social norms. The greater openness of the Bank to GSM contact indicates that its future as a MEI is more secure than the IMF and WTO. These latter institutions need to give greater attention to their relationships with civil society and social movements. This may imply some policy compromises to the liberal agenda in return for the health of the institution.

2 Does complex multilateralism have a wider applicability?

Does our concept of complex multilateralism have an applicability that goes beyond our case studies of the IMF, World Bank and WTO? Would it be possible to apply it to other multilateral institutions or to the broader concept of regimes? We believe there are reasons that it might. First, we have chosen hard case studies in the sense that these are powerful interstate institutions dealing with issues of central economic concern to many states. These are institutions and issues that states rank high on their agenda whether they are developing states seeking to improve their economic plight or developed states seeking value for money or commercial advantage for their firms. If we have found evidence of a change in governance in these institutions the chances are high that it is happening in other places as well.

Second, a casual glance at other areas seems to mirror developments we have charted. The debate surrounding the Multilateral Agreement on Investment (MAI) at the OECD exhibits similar characteristics to those of this study (Mayne and Picciotto 1999; Strom 1998). An example in the security field is the International Landmines Convention banning landmines signed in Ottawa on 3 December 1997 (Price 1998; Tomlin, Cameron and Lawson 1998). The campaign to ban landmines was led by numerous groups in global civil society. This is evidence of the type of activity described as new multilateralism. Local groups of citizens from around the word united to pressure state decision makers into adopting more people-friendly policies. However, for implementation the treaty relies on the signature and enforcement of states. Their crucial role is highlighted by the decision of three great powers (United States, China and Russia) not to be influenced by the public campaign for reasons of national security. Multilateralism has become more complex, but it has not changed beyond recognition.

In the event that further research finds our assumption that complex multilateralism does not have wider applicability we would still argue for its significance on the basis of these case studies. This is because of the relationship between the iron triangle of liberalism (IMF–World Bank–WTO) and other elements of global governance. The liberalisation trinity are taking on an increasingly significant governance role to the detriment of other multilateral institutions. This is most clearly seen in the struggle to define the role of the WTO. It has expanded from the old GATT competencies of tariff reduction in goods into services and non-tariff barriers. It has moved beyond state policies to take up the issue of the behaviour of firms. An interesting example is the WTO working group on competition policy which is meant to ensure that companies behave in particular ways. Another is the agreement on intellectual property rights which is designed to defend the advantages of Northern TNCs. Similarly, the issue of investment has been brought into the WTO. This activity marginalises the importance of institutions such as the World Intellectual Property Organisation and the United Nations Conference on Trade and Development (UNCTAD). For example, although developing countries claimed that investment policy should be discussed in the context of UNCTAD, it is possible that an agreement first negotiated at the OECD will find its way into the WTO.

Similar examples could be made with regard to the rest of the UN system. Provisions for health or child care advocated by UNICEF or the World Health Organisation must exist in the context of IMF/World Bank structural adjustment prescriptions. Organised labour's attempt to have a social clause incorporated in the WTO was an acknowledgement of the failure of the ILO and a need to influence the institutions where power can be wielded most easily. This suggests a weakening of other aspects of the UN system. In addition, the large influence exercised by OECD states in the trinity suggest that the rising importance of MEIs will frustrate attempts at more equity based institution building.

233

3 What are the implications for understanding international organisation and international relations?

Our study lends some support to theoretical approaches that try to understand world order, international relations and multilateral organisation in a manner which integrates political activity at the national, international and global levels and pays attention to the role of groups across and within society. The activity of MEIs in our study indicates a growing awareness amongst officials that the stability of the international system which they are trying to construct rests on foundations in domestic civil societies and emerging global civil society. This goes beyond a sense that transnational relations will have an impact on state policies (Keohane and Nye 1972, Risse-Kappen 1995). It also goes beyond the view that domestic interest groups matter to the conduct of international policy because they influence states (Milner 1997). Our study has stressed the link between forms of international institution and social movements in which the state is just one area of contact and struggle (albeit an important one). The MEI–GSM relationship can be direct and need not be mediated by the state. Social forces within and across state borders are a factor in determining the nature of international order and organisation (Cox 1981; 1987). Attempts to explain developments which ignore this are incomplete.

The study also finds some evidence to support approaches that attempt to link changes in economic organisation with forms of governance (Murphy 1994). Complex multilateralism is a product of an increasingly interconnected global political economy. Structural changes such as the liberalisation of economies, globalisation of financial markets, and innovation in information technology are driving changes in regulatory forms and governance. These changes in governance are not yet complete. Complex multilateralism may be a temporary stepping stone to a more elaborate form of global governance or it may be an imperfect answer to a perplexing problem.

References

AAWORD, 1992. 'The Experience of the Association of African Women for Research and Development (AAWORD),' *Development Dialogue*, 1–2: 101–13 (New York: UN)

Abugre, Charles and Nancy Alexander, 1997. *NGOs and the International Monetary and Financial System*, Washington, DC: unpublished manuscript (24 July)

AFL–CIO, 1998. Testimony of George Becker for the AFL–CIO before the House of Representatives Banking and Financial Services Committee (3 February)

Alexander, Nancy, 1996. *Gender Justice and the World Bank*, Silver Spring, Md: Bread for the World Institute (September)

Alexander, Robin, 1994. 'The Emergence of Cross-Border Labor Solidarity,' *NACLA Report on the Americas*, 28 (1) (July/August): 42–8

Alger, Chadwick F., 1997. 'Transnational Social Movements, World Politics and Global Governance,' in Smith, Chatfield and Pagnucco, 1997, pp. 260–75

ALU, 1995. 'Towards a UN Labour Rights Convention,' and 'Conclusions of the National Consultation Concerning the Social Clause in World Trade Agreements,' *Asian Labour Update*, November 1995 – March 1996: 11–12, 17

1996. 'Global Business Unionism,' *Asian Labour Update*, August–October: 4

Annan, Kofi, 1999. 'Address of Secretary-General Annan to the World Economic Forum in Davos, Switzerland' (January 31), UN Press Release SG/SM/6881

Antrobus, Peggy, 1988. *The Impact of Structural Adjustment Policies on Women: The Experience of Caribbean Countries*, Santo Domingo: INSTRAW

Arrighi, Giovanni, Terrance K. Hopkins and Immanuel Wallerstein, 1989. *Antisystemic Movements*, London: Verso

Baldwin, Robert E., 1985. *The Political Economy of U.S. Import Policy*, Cambridge, Mass: MIT Press

Bandow, D., 1998. 'Kill the IMF,' *Fortune*, 25 March: 40

References

Bandow, D. and I. Vásquez (eds.), 1994. *Perpetuating Poverty: The World Bank, the IMF, and the Developing World*, Washington, DC: Cato Institute

Bangura, Yusuf, 1997. 'Policy Dialogue and Gendered Development: Institutional and Ideological Constraints,' Discussion Paper 87, Geneva: UNRISD

Bellmann, Christophe and Richard Gerster, 1996. 'Accountability in the World Trade Organisation,' *Journal of World Trade*, December: 31–74

Bhatnagar, Bhuvan, 1991. 'Non-Governmental Organisations and World Bank-Supported Projects in Asia: Lessons Learned,' Asia Technical Department Departmental Papers Series 2 (May), Washington, DC: World Bank

Bichsel, A., 1996. 'NGOs as Agents of Public Accountability and Democratisation in Intergovernmental Forums,' in W.M. Lafferty and J. Meadowcroft (eds.), *Democracy and the Environment: Problems and Prospects*, Cheltenham: Elgar, pp. 234–55

Biersteker, Thomas J., 1992. 'The Triumph of Neoclassical Economics,' in Rosenau and Czempiel (eds.), pp. 102–31

Blackden, Mark C. and Elizabeth Morris-Hughes, 1993. *Paradigm Postponed: Gender and Economic Adjustment in Sub-Saharan Africa*, Washington DC: Technical Department, Africa Region, World Bank (August)

Blair, Harry, 1997. 'Donors, Democratisation and Civil Society: Relating Theory to Practice,' in Hulme and Edwards (eds.), pp. 23–42

Boote, A.R. and K. Thugge, 1997. 'Debt Relief for Low-Income Countries: The HIPC Initiative,' IMF Pamphlet Series 51, Washington, DC; http://www.imf.org/external/np/exr/facts/hipc.htm.

BothENDS, 1995. *Annual Report 1994*, Amsterdam: BothENDS

Boulding, Elsie, 1993. *Women's Movements and Social Transformation in the Twentieth Century*, Meigaku, Japan: International Peace Research Institute Meigaku

Bramble, Barbara J. and Gareth Porter, 1992. 'NGOs and the Making of US International Environmental Policy,' in Hurrell and Kingsbury (eds.), pp. 313–53

Bread for the World, 1996. 'Downsizing the World Bank,' *News and Notices for World Bank Watchers*, 15 (November) (Silver Spring, Md: Bread for the World Institute)

    1997a. *News and Notices for World Bank Watchers*, 17 (April) (Silver Spring, Md: Bread for the World Institute)

    1997b. *News and Notices for World Bank Watchers*, 19 (December) (Silver Spring, Md: Bread for the World Institute)

    1997c. *News and Notices for World Bank Watchers*, 16 (January) (Silver Spring, Md: Bread for the World Institute)

Brecher, Jeremy, John Brown Childs and Jill Culter (eds.), 1993. *Global Visions: Beyond the New World Order*, Boston: South End Press

Brew, Jo, 1998. 'WTO, European Union Trade Policy and Women's Rights,' Paper presented to Globalism and Social Policy Programme (GASSP) Seminar 10–12 December

236

Bridges Weekly Trade News Digest, 1998. 'Clinton Endorses Call for High-Level WTO Meeting on Trade-Environment and Calls for WTO Openness,' *Bridges Weekly Trade News Digest*, 2 (18) (18 May)

Brown, William Adams, 1950. *The United States and the Restoration of World Trade*, Washington, DC: Brookings Institution

Bull, Hedley and Adam Watson, 1994. *The Expansion of International Society*, Oxford: Oxford University Press

Bullen, Sally and Brennan Van Dyke, 1996. *In Search of Sound Environment and Trade Policy: A Critique of Public Participation in the WTO*, Geneva: Center for International Environmental Law

Busch, Gary, 1983. *The Political Role of International Trade Unions*, London: Macmillan

Castells, Manuel, 1996. *The Rise of the Network Society*, Oxford: Blackwell

Cato Institute, 1998. http://www.cato.org/research/glob-st.html

Center of Concern, 1998. http://www.igc.org/coc/global.htm

Cernea, Michael, 1987. 'Nongovernmental Organisations and Local Development,' World Bank Discussion Paper 40, Washington, DC

Charnovitz, Steve, 1996. 'Participation of Nongovernmental Organisations in the World Trade Organisation,' *University of Pennsylvania Journal of International Economic Law*, 7 (1): 331–57

1997. 'Two Centuries of Particpation: NGOs and International Governance,' *Michigan Journal of International Law*, 18 (2) (Winter): 183–286

Charnovitz, Steve and John Wickham, 1995. 'NGOs and the Original International Trade Regime,' *Journal of World Trade*, October: 111–22

Clark, Anne Marie, Elisabeth J. Friedman and Kathryn Hochstetler, 1998. 'The Sovereign Limits of Global Civil Society: A Comparison of NGO Participation in UN World Conferences on the Environment, Human Rights, and Women,' *World Politics*, 51 (1) (October): 1–35

Commission on Global Governance, 1995. *Our Global Neighbourhood: The Report of the Commission on Global Governance*, Oxford: Oxford University Press

Congressional Quarterly Almanac, 1994. 'Foreign Aid Bill Clears Easily,' *Congressional Quarterly Almanac*, 50: 505–12

Connolly, William E., 1991. 'Democracy and Territoriality,' *Millennium*, 20 (3) (Winter): 463–84

Cornia, G.A., R. Jolly and Frances Stewart (eds.), 1987–8. *Adjustment with a Human Face*, 2 vols., Oxford: Clarendon/UNICEF

Cox, Robert W., 1969. 'The Executive Head: An Essay on Leadership in International Organisation,' *International Organisation*, 23 (2) (Spring): 205–30

1977. 'Labor and Hegemony,' *International Organisation*, 31 (3) (Summer): 385–424

1981. 'Social Forces, States and World Orders: Beyond International Relations Theory,' *Millennium*, 10 (2) (Summer): 126–55

1987. *Production, Power and World Order: Social Forces in the Making of History*, New York: Columbia University Press

References

Cox, Robert (ed.), 1997. *The New Realism: Perspectives on Multilateralism and World Order*, Basingstoke: Macmillan/United Nations University Press

Cox, Robert W. and Harold K. Jacobson (eds.), 1974. *The Anatomy of Influence: Decision Making in International Organisation*, New Haven: Yale University Press

Croome, John, 1995. *Reshaping the World Trading System*, Geneva: World Trade Organisation

Cruz, W. and R. Repetto, 1992. *The Environmental Effects of Stabilisation and Structural Adjustment Programs: The Philippines Case*, Washington, DC: World Resources Institute

Culter, A. Claire, Virginia Haufler and Tony Porter (eds.), 1999. *Private Authority and International Affairs*, Albany: State University of New York

Dalton, Russell J., 1994. *The Green Rainbow: Environmental Groups in Western Europe*, New Haven and London: Yale University Press

Das, Bhagirath Lal, 1998a. *An Introduction to the WTO Agreements*, London and Penang: Zed Books and Third World Network

　1998b. *The WTO Agreements: Deficiencies, Imbalances and Required Changes*, London and Penang: Zed Books and Third World Network

Dayal, Ashvin and Maitrayee Mukhopadhyay, 1995. 'Economic Liberalisation and Women: An Overview of Assumptions, Theory, and Experience,' *AGRA South 1995: Gender and Structural Adjustment*, Oxford: Oxfam

de la Court, Thijs, 1990. *Beyond Bruntland: Green Developments in the 1990s*, London and New Jersey: Zed Books; New York: New Horizons Press

de Vries, M., 1986. *The IMF in a Changing World, 1945–85*, Washington, DC: IMF

Deacon, Bob, Michelle Hulse and Paul Stubbs, 1997. *Global Social Policy: International Organisations and the Future of Welfare*, London: Sage

Denters, E., 1996. *Law and Policy of IMF Conditionality*, Dordrecht: Kluwer

Destler, I.M., 1986. *American Trade Politics: System Under Stress*, Washington, DC: Institute for International Economics

DGAP, 1995. *Structural Adjustment and the Spreading Crisis in Latin America*, Washington, DC: Development GAP

　1996a. *Democratic Alternatives to Structural Adjustment in the Americas*, Washington, DC: Development GAP

　1996b. *Women Standing up to Adjustment in Africa: A Report of the African Women's Economic Policy Network*, Washington, DC: Development GAP

Dhonte, P. and I. Kapur, 1997. 'Toward a Market Economy: Structures of Governance,' IMF Working Paper 97/11, Washington, DC: IMF

Dobson, Andrew, 1990. *Green Political Thought*, London: Routledge

Drake, C, 1994. 'The United Nations and NGOs: Future Roles,' in G.J. Demko and W.B. Wood (eds.), *Reordering the World: Geopolitical Perspectives on the Twenty-First Century*, Boulder: Westview, pp. 243–67

Dubro, Alec and Mike Konopacki, 1995. *The World Bank: A Tale of Power, Plunder and Resistance*, France: Public Services International

Eckersley, Robyn, 1994. *Environmentalism and Political Theory*, London: UCL Press

Economic and Social Research Council (ESRC), 1995. 'Call for Phase 2 Proposals on Structures of Global Governance,' London: ESRC (February)

Elson, Diane, 1991. 'Male Bias in Macro Economics: The Case of Structural Adjustment,' in Diane Elson (ed.), *Male Bias in the Development Process*, Manchester: Manchester University Press

Enders, Alice, 1996. 'Openness and the WTO: A Draft IISD Working Paper,' Winnipeg: Institute for Sustainable Development

Esty, Daniel, 1994. *Greening the GATT*, Washington, DC: Institute for International Economics

    1997. *Why the World Trade Organisation Needs Environmental NGOs*, Geneva: International Center for Trade and Sustainable Development

EURODAD, 1995. *EURODAD 1994 Annual Report* (mimeo)

    1996a. *Annual Report*, available at http://www.oneworld.org/eurodad/

    1996b. *EURODAD Multilateral Debt Update* (15 October)

    1996c. *EURODAD 1995 Annual Report* (mimeo)

    1997. *Solagral Seminar on Financial Markets* (Paris, 3–4 October) (unpublished minutes)

    1998a. 'The HIPC Debt Initiative: Any Impact on Poverty? Uganda, Mozambique and Nicaragua,' Brussels: EURODAD Infosheet

    1998b. 'Letters to the Managing Director of the IMF, the Chair of the IMF Interim Committee, and all Executive Directors of the IMF' (2–3 July)

Fallon, Peter and Zafiris Tzannatos, 1998. *Child Labour: Issues and Directions for the World Bank*, Washington, DC: World Bank

Far Eastern Economic Review, 1996. 'Indonesia: Driven by Dissent,' *Far Eastern Economic Review*, 26 December: 14–15

Feinberg, R.E. and V. Kallab, 1985. *Adjustment Crisis in the Third World*, Washington, DC: Overseas Development Council

Feldstein, Martin, 1998. 'Refocusing the IMF,' *Foreign Affairs*, 77 (2) (March/April): 20–33

Felice, William, 1997. 'The Copenhagen Summit: A Victory for the World Bank?' *Social Justice*, 24 (1): 107–19

Fifty Years Is Enough, 1999. http://www.50years.org

Finlayson, Jock A. and Mark W. Zacher, 1981. 'The GATT and the Regulation of Trade Barriers: Regime Dynamics and Functions,' *International Organisation*, 35 (4) (Autumn): 273–314

Fischer, Stanley, 1998. 'In Defence of the IMF,' *Foreign Affairs* July/August: 103–6

Floro, M.S., 1994. 'The Dynamics of Economic Change and Gender Roles, Export Cropping in the Philippines,' in Sparr (ed.), pp. 116–33

FOE, 1996a. *Fact Sheet: International Monetary Fund*, September, Friends of the Earth

    1996b. 'A Call to Close the Committee on Trade and the Environment,' Friends of the Earth Briefing Paper (December), Amsterdam: Friends of the Earth

FOE-US, 1998. Letter to the Executive Director for the USA (July)

References

Folbre, Nancy, 1986. 'Hearts and Spades: Paradigms of Household Economics,' *World Development*, 14 (2): 245–55

Ford, Lucy H., 1998. 'The Global Enclosure: Social Movements and the Globalisation of Environmental Management,' Paper prepared for the Convention of the International Studies Association (17–21 March), Minneapolis

Fox, Jonathan A. and David L. Brown (eds.), 1998. *The Struggle for Accountability: The World Bank, NGOs and Grassroots Movements*, Cambridge, Mass: MIT Press

Gale, Fred. 1998. 'Cave "Cave! Hic dragones": a Neo-Gramscian Deconstruction and Reconstruction of International Regime Theory,' *Review of International Political Economy*, 5 (2) (Summer): 252–83

Gandhi, V.P. (ed.), 1996. *Macroeconomics and the Environment*, Washington, DC: IMF

Garner, Robert, 1996. *Environmental Politics*, London: Harvester Wheatsheaf

GATT, 1992. *Trade and Environment Report*, Geneva: GATT Secretariat

  1993a. 'Bulletin – Trade and Environment,' GATT Doc.TE 001 (1 April)

  1993b. 'Bulletin – Trade and the Environment,' GATT Doc. TE 002 (July)

  1994. 'Report on the GATT Symposium on Trade, Environment, and Sustainable Development,' GATT Doc. TE 008 (28 July)

Germain, Randall and Michael Kenny, 1998. 'International Relations Theory and the New Gramscians,' *Review of International Studies* 24 (1) (January): 3–21

Gerster, R., 1982. 'The IMF and Basic Needs Conditionality,' *Journal of World Trade Law*, 16 (6) (November/December): 497–517

  1993. 'Proposals for Voting Reform Within the International Monetary Fund,' *Journal of World Trade*, 27 (3) (June): 121–36

Gilbert, Christopher L., Raul Hopkins, Andrew Powell and Amian Roy, 1996. 'The World Bank: Its Functions and Its Future,' Global Economic Institutions Working Paper 15 (July)

Gill, Stephen, 1990. *American Hegemony and the Trilateral Commission*, Cambridge: Cambridge University Press

Gill, Stephen, (ed.), 1997, *Globalisation, Democratisation and Multilateralism*, Basingstoke: Macmillan/United Nations University Press

Goetz, Anne Marie (ed.), 1997. *Getting Institutions Right for Women in Development*, London: Zed Books

Goetz, Anne Marie, Simon Maxwell and Henry Maniyire, 1994. *Poverty Assessment and Public Expenditure: Country Field Study – Uganda*, Brighton: Institute of Development Studies

Gordenker, Leon and Thomas G. Weiss, 1996. 'Pluralizing Global Governance: Analytical Approaches and Dimensions,' in Weiss and Gordenker (eds.), 17–47

Gordon, D.F. and C. Gwin, 1998. 'Poor Country Debt Relief: Taking the Hiccups out of HIPC,' ODC Briefing Paper, Washington, DC

Government of Kenya, 1996. *Economic Reforms for 1996–1998: The Policy Framework Paper*, Nairobi: Government of Kenya

240

Griesgraber J.M. and B.G. Gunter (eds.), 1995. *Promoting Development: Effective Global Institutions for the Twenty-First Century*, London: Pluto
    1996 *The World's Monetary System: Toward Stability and Sustainability in the Twenty-First Century*, London: Pluto

Guitián, M., 1992. *The Unique Nature of the Responsibilities of the International Monetary Fund*, Washington, DC: IMF

Gupta, S., K. Miranda and I. Parry, 1993. 'Public Expenditure Policy and the Environment: A Review and Synthesis,' IMF Working Paper 93/27, Washington, DC

Hall, John A. (ed.), 1995. *Civil Society: Theory History Comparison*, Cambridge: Polity Press

Hanlon, J., 1997. 'Dublin and Maputo Challenges to the IMF,' in *Common Cause: Challenging Development Strategies: The International Monetary Fund and the World Bank*, Dublin: Irish Mozambique Solidarity/Debt and Development Coalition, pp. 24–5

Hansenne, M., 1996. 'Trade and Labour Standards: Can Common Rules be Agreed?' Address by Director-General, ILO to 464th Wilton Park Conference (Sussex, 6 March)

Harris, Bob, 1996. 'The United Nations, NGOs and Global Governance,' Statement by Bob Harris of Education International at a UN–NGO Global Governance Conference, *Development Dossiers* (August): 40–1

Harrod, Jeffrey, 1992. *Labour and Third World Debt*, Brussels: ICEF

Hasenclever, Andreas, Peter Mayer and Volker Rittberger, 1997. *Theories of International Regimes*, Cambridge: Cambridge University Press

Herfkens, Eveline, 1994. 'Statement by Eveline Herfkens,' unpublished memo to the Executive Board of the IBRD, IDA, IFC (13 April), Washington, DC

Hino, Toshik, 1996. 'A Tale of Two Projects: Lessons Drawn From World Bank–NGO Partnerships,' PSP Discussion Paper Series (April), Washington, DC: World Bank

Horta, Korinna, 1996. 'The World Bank and the International Monetary Fund,' in Werksman (ed.), pp. 131–47

Hulme, David and Michael Edwards (eds.), 1997. *NGOs, States and Donors*, London: Macmillan

Hunter, David and Lori Udall, 1994. 'The World Bank's New Inspection Panel: Will it Increase the Bank's Accountability?' CIEL Issue Brief 1 (April), Washington, DC

Hurrell, Andrew and Benedict Kingbury (eds.), 1992. *The International Politics of the Environment*, Oxford: Clarendon Press

ICFTU, 1995. *Rethinking the Role of the IMF and World Bank: ICFTU Proposals to the Annual Meetings of the Board of Governors of the IMF and World Bank* (10–12 October), Washington
    1996a. *A Users' Guide to the UN Social Summit*, Brussels: ICFTU
    1996b. *International Workers' Rights and Trade: The Need for Dialogue*, Brussels: ICFTU

1996c. *The Global Market: Trade Unionism's Greatest Challenge*, Brussels: ICFTU

1996d. Seminar on 'Follow up to the World Social Summit for Development,' Organised by ICFTU, UNDP and ILO (Brussels 29 March)

1996e. 'International Labour Standards and Trade,' Address by Bill Jordan, General Secretary of the ICFTU, to the ICFTU Conference on Labour Standards (Singapore, 6 December)

1997. 'Internationally-Recognized Core Labour Standards in Fiji,' Report for the WTO General Council Review of the Trade Policies of Fiji (Brussels, 9–10 April)

1998. 'ICFTU Welcomes ILO Declaration on Fundamental Principles and Rights at Work,' ICFTU Press Release, 19 June

1999a. 'Social Policy, Good Governance, Core Labour Standards and Development,' Discussion Paper for the Meeting on 20 January 1999 between the ICFTU and Executive Directors and Staff of the World Bank, Brussels: ICFTU

1999b. 'Statement to the High-Level Symposia of the World Trade Organisation (WTO) on Trade and Environment and Trade and Development,' 15–16, 17–18 March, Brussels: ICFTU

IDS, 1994. *Poverty Assessment and Public Expenditure Study for the SPA Working Group on Poverty and Social Policy*, Brighton: Institute of Development Studies for the ODA and SIDA (July)

IISD, 1996. *The World Trade Organisation and Sustainable Development*, Winnipeg: International Institute for Sustainable Development

ILO, 1994. *Constitution of the International Labour Organisation and Standing Orders of the International Labour Conference*, Geneva: International Labour Office

1997a. *The ILO, Standard Setting and Globalisation: Report of the Director-General*, Geneva: International Labour Office

1997b. 'Employers: After Singapore, the ILO Must Act, and Quickly,' *World of Work: The Magazine of the ILO*, 20 (June): 14

1998a. 'ILO Declaration on Fundamental Principles and Rights at Work,' *International Labour Conference 86th Session* (June), Geneva

1998b. 'Fundamental Rights Declaration Clears Final Hurdle, ILO Conference Seeks End to Child Labour Abuses,' *International Labour Organisation Press Release*, 18 June

ILRF, 1996. 'Rugmark After One Year: Appraisal of a New Effort at Social Marketing in the Interest of Children,' Washington: International Labor Rights Fund

Imber, Mark F., 1989. *The USA, ILO UNESCO and IAEA: Politicisation and Withdrawal in the Specialized Agencies*, London: Macmillan

IMF, 1966. *Annual Report 1966*, Washington, DC: International Monetary Fund; http://imf.org/external/np/ext/facts/glance.htm

1989. 'The Technical Assistance and Training Services of the International Monetary Fund,' Pamphlet Series 43, Washington: International Monetary Fund

1990. *Functions and Organisation of the Staff Financial Year 1991*, Washington, DC: IMF Budget and Planning Division

1992. IMF Speeches 92/14

1993. 'Seminar Explores Links between Macro Policy and the Environment,' *IMF Survey*, 22 (11) (14 June): 177, 187

1994a. 'IMF: 50 Facts (30. IMF Technical Assistance to Member Countries),' Washington, DC: IMF External Relations Department; http://imf.org/external/np/ext/facts/tech.htm

1994b. 'Interim Committee Declaration on Cooperation to Strengthen the Global Expansion' (2 October)

1995a. 'Social Dimensions of the IMF's Policy Dialogue,' Pamphlet Series 47, Washington, DC: IMF

1995b. 'Financial Organisation and Operations of the IMF,' Pamphlet Series 45, 4th edn., Washington, DC: IMF Treasurer's Department

1995c. 'Address by the Managing Director of the International Monetary Fund to the UN World Summit for Social Development,' (7 March) Copenhagen

1995d. 'Linking Macroeconomics and the Environment,' *IMF Survey*, 24 (11) (5 June): 172–5

1995e. 'Growth and Income Equity: A Role for the IMF?' *IMF Survey*, 24 (12) (19 June): 189–91

1995f. 'Gender Issues in Economic Adjustment Discussed at UN Conference on Women,' *IMF Survey*, 24 (18) (25 September): 287f.

1996a. *Annual Report 1996*; http://www.imf.org/external/np/obp/orgcht.htm

1996b. 'The IMF Opens Its Archives,' *IMF Survey*, 25 (3) (5 February): 44–5

1996c. 'Fiscal Issues Are a Growing Concern of the IMF,' *IMF Survey*, 25 (6) (19 March)

1996d. IMF Press Release 96/17, 15 April

1996e. IMF Press Release 96/18, 16 April

1996f. IMF Press Release 96/19, 17 April

1996g. *IMF Survey*, 25 (11) (3 June)

1996h. IMF Press Release 96/32, 14 June

1996i. 'The Impacts of Globalisation and Regional Integration on Workers and Their Trade Unions' (by Michel Camdessus, 26 June), Brussels: ICFTU 16th World Congress

1996j. 'IMF Reinforces Evaluation,' *IMF Survey*, 25 (15) (29 July): 254

1996k. IMF Press Release 96/47, 19 September

1996l. 'Social Dimensions of the IMF's Policy Dialogue,' IMF Fact Sheet, 24 September

1997a. *Annual Report 1997*, Washington, DC: IMF

1997b. *Good Governance: The IMF's Role*, Washington, DC: IMF

1997c. 'IMF Executive Board Adopts New Arrangements to Borrow,' *IMF Survey*, 26 (3) (10 February): 33–4; http://imf.org/external/np/ext/facts/nab.htm

1997d. *IMF Survey*, 26 (9) (12 May)

1997e. 'Meeting with Church Leaders Highlights Strategy beyond Debt Reduction,' *IMF Survey*, 26 (13) (7 July): 208

References

1997f. 'IMF Adopts Guidelines Regarding Governance Issues,' *IMF Survey,* 26 (15) (5 August): 233–8

1998a. IMF News Brief 98/27

1998b. *Report of the Group of Independent Persons Appointed to Conduct an Evaluation of Certain Aspects of the Enhanced Structural Adjustment Facility,* Washington, DC: IMF

1998c. Managing Director's speech to Transparency International (21 January); http://www.imf.org/external/np/speeches/1998/012198.htm

1998d. IMF Press Release 98/2, 6 February

1998e. 'Good Governance has become Essential in Promoting Growth and Stability,' *IMF Survey,* 27 (3) (9 February): 36–8

1998f. 'IMF Study Group Report: Transparency and Evaluation' (April), Washington, DC: mimeo

1998g. *IMF Survey,* 27 (8) (27 April)

1998h. 'Debate on Equity Invites Diverse Perspectives, Generates Pragmatic Prescriptions,' *IMF Survey,* 27 (12) (22 June): 189–93

1998i. 'IMF Announces External Evaluation of Its Surveillance Role,' *IMF Survey,* 27 (13) (6 July): 218

1998j. *Annual Report 1998,* Washington, DC: IMF

1998k. http://www.imf.org/external/np/exr/facts/hipc.htm

IUCN, 1996. *The 'Trade and Environment' Agenda: Survey of Major Issues and Proposals. From Marrakesh to Singapore,* Bonn: IUCN

Jackson, John H., 1998. *The World Trade Organisation: Constitution and Jurisprudence,* London: Royal Institute of International Affairs

James, H., 1996. *International Monetary Cooperation since Bretton Woods,* New York: IMF/Oxford University Press

John Paul II, 1995. *Ecclesia in Africa,* papal encyclical, September

Jones, Adam, 1994. 'Wired World: Communication Technology, Governance and Democratic Uprisisng,' in Edward Commor (ed.), *The Global Political Economy of Communication,* New York: St. Martin's Press, pp. 145–64

Jordan, L., 1996. 'The Bretton Woods Challengers,' in Griesgraber and Gunter (eds.), pp. 75–88.

Jubilee 2000 Campaign, 1999a. http://www.j2000usa.org

1999b. http://www.oneworld.org/jubilee2000

Kapur, Devesh, 1998. 'The IMF: A Cure or a Curse?' *Foreign Policy,* 111 (Summer): 114–29

Kardam, Nuket, 1991. *Bringing Women In: Women's Issues in International Development Programs,* Boulder: Lynne Reinner

Keck, Margaret and Kathryn Sikkink, 1998. *Activists Beyond Borders; Advocacy Networks in International Politics,* Ithaca: Cornell University Press

Keohane, Robert and Joseph Nye, 1972. *Transnational Relations and World Politics,* Cambridge, Mass.: Harvard University Press

1977. *Power and Interdependence: World Politics in Transition,* Boston: Little, Brown and Company

1987. 'Power and Interdependence Revisited,' *International Organization*, 41 (4) (Autumn): 725–53

Killick, T. (ed.), 1982. *Adjustment and Financing in the Developing World: The Role of the International Monetary Fund*, Washington, DC: IMF (published proceedings of an IMF-ODI seminar in October 1981)

Kock, Karin, 1969. *International Trade Policy and the GATT 1947–1967*, Stockholm: Almqvist & Widsell

Kopits, G. and J. Craig, 1998. 'Transparency in Government Operations,' IMF Occasional Paper 158, Washington, DC: IMF

Krause, Keith and Andy W. Knight (eds.), 1994. *States, Society and the UN System: Changing Perspectives on Multilateralism*, Tokyo: United Nations Press

Kusago, Takayoshi and Zafiris Tzannatos, 1998. 'Export Processing Zones: A Review in Need of an Update,' Social Protection Discussion Paper 9802 (January)

Lindblom, Charles, 1977. *Politics and Markets*, New York: Basic Books

Lipow, Arthur, 1996. *Power and Counterpower: The Union Response to Global Capital*, London: Pluto

Lipschutz, Ronnie D., 1992. 'Reconstructing World Politics: The Emergence of Global Civil Society,' *Millennium*, 21 (3) (Winter): 389–420

Lorwin, Lewis L., 1973. *The International Labor Movement*, Westport: Greenwood Press

Malena, Carmen, 1995. *Working with NGOs: A Practical Guide to Operational Collaboration between the World Bank and Non-governmental Organisations* (March), Washington, DC: World Bank Operations Policy Department
1996. *Working with NGOs: A Toolkit for World Bank Field Offices* (March), Washington, DC: World Bank NGO Unit, PSP

Martin, Lisa L. and Beth A. Simmons, 1998. 'Theories and Empirical Studies of International Institutions,' *International Organisation*, 52 (4) (Autumn): 729–57

Martin, M., 1993. *Catalyst or Debt Collector: The IMF's Role in Aid and Debt Talks: Time for Change*, London: External Finance for Africa

Maucher, Helmut, 1997. *Financial Times Exporter* (December)

Mauro, P., 1997. 'Why Worry about Corruption?' Economic Issues Series, 6, Washington, DC: IMF

Mayne, Ruth and Sol Picciotto (eds.), 1999. *Regulating International Business – Beyond the MAI*, Basingstoke: Macmillan

Mayoux, Linda, 1998. 'Gender Accountability and NGOs: Avoiding the Black Hole,' in Miller and Razavi (eds), pp. 172–93

McCormick, John, 1989. *The Global Environment Movement*, London: Belhaven Press

McDowell, L. and G. Court, 1994. 'Gender Divisions of Labour in the Post-Fordist Economy: The Maintenance of Occupational Sex Segregation in the Financial Services Sector,' *Environment and Planning A*, 26 (9) (September): 1397–418

References

Meyer, C.A., 1995. 'Opportunism and NGOs: Entrepeneurship and Green North–South Transfers,' *World Development* (August): 1277

Miller, Carol and Shahra Razavi (eds.), 1998. *Missionaries and Mandarins: Feminist Engagement with Development Institutions*, London: Intermediate Technology

Milner, Helen V., 1988. *Resisting Protectionism: Global Industries and the Politics of International Trade*, Princeton: Princeton University Press

1997. *Interests, Institutions and Information: Domestic Politics and International Relations*, Princeton: Princeton University Press

Mistry, P.S., 1994. *Multilateral Debt: An Emerging Crisis?*, The Hague: FONDAD

1996. *Resolving Africa's Multilateral Debt Problem: A Response to the IMF*, The Hague: FONDAD

Mohanty, Chandra Talpade, 1991. 'Under Western Eyes: Feminist Scholarship and Colonial Discourses,' in Chandra Mohanty, Anna Russo and Lourdes Torres (eds.), *Third World Women and the Politics of Feminism*, Bloomingdale: Indiana University Press, pp. 51–80

Moody, Kim, 1997. *Workers in a Lean World: Unions in the International Economy*, London: Verso

Mort, Jo (ed.), 1998. *Not Your Father's Union Movement: Inside the AFL–CIO*, London: Verso

Murphy, Craig N., 1994. *International Organisation and Industrial Change: Global Governance Since 1850*, Cambridge: Polity Press

Muzondo, T.R. *et al.*, 1990. 'Public Policy and the Environment: A Survey of the Literature,' IMF Working Paper 90/56, Washington, DC

Nelson, Paul, 1995. *The World Bank and Non-Governmental Organisations*, London: Macmillan

1996. 'Internationalising Economic and Environmental Policy: Transnational NGO Networks and the World Bank's Expanding Influence,' *Millennium* (July): 605–633

O'Brien, Robert, 1998. 'Shallow Foundations: Labour and the Selective Regulation of Free Trade,' in Gary Cook (ed.), *The Economics and Politics of International Trade*, London: Routledge, pp. 105–24

ODA/ICRW, 1995. *Women's Issues in World Bank Lending: A Preliminary Summary of Findings*, draft report (August), Washington DC: Overseas Development Council/International Center for Research on Women

OECD, 1996. *Trade, Employment and Labour Standards: A Study of Core Workers' Rights and International Trade*, Paris: Organisation for Economic Cooperation and Development

Ogley, Roderick C., 1969. 'Towards a General Theory of International Organisation,' *International Relations*, 3: 599–619

Osunsade F.L. and P. Gleason, 1992. *IMF Assistance to Sub-Saharan Africa*, Washington, DC: IMF

Oxfam, 1995. *A Case for Reform: Fifty Years of the IMF and World Bank*, Oxford: Oxfam Insight

1998. 'Lack of Political Will Is Causing Poor Country Debt Relief to Fail,' Oxfam International Press Release, 14 April

Pepper, David, 1996. *Modern Environmentalism*, London: Routledge

Pescatore, Pierre, 1993. 'The GATT Dispute Settlement Mechanism,' *Journal of World Trade*, 27 (1) (February): 5–20

Petersmann, Ernst-Ulrich, 1997. *The GATT/WTO Dispute Settlement System: International Law, International Organisations and Dispute Settlement*, London: Kluwer Law International

Peterson, M.J., 1992. 'Transnational Activity, International Society and World Politics,' *Millennium*, 21 (3) (Winter): 371–89

Piddington, Kenneth, 1992. 'The Role of the World Bank,' in Hurrell and Kingsbury (eds.), pp. 212–17

Price, John, 1945. *The International Labour Movement*, London: Oxford University Press and RIIA

Price, Richard, 1998. 'Reversing the Gun Sights: Transnational Civil Society Targets Land Mines,' *International Organisation* 52 (3) (Summer): 613–44

Princen, Thomas and Mathias Finger, 1994. *Environmental NGOs in World Politics*, London: Routledge

Quadir, Fahimul and Timothy M. Shaw, 1996. 'Relations between Non- and Inter-Governmental Organisations: Comparing the United Nations System and the World Bank,' Paper presented to the ISA Conference, San Diego, USA 16–20 April

Radosh, Ronald, 1969. *American Labor and United States Foreign Policy*, New York: Random House

Raffer, K. and H.W. Singer, 1996. *The Foreign Aid Business: Economic Assistance and Development Co-operation*, Cheltenham: Elgar

Rao, Aruna and David Kelleher, 1997. 'Engendering Organisational Change: The BRAC Case,' in Goetz (ed.), pp. 123–39

Raustiala, Kal, 1997. 'States, NGOs and International Environmental Institutions,' *International Studies Quarterly*, 41 (4) (December): 719–40

Razavi, Shahra and Carol Miller, 1995. 'Gender Mainstreaming: A Study of Efforts by the UNDP, the World Bank and the ILO to Institutionalise Gender Issues,' Occasional Paper 4 (August), Geneva: UNRISD

Reed, D. (ed.), 1992. *Structural Adjustment and the Environment*, Boulder: Westview

1996. *Structural Adjustment, the Environment and Sustainable Development*, London: Earthscan

Rich, Bruce, 1994. *Mortgaging the Earth: The World Bank, Environmental Impoverishment and the Crisis of Development*, London: Earthscan

1995. 'Statement of Bruce Rich on Behalf of the Environmental Defense Fund, National Wildlife Federation, Sierra Club, Greenpeace,' before The House Committee on Banking and Financial Services Subcommittee on Domestic and International Monetary Policy Concerning The World Bank: Effectiveness and Needed Reforms (27 March)

References

Risse-Kappen, Thomas (ed.) 1995. *Bringing Transnational Relations Back In*, Cambridge: Cambridge University Press

Rosenau, James N. and Ernst-Otto Czempiel (eds.), 1992. *Governance Without Government: Order and Change in World Politics*, Cambridge: Cambridge University Press

Rowlands, Ian, 1992. 'The International Politics of the Environment and Development: The Post-UNCED Agenda,' *Millennium*, 21 (2): 209–24

Ruggie, John Gerard, 1982. 'International Regimes, Transactions, and Change: Embedded Liberalism in the Postwar Economic Order,' *International Organisation*, 36 (2) (Spring): 379–415

Ruggie, John Gerard (ed.), 1993. *Multilateralism Matters: The Theory and Praxis of an Institutional Form*, New York: Columbia University Press

Rupert, Mark E., 1995. '(Re) Politicizing the Global Economy: Liberal Common Sense and Ideological Struggle in the US NAFTA Debate,' *Review of International Political Economy*, 2 (4) (Autumn): 658–92

Saito, Katrine, 1992. *Raising the Productivity of Women Farmers in Sub-Saharan Africa*, Overview Report, Washington, DC: World Bank, Women in Development Division, Population and Human Resources Department

Sakamoto, Yoshikazu (ed.), 1994. *Global Transformation: Challenges to the State System*, Tokyo: United Nations University Press

Salmen, Lawrence F. and A. Page Eaves, 1989. 'World Bank Work with Nongovernmental Organisations,' Policy, Planning and Research Working Paper 305, Washington, DC: World Bank

  1991. 'Interactions between Nongovernmental Organisations, Governments, and the World Bank: Evidence from Bank Projects,' in Samuel Paul and Arturo Israel (eds.), *Nongovernmental Organisations and the World Bank: Cooperation for Development*, Washington, DC: World Bank, pp. 94–133

SAPRIN 1999a. http://www.igc.org/dgap/saprin

  1999b. http://worldbank.org/html1/prddr/sapri/saprihp.htm

Schadler, S. (ed.), 1995. 'IMF Conditionality: Experience under Stand-By and Extended Arrangements. Part II: Background Papers,' IMF Occasional Paper 129, Washington, DC

Schadler, S., A. Bennett, M. Carkovic, L.-D. Mireaux, M. Mecagni, J.H.J. Morsink and M.A. Savastano, 1995. 'IMF Conditionality: Experience under Stand-By and Extended Arrangements. Part I: Key Issues and Findings,' IMF Occasional Paper 128, Washington, DC

Schadler, S. (study director), H. Bredenkamp (principal author) *et al.*, 1997. 'The ESAF at Ten Years: Economic Adjustment and Reform in Low-Income Countries,' IMF Occasional Paper 156, Washington, DC

Schadler, S., F. Rozwadowski, S. Tiwari and D.O. Robinson 1993. 'Economic Adjustment in Low-Income Countries: Experience under the Enhanced Structural Adjustment Facility,' IMF Occasional Paper 106, Washington, DC

Schartzman, S., 1986. *Bankrolling Disasters*, Washington, DC: Sierra Club

Schechter, Michael (ed.), 1998a. *Future Multilateralism: The Political and Social Framework*, Basingstoke: Macmillan/United Nations University Press

1998b *Innovation in Multilateralism*, Basingstoke: Macmillan/United Nations University Press

Schlagenhof, Markus, 1996. 'Trade Measures Based on Environment Processes and Production Methods,' *Journal of World Trade*, December: 123–55

Scholte, Jan Aart, 1997. 'Global Capitalism and the State,' *International Affairs*, 73 (3): 427–52

1999a. 'Civil Society and a Democratisation of the International Monetary Fund,' in S.O. Vandersluis and P. Yeros (eds.), *Poverty in World Politics: Whose Global Era?*, London: Macmillan, pp. 91–116

1999b. ' "In the Foothills": Relations between the IMF and Civil Society,' in R. Higgott and A. Bieler (eds.), *Non-State Actors and Authority in the Global System*, London: Routledge, pp. 256–73

Scott, Alan, 1990. *Ideology and the New Social Movements*, London: Routledge

Sen, Gita and Caren Grown, 1987. *Development, Crises, and Alternative Visions: Third World Women's Perspectives*, New York: Monthly Review Press

Serageldin, Ismail, 1996. 'Making Development Sustainable,' in Serageldin and Steers (eds.), pp. 1–5

Serageldin, Ismail and Andres Steers, 1996 (eds.), *Making Development Sustainable*, Washington, DC: World Bank

Shaw, Linda, 1997. 'The Labor Behind the Label; Clean Clothes Campaigns in Europe,' in Andrew Ross (ed.), *No Sweat: Fashion, Free Trade and the Rights of Garment Workers*, New York: Verso, pp. 215–20

Shaw, Martin, 1994a. 'Civil Society and Global Politics: Beyond a Social Movements Approach,' *Millennium*, 23 (3): 647–67

1994b. *Global Society and International Relations: Sociological Concepts and Political Perspectives*, Cambridge: Polity Press

Shihata, Ibrahim F.I., 1992. 'The World Bank and Non-Governmental Organisations,' *Cornell International Law Journal*, 25 (3): 623–41

Shrybman, Steven, 1990. 'International Trade and the Environment: An Environmental Assessment of the General Agreement on Tariffs and Trade,' *The Ecologist*, 20 (1): 30–4

Siddarth, Veena, 1995. 'Gendered Participation: NGOs and the World Bank,' *IDS Bulletin*, July (Brighton: Institute of Development Studies)

1996. 'Gender Advocacy and the World Bank,' unpublished manuscript

Sinclair, Timothy J., 1994. 'Passing Judgement: Credit Rating Processes as Regulating Mechanisms of Governance,' *Review of International Political Economy*, 1 (1) (Spring): 133–60

Skilton, T.E., 1993. 'GATT and the Environment in Conflict – the Tuna–Dolphin Dispute and the Quest for an International Conservation Strategy,' *Cornell International Law Journal*, 26 (2): 455–94

Sklair, Leslie, 1994. 'Global Sociology and Global Environmental Change,' in Michael Redclift and Ted Benton (eds.), *Social Theory and the Global Environment*, London: Routledge, pp. 210–12

1997. 'Social Movements for Global Capitalism,' *Review of International Political Economy*, Autumn: 514–38

Smith, Jackie, Charles Chatfield and Ron Pagnucco, 1997. *Transnational Social Movements and Global Politics: Solidarity Beyond the State*, Syracuse: Syracuse University Press

Somers, J., 1997. 'Breaking the Consensus: Ireland and the IMF's Enhanced Structural Adjustment Facility: A Case Study,' in *Common Cause: Challenging Development Strategies: The International Monetary Fund and the World Bank*, Dublin: Irish Mozambique Solidarity/Debt and Development Coalition, pp. 34–7

Soros, George, 1997. 'The Capitalist Threat,' *Atlantic Monthly*, February: 45–58

South Letter, 1997. 'How to Achieve Labour Standards: A NAM response to the ILO Director General's Report on The ILO, Standard Setting and Globalisation,' *South Letter*, 28 (1–2): 16–18

Sparr, Pamela (ed.), 1994. *Mortgaging Women's Lives: Feminist Critiques of Structural Adjustment*, London: Zed Books

Spooner, Dave, 1989. *Partners or Predators: International Trade Unionism and Asia*, Hong Kong: Asia Monitor Resource Centre

Ssemogerere, G. with M. Sengendo and R. Kiggundu, 1995. *Women and Structural Adjustment: A Case Study of Arua District, Uganda*, Kampala: Uganda Women's Network

Staudt, Kathleen, 1997. *Women, International Development, and Politics: The Bureaucratic Mire*, Philadelphia: Temple University Press

Stern, Nicholas with Francisco Ferreira, 1993. 'The World Bank as Intellectual Actor,' LSE and STICERD, DEP 50 (November)

Stiglitz, Joseph E., 1998. 'Towards a New Paradigm for Development: Strategies, Policies and Processes,' Ninth Raul Prebisch Lecture, 19 October, UNCTAD

Stopford, John and Susan Strange, 1991. *Rival States, Rival Firms*, Cambridge: Cambridge University Press

Stotsky, J.G., 1996. 'Gender Biases in Tax Systems,' IMF Discussion Paper 96/99, Washington, DC

Strange, Susan, 1996. *The Retreat of the State: The Diffusion of Power in the World Economy*, Cambridge: Cambridge University Press

Strom, N., 1998. 'Taking Stock of the NGO Activity on MAI,' *ICDA Journal*, 6 (1): 60–4

Tanzi, V., 1998. 'Corruption around the World: Causes, Consequences, Scope, and Cures,' IMF Working Paper 98/63, Washington, DC

Taylor, Lucy, 1996. 'Exploring Civil Society in Post Authoritarian Regimes,' in Ian Hampsher-Monk and Jeffery Stanyer (eds.), *Contemporary Political Studies 1996*, vol. II, Glasgow: Proceedings of the Annual Conference of the Political Studies Association, Political Studies Association of the United Kingdom, pp. 778–85

Thiele, Leslie Paul, 1993. 'Making Democracy Safe for the World: Social Movements and Global Politics,' *Alternatives*, 18 (3) (Summer): 273–305

Thompson, Karen Brown, 1997. 'Women's Rights and the United Nations: Reflections of Gender in International Institutions,' Paper presented to the Annual Meeting of the American Political Science Association (28–31 August), Washington DC

Tinker, Irene, 1990. 'The Making of a Field: Advocates, Practitioners, and Scholars,' in Irene Tinker (ed.), *Persistent Inequalities: Women and World Development*, Oxford: Oxford University Press

Tomlin, Brian, Maxwell Cameron and Robert Lawson, 1998. *To Walk Without Fear: The Global Movement to Ban Landmines*, Toronto: Oxford University Press

Torfs, M., 1996. *The IMF Handbook: Arming NGOs with Knowledge*, Brussels: Friends of the Earth Europe

TWN, 1996. 'Joint NGO Statement on Issues and Proposals for the WTO Ministerial Conference' (8 December), Singapore: Third World Network

UAW, 1998. UAW International Executive Board Resolution on US Contributions to the International Monetary Fund (18 February)

Udall, L., 1998. 'The World Bank and Public Accountability: Has Anything Changed?' in Fox and Brown (eds.), pp. 390–436

Uimonen, Peter and John Whalley, 1997. *Environmental Issues in the New World Trading System*, London: Macmillan

UNCTAD, 1989. *Trade and Development Report 1989*, New York: United Nations Conference on Trade and Development

UNDP, 1995. *UNDP Human Development Index*, Oxford: Oxford University Press

UNGLS, 1996a. 'Social Priorities of Civil Society: Speeches by Non-Governmental Organisations at the World Summit for Social Development,' *Development Dossiers* (July), Geneva

1996b. 'The United Nations, NGOs and Global Governance,' *Development Dossiers* (August), Geneva

1997. *The NGLS Handbook of UN Agencies, Programmes and Funds Working for Economic and Social Development*, New York: NGLS

USGAO, 1998. 'International Monetary Fund: Observations on Its Financial Condition,' Washington, DC: US Government General Accounting Office

USTR, 1996. 'Draft of Remarks by Acting USTR Charlene Barshefsky before the ICFTU Conference on International Labour Standards and Trade' (8 December), Singapore: Office of the United States Trade Representative

Vallely, P., 1996. 'How to Make the Poor Poorer,' *The Tablet*, 24 February: 248–50

Van Dyke, Brennan L. and John Barlow Weiner, n.d. *An Introduction to the WTO Decision on Document Restriction*, Geneva: International Centre for Trade and Sustainable Development/Center for International Environmental Law

Van Holthoon, Frits and Marcel van der Linden (eds.), 1988. *Internationalism in the Labour Movement 1830–1940*, Vols I and II, Leiden: E.J. Brill

Van Leeuwen, 1996. Statement by Fred van Leeuwen, General Secretary of Education International, ICFTU World Congress, Brussels (27 June)

Vander Stichele, Myriam, 1996. 'Discussion Note on Establishing Relations Between The World Trade Organisation (WTO) and Non-governmental Organisations (NGOs)' (December), Brussels: Transnational Institute

1998. 'Towards a World Transnationals' Organisation?' The World Trade Organisation Series, 3, Amsterdam: Transnational Institute

Wade, Robert, 1997. 'Development and Environment: Marital Difficulties at the World Bank,' Global Economic Institutions Working Paper Series, ERSC, 29 (July), London

Wade, Robert and Frank Verneroso, 1998. 'The Gathering World Slump and the Battle over Capital Controls,' *New Left Review*, 231 (September/October): 13–42

Walker, R.B.J., 1993. *Inside/Outside: International Relations as Political Theory*, Cambridge: Cambridge University Press

1994. 'Social Movements and World Politics,' *Millennium*, 23 (3): 669–700

Walton, J. and D. Seddon, 1994. *Free Markets and Food Riots: The Politics of Global Adjustment*, Oxford: Blackwell

Wapner, Paul, 1995. 'Politics beyond the State: Environmental Activitism and World Civic Politics,' *World Politics*, 47 (April): 311–40

1996. *Environmental Activism and World Civic Politics*, Albany: State University of New York Press

Wappenhans, W.A., 1992. *Report of the Portfolio Management Task Force*, Washington, DC: World Bank

Watkins, K. *et al.*, 1995. *The Oxfam Poverty Report*, Oxford: Oxfam UK & Ireland

WCL, 1995. 'World Confederation of Labour: A Spiritualistic Concept,' Brussels: WCL

Weiner, John Barlow and Brennan Van Dyke, n.d. *A Handbook for Obtaining Documents From the World Trade Organisation*, Geneva: International Centre for Trade and Sustainable Development/Center for International Environmental Law

Weiss, T.G. and L. Gordenker (eds.), 1996. *NGOs, the UN and Global Governance*, Boulder and London: Lynne Rienner

Werksman, J. (ed.), 1996. *Greening International Institutions*, London: Earthscan

Wignaraja, Ponna (ed.), 1993. *New Social Movements in the South: Empowering the People*, London: Zed Books

Wilcox, Clair, 1949. *A Charter for World Trade*, New York: Macmillan

Willetts, Peter (ed.), 1996. *'The Conscience of the World'. The Influence of Non-Governmental Organisations in the UN System*, London: Hurst & Company

Williams, Marc, 1993. 'International Trade and the Environment: Issues, Perspectives and Challenges,' *Environmental Politics*, 2 (4): 80–97

1994. *International Economic Institutions and the Third World*, Hemel Hempstead: Wheatsheaf

1998. 'Aid, Sustainable Development and the Environmental Crisis,' *International Journal of Peace Studies*, 3 (2) (July): 19–33

Wilson, Francis Graham, 1934. *Labor and the League System: A Study of*

International Labor Organisation in Relation to International Administration, Stanford: Stanford University Press

Wirth, David A., 1998. 'Partnership Advocacy in the World Bank Environmental Reform,' in Fox and Brown (eds.), pp. 51–79

Woestman, L., 1994. *Male Chauvinist SAPs: Structural Adjustment and Gender Policies*, Brussels: EURODAD/WIDE

Wolf, Martin, 1990. 'What we Need from the Uruguay Round,' *World Today*, 46 (3) (March): 43–6

Wolfensohn, James D., 1995. *New Directions and Partnerships*, Washington, DC: World Bank

Women's Environment and Development Organization (WEDO), 1997. 'Women's Eyes Bore into the Bank,' *News and Views*, 10 (2) (September): 4–5

Women's Eyes on the World Bank (US Chapter), 1997. 'Gender Equality and the World Bank Group: A Post-Beijing Assessment,' Executive Summary (May), Washington DC: Oxfam America

Wood A. and C. Welch, 1998. *Policing the Policemen: The Case for an Independent Evaluation Mechanism for the IMF*, Bretton Woods Project, London and FOE-US, Washington

World Bank, 1989. Operational Directive 14.70 (August)

1990. *Analysis Plan for Understanding the Social Dimensions of Adjustment*, Washington, DC: World Bank Africa Region

1991. *The Conable Years at the World Bank: Major Policy Addresses of Barber B. Conable 1986–1991*, Washington, DC: World Bank

1992. *World Development Report 1992*, Oxford: Oxford University Press

1993a. *The East Asian Miracle: Economic Growth and Public Policy*, Oxford: Oxford University Press

1993b. *Getting Results: The World Bank's Agenda for Improving Development Effectiveness* (July), Washington, DC: World Bank

1994a. *Governance: The World Bank's Experience*, Washington, DC: Operations Policy Department

1994b. *The World Bank: Policy on Disclosure of Information* (March), Washington, DC: World Bank

1994c. 'The Gender Dimension of Development,' Operational Directive 4.20, *The World Bank Operational Manual: Operational Policies* (April), Washington, DC: World Bank

1994d. *Closing the Gender Gap: Investing in and Releasing the Economic Potential of Women* (June), Washington, DC: Revised Initiating Memorandum

1994e. 'Gender and Economic Adjustment in Sub-Saharan Africa,' *Findings* (June), Washington, DC: World Bank; Africa Technical Department

1994f. *Gender Issues in Bank Lending: An Overview*, Report 13246 (June), Washington, DC: World Bank Operations and Evaluation Division

1994g. *Gender Issues in Bank Lending: An Overview* (30 June 30), Washington, DC: Operations Evaluation Department

1994h. *The World Bank and Participation* (September), Washington, DC: World Bank Operations Policy Department

1995a. *Mainstreaming the Environment*, Washington, DC: World Bank

1995b. *World Development Report 1995: Workers in an Integrating World*, Oxford: Oxford University Press

1996a. *Implementing the World Bank's Gender Policies*, Washington, DC: World Bank, Gender Analysis and Policy

1996b. *NGOs and the World Bank: Incorporating FY 94 Progress Report on Cooperation between the World Bank and NGOs*, Washington, DC: Poverty and Social Policy Department

1996c. *The World Bank's Partnership with Nongovernmental Organisations*, Washington, DC: World Bank, Participation and NGO Group; Poverty and Social Policy Department

1996d. *NGOs and the Bank: Incorporating FY 95 Progress Report on Cooperation Between the World Bank and NGOs* (June), Washington, DC: World Bank, Poverty and Social Policy Department

1997a. 'Report on the Second Annual Meeting, The World Bank External Gender Consultative Group' (Draft), Washington, DC: World Bank, Gender Sector Board, PREM

1997b. *World Development Report 1997: The State in a Changing World*, Oxford: Oxford University Press

1997c. *Implementing the World Bank's Gender Policies*, Progress Report No. 2 (June), Washington, DC: World Bank

1998a. *Partnerships for Development: A New World Bank Approach*, Washington, DC: World Bank

1998b. 'Report and Recommendation of the President of the International Bank for Reconstruction and Development to the Executive Directors on a Proposed Structural Adjustment Loan in an Amount Equivalent to US $2.0 Billion to the Republic of Korea' (19 March)

World Commission on Environment and Development, 1987. *Our Common Future* (the Bruntland Report), Oxford: Oxford University Press

WTO, 1996a. 'Procedures for the Circulation and Derestriction of WTO Documents,' World Trade Organisation WT/L/160/Rev.1, 22 July, Geneva

1996b. 'Guidelines for Arrangements on Relations with Non-Governmental Organisations,' World Trade Organisation WT/L/162, 23 July, Geneva

1996c. 'Draft Singapore Ministerial Declaration,' (13 December), Singapore

1998. 'Ruggiero Announces Enhanced WTO Plan for Cooperation with NGOs,' WTO Press Release 107, 17 July

WWF, 1996a. *The Relationship between the Provisions of the Multilateral Trading System and Trade Measures for Environmental Purposes, including those pursuant to Multilateral Environmental Agreements (MEAs)*, Geneva: World Wildlife Fund Legal Briefing 2, (2 January)

1996b. *Expert Panel on Trade and Sustainable Development. Report of First Meeting*, Geneva: WWF (November)

1996c. *The WTO Committte on Trade and the Environment – Is It Serious?*, Geneva: WWF (December)

WWW, 1996. 'WTO is Gender Blind,' Women's Caucus (12 December), Singapore: WTO meeting

1997. 'World Trade and the Rights of Women,' Women Working World Wide Bulletin 2 (January)

Yeo, C.T., 1996. 'Concluding Remarks by H.E. Mr. Yeo Cheow Tong,' Chairman of the Ministerial Conference, Minister for Trade and Industry of Singapore (13 December)

Index

CAMBRIDGE STUDIES IN INTERNATIONAL RELATIONS